Not So Abnormal Psychology

Not So Abnormal Psychology

A Pragmatic View of Mental Illness

Ronald B. Miller

American Psychological Association

Washington, DC

Published by
American Psychological Association
750 First Street, NE
Washington, DC 20002
www.apa.org

To order
APA Order Department
P.O. Box 92984
Washington, DC 20090-2984
Tel: (800) 374-2721; Direct: (202) 336-5510
Fax: (202) 336-5502; TDD/TTY: (202) 336-6123
Online: www.apa.org/pubs/books
E-mail: order@apa.org

In the U.K., Europe, Africa, and the Middle East, copies may be ordered from
American Psychological Association
3 Henrietta Street
Covent Garden, London
WC2E 8LU England

Typeset in Goudy by Circle Graphics, Inc., Columbia, MD

Printer: Edwards Brothers, Lillington, NC
Cover Designer: Minker Design, Sarasota, FL

The opinions and statements published are the responsibility of the authors, and such opinions and statements do not necessarily represent the policies of the American Psychological Association.

Library of Congress Cataloging-in-Publication Data

Miller, Ronald B., 1948- , author.
  Not so abnormal psychology : a pragmatic view of mental illness / by Ronald B. Miller.
    p. ; cm.
  Includes bibliographical references and index.
  ISBN 978-1-4338-2021-2 — ISBN 1-4338-2021-8
  I. American Psychological Association, issuing body. II. Title.
  [DNLM: 1. Mental Disorders. 2. Psychopathology—methods. WM 140]
  RC454
  616.89—dc23
                          2015007659

British Library Cataloguing-in-Publication Data

A CIP record is available from the British Library.

Printed in the United States of America
First Edition

http://dx.doi.org/10.1037/14693-000

CONTENTS

PREFACE

Traditionally, the abnormal psychology textbook is structured around the diagnostic categories in the American Psychiatric Association's diagnostic reference work, the *Diagnostic and Statistical Manual of Mental Disorders* (5th ed.; *DSM–5*; American Psychiatric Association, 2013). Chapters describe and explain the various "mental disorders" and their treatment in terms of the culturally dominant biomedical model, augmented by that theory from contemporary clinical psychology that is also most consistent with culturally dominant views, namely, the cognitive–behavioral approach to diagnosis and treatment. Humanistic, psychodynamic, community, and family systems models for understanding and treating such disorders are introduced but rarely mentioned after an introductory chapter on theories, because they are said to have little traditional empirical support.

This is not a bad pedagogical strategy if one wishes to train students for careers doing research in abnormal/clinical psychology on the abstract principles of developmental psychopathology or behavior change. However, if one wants to prepare students to think effectively in the realm of clinical practice, one has to start with the concepts and theories that have emerged from the realm of clinical practice itself, augmented as necessary by the work of pure theoreticians or scientists. In this book, I draw heavily on the concepts and theories in the clinical practice traditions in psychology that I have found in almost 40 years of practice to have pragmatic value—namely, the humanistic, psychodynamic, community, and family systems approaches to clinical work. I have spent 3 decades immersed in various aspects of theoretical and philosophical psychology focusing on issues in the philosophy of science, the moral judgments implicit in psychological theories, the role of case studies in developing the knowledge base of clinical practice, and the politics of mental health. In so doing, I have sought to understand why these approaches that made so much sense to me came to be supplanted, broadly within psychology, by the biomedical and cognitive–behavioral approaches that are governed by scientific theory.

In Chapter 1, I acknowledge the literatures in these areas that have heavily influenced my thinking, so much so that in writing this introductory textbook, I have often been hard-pressed to identify which ideas and arguments from these traditions are best attributed to which authors and which are part of the intellectual climate in which I have operated for so long. I acknowledge my indebtedness to these academic and intellectual communities and hope those who may not have been cited will forgive any oversight on my part and be pleased to see an introductory textbook in abnormal psychology fairly representing points of view that undergraduate students have long been denied access to. Because the predominant biomedical model cannot be ignored, I have carefully reviewed the literature on the genetic, physiological, and neuroscience aspects of mental disorders, and the effectiveness of treatment with pharmaceutical drugs, looking particularly at the quality of research rather than simply the frequency of citations in the literature.

One can take a traditional course in abnormal psychology without having gained much practical knowledge about how to understand the psychological difficulties in one's own life or how to effectively address such difficulties in the lives of one's loved ones. This comes as no surprise when one understands that often at large research universities, the individuals teaching such courses have a purely theoretical interest in understanding such disorders and little knowledge or interest in the practical task of actually being therapeutic when working with such clients (patients). Attending to the immediate suffering of "mental patients" or psychotherapy clients in the here and now is all too often of little interest or import.

This is a tremendous squandering of psychology's resources. It is also a tragic lost opportunity to improve the lives of the million or more college students each year who take a course in abnormal psychology and who ought to emerge from this course with a pragmatic understanding of themselves and how to cope with the psychological stressors and problems so typical of late adolescence and young adulthood. This is a critical developmental period during which those students who are overwhelmed with new responsibilities, environments, and work demands often are at increased risk of depression, anxiety, substance abuse, self-harm, and first psychotic breaks.

The goal of this volume is to be such a text—to provide undergraduate students (and other interested readers) with an introduction to abnormal psychology that is theoretically grounded and historically informed, while at the same time promoting the understanding of self and others that is critical to emotional health and well-being. To this end, I freely discuss the kind of personal struggles I have encountered both as a child and later as an aspiring psychologist, and I have integrated case studies into each chapter as a way of acknowledging that the subject matter of the book is the challenge all of us face as we attempt to make a life for ourselves, care for those we love, and navigate the complex physical and social environments that we inhabit. Deeply troubling states of mind, emotions, and behavior patterns are not abstract scientific entities, but are instead the lived experiences of human suffering. My unabashed goal is for readers to both know more about abnormal psychology as a subdiscipline of psychology proper and to know more about themselves and the people they care about in a manner that eases some of the pain of human existence, especially that of being a young or emerging adult in our highly stressful society. Consequently, I have focused the case studies whenever possible on college students to illustrate the application of concepts and strategies that are applicable across the life span.

I am indebted to the good people of Saint Michael's College for the opportunity to teach and write on topics related to this book over a period of 30 years. The department of psychology's administrative assistant, Diana Hoppe, provided technical support and kept the master's program in clinical psychology that I direct functioning smoothly while I was preoccupied at times with this project. In those times when the preoccupation became burdensome, the encouragement of my longtime colleague Dr. Susan Kuntz proved invaluable, as did that of Tara Arcury, assistant to the president, who also offered technical assistance with the manuscript. The following graduate students provided assistance in reviewing scientific and clinical literature for this project: Meaghan Pilling, Kristin Robideau, Jennifer Moore, Monica Lawson, Jennifer Signet, Frank Huseman, and Griffin Thayer. More recently, as I began using the book's chapters in my abnormal psychology course, I appreciate the efforts of more than 100 of my recent undergraduate students at Saint Michael's College who provided useful critical feedback to the author of their textbook.

I have learned a great deal from the many individuals and families who bestowed their trust in me over the past 40 years in my role as a clinical practitioner. In addition to the tremendous meaning that clinical work brings into my life, I have drawn on these experiences heavily in authoring this textbook, though always with an eye to the critical centrality of confidentiality in the therapeutic process. Cases of my own discussed in this book have been heavily disguised to conceal the identity of the individuals and families involved. This has been done in a manner to preserve the clinical integrity of a case so that no essential psychological process or outcome that would affect the reader's judgment of the case has been altered. In some instances, similar elements from the life histories of several case subjects were combined to provide the necessary level of detail while preserving confidentiality.

One learns a great deal from listening to the life histories of one's clients, but even more if one has trusted colleagues with whom one can consult on how to understand and improve the therapeutic relationship. I have been truly blessed in this regard to have had the opportunity to work with a marvelously talented clinical social worker and play therapist, Naomi P. Shapiro, LICSW, with whom I have shared not only a practice but also a life. Much of the clinical perspective presented in this volume has evolved in the context of our relationship—practicing, teaching, and raising a family together. The chapter on psychological suffering in childhood is largely a result of what I have learned from her about the amazing power of play therapy when practiced by a person who truly loves children and loves life. We have been blessed with two wonderful children of our own, Ari Shapiro-Miller and Maya Shapiro-Miller, now grown into adulthood and pursuing careers in the educational and mental health worlds. I have relied on their love and support as I endeavored to complete this project. As the member of the family who had most recently been a college student, Maya provided feedback on how accessible a student taking a first course in abnormal psychology would find the material. I counted on her for the unvarnished truth, and she never let me down.

Thanks too, are due to my friend Craig Lawrence, for his encouragement and incisive editorial suggestions, and to Bertram P. Karon, a mentor and friend these last 30 years who took time from his arduous schedule to review the entire manuscript, and whose professional and personal courage and generosity have inspired several generations of clinical psychology students and colleagues. Finally, I am appreciative of the diligent efforts of the American Psychological Association staff, Mary Lynn Skutley, Linda Malnasi McCarter, and Tyler Aune, as well as the several anonymous reviewers who provided excellent feedback on an earlier draft. I believe the book was greatly improved because of their collective efforts. Of course, in all instances where I benefited from the writings and feedback of others in this process, I both gratefully acknowledge their assistance and take full responsibility for the interpretations of the literature and views expressed here.

Not So Abnormal
Psychology

1

THE PERSONAL ALLURE OF A BEHAVIORAL SCIENCE

Psychology is a hybrid subject. With its basic concepts and theories rooted in ancient religions and philosophy, its branches reaching into experimental biology, physiology, pharmacology, anthropology, sociology, and even biography, psychology's theories and data are diverse, inconsistent, and at times contradictory. Attempts to produce an integrated comprehensive theory remain elusive. In its place we find an array of mini-theories tied to specific subareas of the field (e.g., cognitive, developmental, physiological, or social psychology). Although we remain intrigued, compelled to search for answers to the riddle of ourselves and others, we can often feel more than a bit overwhelmed by the task.

Nowhere is this truer than in the subdiscipline of abnormal psychology. Its topics directly affect our quality of life both as individuals and as a society, sometimes even in life-and-death ways. Multiple professions draw on and in turn influence our view of abnormal psychology (e.g., psychology, psychiatry, social work, counseling, nursing, special education). Within and across

http://dx.doi.org/10.1037/14693-001
Not So Abnormal Psychology: A Pragmatic View of Mental Illness, by R. B. Miller

these professions, competing theories, treatments, and public policy positions vie for dominance. Increasingly there are consumer advocacy or self-help groups that offer an alternative to professional services, often motivated by a deep disappointment with services that had been received. Alcoholics Anonymous, Survivors of Psychiatry (A. J. Joseph, 2013), the recovery movement for persons with "serious mental illness" (Roe & Davidson, 2008), and the Son-Rise Program (Kaufman, 1995) for parents and their autistic children all claim insights and knowledge ignored by the mainstream mental health professions.

As one examines the subdiscipline of abnormal psychology, one stark division is striking: the struggle between clinical research scientists and clinical practitioners over the right to claim expert knowledge in the field. This schism in the field is often referred to as the *scientist–practitioner gap* (Stricker & Trierweiler, 2006), though Saltzman and Norcross (1990) may have more aptly described the situation as the "therapy wars." Both sides of this division have their own theories, kinds of data, research methods, professional literature, networks, and associations. Sometimes they collaborate, but more often than not they operate in parallel universes, except in competing for research funding, tenure positions in academic departments, contracts from employers, reimbursements from insurance companies for their services, and publishing outlets for their writings (Sternberg, 2005).

In seeking legitimacy for our psychological expertise and knowledge, we psychologists rarely acknowledge our own humanity even when it is revealed by our professional conflicts and rivalries. We are reluctant to acknowledge in ourselves the same irrational forces that we attempt to explain in our research populations or that we attempt to treat in our clinical and counseling practices. But to understand anxiety, interpersonal conflict, perfectionism, paranoia, dependency, narcissism, and so forth, we must start with ourselves.

Honest self-examination has its roots in philosophy (the Delphic oracle of ancient Greece who admonished all who would enter her temple to "First, know thyself"), the Catholic confessional (Saint Augustine of Hippo's autobiographical Confessions c. 400 AD), and pastoral counseling (Boston's Emmanuel movement c. 1905). It was adopted by the founder of psychoanalysis, Sigmund Freud (1920/1966), in his method of "free association" and later amplified in humanistic psychology's (Jourard, 1964; Rogers, 1951) focus on self-awareness and self-disclosure. Contemporary interest in Buddhist mindfulness practices in cognitive–behavior therapies reflects a similar orientation, requiring us to be accepting of all of our thoughts, images, feelings, and memories (Hayes, Follette, & Linehan, 2004). Granted, each of these traditions has many institutional differences and varied practices and traditions, but they share a core component: The individual must pay attention to, and become responsible for, his or her inner experience.

In understanding ourselves, where we come from, and where we are heading, we acquire self-knowledge that ultimately allows us to both live well and effectively be of assistance to others. This self-understanding is our touchstone for the practical validity of psychological knowledge. It is a capacity that resides within each of us. In a discipline in which clinical theories often disagree and research results often conflict, we have no choice but to return to our own self-understanding. In working with others, it permits us to ask: When have I come closest to experiencing the kind of pain or exhibiting the kind of extreme behavior that I am seeing in this person? What else was going on in my life when I felt or acted this way? What helped me to move through that time into a better place?

In this way we build an empathetic understanding of those around us, and we begin to experience firsthand the renowned 20th-century American psychiatrist Harry Stack Sullivan's (1968) well-known dictum: We "are much more simply human than otherwise" (p. 32). No matter how strange, bizarre, or seemingly inhuman another person's actions are, we should regard such an individual as first a fellow human being and not, for example, as a "bipolar disorder," "psychotic schizophrenic," "oppositional defiant child," or "borderline personality." When we label and categorize people in this manner, we subtly but radically shift our focus from a person who is like us when we are overwhelmed, to an overwhelming person to be around—a slippery slope on the road to nonpersonhood.

A lack of openness to self-awareness inhibits not only our ability to progress as a discipline but also our ability to be helpful to others. When we believe that our technical expertise and professionalism are the only critical elements in providing beneficial treatment, we risk devaluing the self-respect and autonomy of the person who is suffering. No matter how many helpful services or treatments we decide to offer such a person to "fix" the problem, this help often comes at a heavy price—a loss of control and responsibility on the client's part for his or her own life.

NAMING THE DISCIPLINE

The topic of study before us is psychological suffering. On the face of it, this appears straightforward, yet the divisions in the discipline affect everything in our field, even the most basic question of how to label and define the subject matter to be studied. When this topic is taught in medical or nursing settings, psychological suffering is most often referred to as *psychiatric* or *mental* disorder (connoting that these are parallel to physical and medical disorders). At psychoanalytic training institutes a similar course would be entitled *Psychopathology*, a term that combines the ancient Greek terms *psyche* and *pathos* to describe the suffering of the mind, spirit, or soul. This suggests a discipline that is the psychological equivalent of the study of pathology in medicine—*pathology* being the study of the anatomical and physiological basis of disease. Some medical schools and psychology graduate programs retained the term *psychopathology*, despite no longer teaching a psychoanalytic approach. Terms that were once considered technical or medical, such as *mental illness* or *emotional disturbance*, are no longer considered so, although they are still widely used in everyday language and may be incorporated into various legislative acts or legal rulings.

Nor does the confusing terminology stop there. Harry Stack Sullivan (1953/1968) preferred the more normalizing term *problems in living* to either *psychiatric disorders* or *psychopathology*. With the rise of behaviorism in clinical psychology (in the 1960s), departments renamed their courses and textbooks "Abnormal Behavior" or "Behavior Disorders" and focused on inappropriate, unproductive, or irrational behaviors, in so doing making overt the field's focus on enforcing social expectations and norms. Therefore, as a trained psychologist who teaches a course called Abnormal Psychology, I will refer to this area of study by that name, while keeping the imperfections and potentially pejorative connotations of the term in mind.

In truth, the field of abnormal psychology is as diverse and divisive as our Western societies. *Abnormal psychology, psychopathology, psychiatric disorders*, and *problems in living* are overlapping terms and phrases referring to a key cornerstone in the knowledge base of the various mental health professions (psychology, counseling, social work, psychiatry, psychiatric nursing, and rehabilitation counseling). Every institution and person within society has a considerable stake in how we conceptualize and then act toward or on the individuals and groups whose actions fall under the purview of this field of study, however it is termed. The psychological or psychiatric diagnoses and treatments that emerge out of these fields of study have an impact on how we as individuals or institutions respond when a person violates social norms and expectations. After all, the successful functioning of our society depends on an effective response and resolution of the kinds of psychological suffering and problems in living studied in abnormal psychology.

It is in courses with such titles that future consumers, practitioners, and researchers learn how to think about the nature and meaning of psychological suffering, what questions are important and reasonable to ask, and what the criteria are for deciding what constitutes a good answer. It is only after these fundamental questions are answered that we can attempt to answer the key questions as to what causes this suffering and what can be done to ameliorate it. The effects of this area of study are felt broadly throughout society in families, schools, hospitals, nursing homes, health care clinics, mental health and college counseling centers, courts and prisons, mental health professions, health insurance and pharmaceutical companies, government agencies, the military, and even at times our religious institutions.

I have gradually come to see the subject matter of abnormal psychology not as a study of the various states of mind that disrupt the peaceful states of mind that usually prevail but rather as a study of how we all come to terms with the pervasive aspects of human suffering, particularly that form of human suffering that seems self-inflicted or self-perpetuating. This psychological suffering is multifaceted, including the rational and irrational anxiety and guilt, self-condemnation, hopelessness, helplessness, self-harm, rage, confusion, and paranoia that we are all prone to when life circumstances are sufficiently hostile or horrible. We cannot expect our students to take this difficult journey toward greater self-understanding alone.

MY STORY I: SEEKING THE AUTHORITY OF SCIENCE

When I entered graduate school to become a clinical psychologist over 40 years ago, I was eager to learn the emerging behavioral science answers to the age-old problems that medicine and religion had too often failed to solve. Nor was my interest merely professional or theoretical (as it almost never is for those who study clinical aspects of psychology); I hoped that the answers to certain mysteries from my own life would also be somehow magically revealed once I added scientific theories and data to my own more philosophical perspective. For example, I wondered why in our extended family that four of the five adult males of my parents' generation (whom I knew quite well) were quite successful in their chosen careers, yet seemed troubled in their personal lives. One was a binge drinker, another experienced periodic incapacitating depression, a third had a clandestine affair leading to divorce, and a fourth emotionally and physically abused his wife. The fifth male was always friendly and upbeat and seemed a devoted husband and father. Yet he engaged in underhanded business practices that harmed the career prospects of another member of the group, and they became estranged for many years.

The women in these partnerships fared only somewhat better, though they were all devoted mothers, and several had professional careers. However, one was prone to bouts of depression and withdrawal, a second was obese and died relatively young of heart failure, a third, the subject of the abuse, was chronically depressed and eventually made a serious suicide attempt. Of course, much of this was kept secret beyond each nuclear family, but by the time I left for college, all of these family secrets were more generally known throughout the extended family.

As a child, many of these people were my role models, even my heroes. The reality of what I would learn about the family's dynamics and secrets left me somewhat stunned and confused as a young adult. Yet nothing of these revelations that emerged over time would top the information I was given on a warm spring day in my junior year of high school. My father suggested we go for a ride in the car to have a talk. Because this was not something he had ever suggested before, I anxiously agreed. As it turned out, the purpose of the talk was to provide me with a bit of family history that he and my mother now thought I was old enough to hear, namely, the circumstances of my maternal grandfather's death. I knew he had died when my mother was in grade school and that she had taken it very hard and did not like to talk about it. So I must have learned early not to ask questions, because that is all that I knew of him.

The circumstances were the following. My maternal grandfather was from a large family of Russian–Jewish extraction. After immigrating to the United States in the early 1900s, the family, led by my great-grandfather, had been remarkably successful in the business community. At the height of the Great Depression, his son, my grandfather, had continued to live the high life, well beyond his means. But then, one day, his loans from a major banking institution in the Northeast came due. To avoid bankruptcy, he walked out of a meeting where he had tried and failed to receive an extension on the loan payment due, and shot himself in front of the bank. As an insurance sales-man, the only asset he had remaining was his own life insurance policy, which in those days did not exclude payment in the event of suicide. My mother, walking home from school, encountered a newsboy standing on the street corner hawking papers: "Read all about it: Local businessman shoots himself in front of bank." She arrived home to learn that the newsboy was referring to her father and that he was dead. Being Jewish, the family regarded suicide as the most venal of sins, and they were deeply disgraced; they therefore never discussed him or what he had done. My parents apparently thought that I needed to know this to protect myself should I ever be taunted by peers concerning my family's shameful past. At least, that is what my father said. Of course, no one in the community ever taunted me about my grandfather's death or even mentioned his name. The purpose of this conversation remains almost as much of a mystery as my grandfather's life.

These discoveries and revelations about the members of my family in my middle and late teens were not the only mysteries to be solved. I struggled to find a meaningful role for myself in a society that seemed to be coming apart at the seams: the political assassinations of President Kennedy, and 5 years later his brother Robert Kennedy and Martin Luther King Jr.; a seem-ingly senseless war in Vietnam to which hundreds of thousands of my peers were being sent as draftees (and I might have been too); close friends becom-ing heroin addicts and psychiatric patients, some of whom seemed to become robotic creatures thanks to the medications their doctors prescribed them. Turning away from increasingly dangerous involvement in the politics of protest, I immersed myself in graduate study in philosophy and then clinical psychology.

By the time I entered graduate school in clinical psychology I had convinced myself that I could separate my own doubts about who I was from the political divisions within the country and from the study of psychological disorders and their treatment. I believed I could do this because that is what every graduate program brochure in the research-oriented field of clinical psychology stated—that the science of clinical psychology was a rational enterprise that progressed only when behavioral scientists put aside all personal, moral, or political values and relied on their powers of empirical observation, rationality, and quantitative analysis (i.e., the scientific method). I was instructed that personal feelings, relationships, and moral and political values were part of one's private life, not a part of the science of psychology.

It was only when my first marriage began to unravel in graduate school and I sought psychotherapy at the University Counseling Center that I began to examine my own family experience. In so doing, I recognized the importance of my grandfather's suicide in my own inner turmoil and conflicted relationships with romantic partners. The event and the secrecy surrounding it were key missing pieces in the puzzle of my mother. My mother's veneration of her mother (our Nana) who had survived the blow of her husband's suicide and worked day and night to support her three children now seemed reasonable rather than exaggerated. I also came to understand my mother's idolization of her older brother's substantial success in business, her willingness to overlook the sometimes questionable methods he used toward that end, and her fear that everyone she loved was likely to die suddenly and tragically without warning. (It took me until my late 20s before I realized that I had internalized the very same fear and that it was not simply an inevitable part of being human to have such a belief.) Though I obviously had never met my grandfather, once I was told how he had died, I could begin to also imagine his life, and my mother's, while he lived. I felt a sense of connection to him and his family that I had never had before. The extended family problems that had both contributed to and been exacerbated by his suicide were not thereby solved, but my mother made more sense to me, and I felt more compassion for her and, as a result, also for myself. It is only in Hollywood movies that insight and self-understanding arrive in a single momentous flash (often after a brilliant therapist's interpretation). In life and real psychotherapy, self-understanding is achieved as the result of hard work, with uneven progress, often interrupted by periods of backsliding or regression (Horney, 1942/2013).

Over the years of working clinically with individuals, couples, and families as a psychologist and teaching abnormal psychology to a broad cross section of college and graduate students, I also came to realize that few, if any, families exist without their own mysteries and heartaches. Most families have their secrets (Farberow, 1963), and even when the secrets become known to other family members, we protect our own from public ridicule, humiliation, and at times, even legal prosecution by holding those secrets within the family. As my career evolved, I came to see that most of my colleagues and under-graduate and graduate students were similarly burdened by family mysteries and secrets.

MY STORY II: PERSONAL MEANING VERSUS SCIENTIFIC EXPLANATION

My experience as a client at the University Counseling Center was fun-damentally life-altering. I had been fortunate to have access to a psychologist who was a supportive, nonjudgmental, patient listener who offered insightful observations on my emotional life and interpersonal relationships. He had been trained by a student of Carl Rogers, at the time the leader of humanistic psychology in the United States, and had also been strongly influenced by the interpersonal theory of H.S. Sullivan. However, as a graduate student in a research-oriented clinical psychology doctoral program, I was unsettled by the experience, self-awareness, and new understanding of interpersonal relationships and how I was affected by them. The longer I was in psycho-therapy at the counseling center, the more confusing my role as a graduate student became. Hardly any of the clinical psychology course work examined any of the psychotherapeutic processes I was experiencing as a client. In fact, subjective feelings, memories of important or even traumatic events, and per-ceptions of significant relationships were all described as outside the purview of a psychological science, to be left to the musings of poets, artists, and philoso-phers. To say this was to imply that these topics were not about "real" objective features of our world, but rather shadowy phenomena that our minds deceived us into thinking were of importance in explaining our actions and behaviors. Consequently, in class discussions in which the research literature on the pro-cess and/or outcome of psychotherapy was discussed (e.g., Bergin & Garfield, 1971; Eysenck, 1952), no one was permitted to discuss their own personal life experiences in psychotherapy or whether they felt they had benefitted. Yet, by the end of the second year of graduate school, most of the graduate stu-dents in my class of eight doctoral students had sought assistance from the counseling center, and even the most scientific among us freely shared our amazement at the positive impact it was having on reducing our intense stress and anxiety that had surfaced in graduate school.

The irony of the situation was not lost on us. Several of us had a sense that we might not be able to survive the highly competitive graduate clinical research doctoral program (which 2 years previously we had fought so hard to enter) without the support we were receiving from the counseling center. Yet the faculty of that research program denied in their teaching that our experience in psychotherapy was any more beneficial than the mere passage of time. So we in essence led an intellectual double life, going to our therapy sessions, excitedly talking with one another about our growing self-awareness, and attending classes on how to do research on clinical treatment in which we progressed toward our doctoral degree.

REFLECTION ON CONFLICTING EXPERIENCES

We felt the tension between these two roles (psychotherapy client and research trainee in clinical psychology) intensely, but we did not yet understand it intellectually. At the time, we graduate students simply thought that the clinical practitioners and the clinical research scientists on the faculty just did not like each other much as individuals. We mistook an institutional, professional, and theoretical conflict for a personal one. It was only after years of reflection, literature reviews, and philosophical analysis, along with the emergence of the professional schools movement in clinical psychology (the PsyD or Vail model; Peterson, 1976), that I began to make sense of what had created this tension. I eventually discovered a legitimate, serious, scholarly literature of clinical and counseling psychology that has been excluded from consideration in our graduate programs on the grounds that it was not sufficiently scientific.

Here I briefly identify this literature and many of its most published theorists and researchers. I do this in a more detailed manner than is customary in an introductory chapter because many readers may be skeptical of the claim that there is a rigorous scholarly literature in abnormal psychology that challenges the mainstream view of establishing the knowledge base through strictly empirical and experimental methods. Many of the works cited in this review receive more in-depth discussion in later chapters of the book.

The Survival of Humanistic Psychology

One of my first discoveries was that Carl Rogers's work on what he came to call a *person-centered approach* to clinical and counseling practice, although less prominent in mainstream psychology after the 1970s, remained alive and well in the Society of Counseling Psychology (Division 17 of the American Psychological Association [APA]) and the Society for Humanistic Psychology (Division 32 of the APA) and related organizations (e.g., Bohart & Watson, 2011; Elliot, Greenberg, & Lietaer, 2004; Gendlin, 1996; McLeod, 2010;

O'Hara, 1997; Prouty, 2003; Schneider, Bugental, & Pierson, 2001; Stiles, Barkham, Twigg, Mellor-Clark, & Cooper, 2006; J. C. Watson, Goldman, & Greenberg, 2011). Many of these investigators and practitioners incorporated other humanistic–existential or Gestalt therapy approaches into their work. Although he was not a student of Rogers, Joseph Rychlak (1981) was a leader in both humanistic and philosophical psychology, at the same time incorporating cognitive and psychodynamic elements into his work and remaining committed to experimental investigations of purposeful behavior, what he referred to as *teleosponsivity*. He also coined the terms *intraspective* and *extraspective*, which are useful in directing our attention to the fundamental difference between theories and methods that study our interior, introspective, subjective experience of living—the *intraspective* orientation—and theories and methods that study people by observing their behavioral, physical, and physiological responses to the environment—the *extraspective* orientation.

The Harvard Department of Social Relations Life History Approach

The Harvard Department of Social Relations was created in the hopes of integrating experimental psychology with psychoanalysis, anthropology, and sociology. These were all departments or traditions that claimed insights into the human mind and behavior. Gordon Allport (1937), who had written the first American textbook on personality, and Henry Murray (1943), who had established the Harvard Psychological Clinic and created the Thematic Apperception Test, left the Harvard Psychology Department to join this new department after conflict with the psychology department experimentalists (namely, B.F. Skinner). This group produced an impressive body of work on personality development, narrative research, and abnormal psychology (White, 1992), and that tradition has been continued by Runyan (1982), McAdams (2006), Josselson and Lieblich (1993), and Messer (1986). Others in this tradition who may not identify with its more psychoanalytic aspects but who resonate with the critical importance of systematic case study research in clinical and counseling psychology include Hoshamond (1992), Fishman (1999), Dattilio, Edwards, and Fishman (2010), Edwards (1998), Eells (2007), and McLeod (2010).

Theoretical and Philosophical Psychology

The life history and narrative approach to abnormal psychology described above has received strong support from philosophically oriented psychologists as well. This literature critically examines the philosophy of science that justifies the current mainstream approach to psychology, finding it better suited to the physical sciences than to the study of the human mind and behavior.

This group may be roughly divided into groups by philosophical orientation. Gergen (1985) inspired many social constructionist critiques of the objectivity of science (e.g., Christopher, 2006; Christopher, Wendt, Marecek, & Goodman, 2014; Cushman, 1996; Kirschner, 1996).

A second group has been inspired by European philosophical hermeneutics, which insists that all linguistic terms, including psychological terms, require interpretation of meanings and therefore are not purely objective in a scientific sense. This group includes Freeman (1997); Martin and Sugarman (2000); Polkinghorne (2004); Richardson, Fowers, and Guignon (1999); Sass and Parnas (2003); Slife, Reber, and Richardson (2005); and Sugarman (2005). A third group, influenced by Anglo-American philosophy in their critique of the logical foundations of psychological science, includes Robinson (1995, 2008); Harré (1998); Held (1995, 2007); Osbeck, Nersessian, Malone, and Newstetter (2011). A fourth group, Howard (1986); R. B. Miller (2004); Tjeltveit (1999, 2006); and Woolfolk (1998) is focused on epistemological and ethical issues that are inherent in psychological judgments and therefore differentiate psychological science from the physical sciences.

Although not always in agreement with one another, these authors in philosophical and theoretical psychology critique an exclusively quantitative/experimental approach to psychological theory and research and invite the inclusion of personal meaning, intention, purpose, moral and ethical values, and agency implicit in human behavior as proper subjects for scholarly investigation. Although one may disagree with the conclusions drawn in this body of work, one cannot question that it represents a serious body of scholarship on the question of the nature of psychology as a discipline and the legitimate grounds for knowledge claims in the realm of clinical practice.

Psychoanalytic Psychology

Many of the academic psychologists drafted into the U.S. Armed Forces during World War II were given on-the-job training in psychoanalytic crisis intervention to assist psychiatrists in the care of soldiers who were psychologically traumatized by combat (Herman, 1995). After the war there was a growing interest in psychoanalysis among academic psychologists, especially in metropolitan areas that were home to psychoanalytic training institutes (New York, Philadelphia, Boston, Chicago, Los Angeles, and San Francisco). Eventually a lawsuit sponsored by the APA forced the institutes to allow doctoral psychologists upon graduation to receive training and certification as psychoanalysts. Given the usual disparagement of psychoanalytic theory and research in the mainstream psychological literature during the 20th century, students are often quite surprised to learn that Division 39 (Psychoanalysis) of the APA is one of the largest divisions, with about 2,600 members.

(Division 12, the Society of Clinical Psychology, represents the mainstream scientific view and has a membership of about 3,200; http://www.apa.org/ secure/reporting/comparison-report.aspx).

Psychoanalysis has developed through its international organizations into an impressive network of journals, publishers, training institutes, and practitioners that includes psychiatrists (MDs), psychologists, social workers, and psychiatric nurses. Many psychologists have made important contributions to this literature (e.g., Della Selva, 1996; Eagle, 1989; Fonagy, 2010; Karon, 2004; Karon & VandenBos, 1981; McWilliams, 2011; Messer, 1986, 2013; Mitchell, 1988; Safran, 2012; D. K. Silverman, 2005; L. H. Silverman & Lachmann, 1985; Stolorow, Brandchaft, & Atwood, 1987; Wachtel, 1997).

Phenomenological Psychology

A fifth tradition that honors the exploration of subjective personal experience in academic psychology is often identified with the Departments of Psychology at Duquesne University, the University of Dallas, West Georgia State University, and Seattle University. Developed by Amedeo Giorgi and colleagues from the philosophical phenomenology of Husserl, the 19th-century German philosopher who laid the groundwork for the emergence of existentialism, phenomenological psychology proposes the systematic investigation of the lived experience of human beings through the careful description of psychological states in first-person accounts (e.g., Aanstoos, 2012; Arons, 1993; Burston & Frie, 2006; Churchill, 2006; Fischer, 2000; Giorgi, 2010; Keen, 1970; Valle, 1998; Wertz, 1986; Wertz et al., 2011).

Community and Critical Psychology

A sixth area outside the mainstream Boulder-model clinical psychology comprises those in abnormal and clinical psychology who wish to work in the community in primary prevention or community organization and who thereby encounter resistance from, and conflict with, established political and economic forces (e.g., A. G. Levine & Levine, 2014; M. Levine, Perkins, & Perkins, 2005). Some have also called this *critical psychology* or *critical psychiatry* because of its reliance on Marxist or socialist analysis of the forces at play in the community when working with underserved populations and minorities. These psychologists look at the social, economic, and political implications of psychological practices and whether psychology is a force of social change or a force preserving the status quo (e.g., Fox, 1993; Hare-Mustin, 2004; Hare-Mustin & Marecek, 1988; Laing, 1959; Marecek & Hare-Mustin, 2009; Prilleltensky,1989; Prilleltensky, Prilleltensky, & Voorhees, 2009; Teo, 2009). Recent work by the investigative journalist Robert Whitaker (2005,

2011) has raised similar questions about the politics of mental health in the United States and its control by the powerful guild interest of the American Psychiatric Association, major pharmaceutical companies, and social-economic elites.

MY STORY III: GRADUATE TRAINING IN BEHAVIORAL CLINICAL PSYCHOLOGY

Of course, I had not entered graduate study to undergo psychotherapy or question its philosophy of science but to learn to be a behavioral scientist/ psychologist able to unlock the mysteries of the human mind and thereby provide a service that might reduce the amount of human misery in the world, including my own. In my initial enthusiasm, I immersed myself in the study of physiological psychology, advanced statistics, classical and contemporary learning theory, applied behavioral analysis, and behavior therapy. I scoured the professional literature for case studies revealing how these principles were actually applied in the real world of clinical practice, and marveled at the reports of success with cases that had been previously considered incurable. I was chastened a bit in my enthusiasm by the former chair of the psychology department, J. P. Chaplin, who advised our first-year graduate seminar to always take advantage of any new "miracle" treatment in psychology or psychiatry during the early years of its development—before it lost its effectiveness. That comment, the only one from a department faculty member that implied any skepticism about the behavioral approach we were learning, proved prophetic, and I would find that it applied equally well to other therapeutic fads I would encounter over the ensuing decades.

Over the 5 years I was in graduate school my enthusiasm for behavioral science as a solution to the personal and family problems of humankind waxed and waned. The advantages I personally observed were many and remain with me to do this day:

- Behavioral approaches (Skinner, 1953; Ullmann & Krasner, 1965) placed primary emphasis on how the environment controlled behavior, and so changing behavior was done by changing the environment, not just trying to change the person who was disturbing, or was disturbed in, that environment.
- Unlike many more abstract theories in clinical psychology (particularly psychoanalysis), behavioral theory was clear and straightforward. With some serious work, it could be learned readily by graduate students over a period of 2 or 3 years. When psychology students then taught parents, teachers, caseworkers,

prison guards, and hospital attendants the basic principles of behavioral management, the information was greeted with enthusiasm. It seemed to work.

- On a personal level, I built reinforcement and behavior shaping into my own study schedule, and found it quite useful. Instead of attempting to study in 5 and 6 hour blocks during the day or night (a goal I frequently failed to reach), I would begin by giving myself a reward or reinforcement (a 10-minute study break with a snack) after 2 hours of studying, gradually lengthening the time required to receive the reinforcement to 3 and 4 hours.

- In the consulting room, working with individual clients/patients, Jacobson's (1976) progressive muscle relaxation exercises were often immediately helpful in lessening the subjective anxiety I encountered in many of my early cases. I used these exercises myself, as well, and in about three weeks began to feel a reduction in the anxiety symptoms I had experienced periodically since I was 13 years of age.

- Although the theory of behavioral psychology rejected the medical model of psychiatric treatment involving brain-altering chemicals or electroconvulsive therapy, behaviorists tended to resemble physicians in their relationship with the patient/client. The psychologist, like the physician, was taking responsibility for fixing the problem using scientific theories and prescribing behavior change techniques rather than medication and deserved therefore the same kind of respect and remuneration from patients and society at large. In short, behavioral psychologists could feel like "real doctors," without having gone to medical school.

However, there were problematic areas that I also personally observed:

- Although in theory any learned behavior can be unlearned, given the power to completely control a person's environment, it was rare even in institutional settings for the psychologist to have such power. Even when environmental changes did produce the desired behavioral effect, the behavior often did not generalize to other settings.

- Working with children required reinforcement programs at both home and school, and overstressed parents and teachers frequently found the behavior modification techniques too complicated to implement, even though they understood the principles and wished they were organized enough in their own lives to make them work. Positive, sometimes even almost miraculous, results were often followed by setbacks, even in the main environment where the reinforcement system was implemented.

- Contingencies of reinforcement would over time lose effectiveness, causing an increase in the problem behavior, or the individual would substitute a new problem behavior for the old one (referred to by psychoanalysts as *symptom substitution*).
- Although progressive muscle relaxation was useful, the systematic desensitization procedures that used it to decondition anxiety responses to specific stimuli in the environment often proved unwieldy and ineffective. The psychologist Arnold Lazarus (1976), who developed the technique with the psychiatrist Joseph Wolpe in South Africa (Wolpe, 1969), found that a majority of the patients they had treated developed symptom substitution. This ultimately led Lazarus to offer an alternative to behavior therapy that was broadly eclectic.
- Although it felt quite good to be seen as the "expert" according to the medical model, there was a subtle but ultimately quite profound impact on the therapeutic relationship that was disturbing to me. The amount of control and direction applied to the session by the behavior therapist produced a tendency toward either resistance (to authority) or passivity in one's clients.

I had sincerely hoped that I would come to understand the research methods of psychology through my graduate degree in clinical psychology. I wanted to understand not only what behavioral techniques worked in the clinic but also how the evidence for their effectiveness was established. I threw myself wholeheartedly into becoming a "scientist–practitioner." I participated in three community-based research projects evaluating methods to reduce recidivism using psychoeducational methods in persons arrested for DUI, to decrease absenteeism and acting out at a middle school using a (Skinnerian) token system, and to identify the behavioral characteristics of children at high risk of later symptoms of schizophrenia (funded by the National Institute of Mental Health).

Although the process was invaluable in terms of understanding the difference between research as an idealized process and the reality of everyday complications when doing research in the community, it was also disturbing in a manner that paralleled the classroom discussions we were having with regard to research on the lack of effectiveness of psychotherapy. The research protocols all called for very scripted (i.e., "controlled") interactions with the research participants. For studies like these to have internal validity, they must be designed to provide standardized interactions with the research participants both in terms of clinical assessment and treatment. We did not get to know the people as we would have if we were simply providing a clinical service, but instead we got to know them by observing and measuring their behaviors with formal standardized instruments or by providing them with a previously designed clinical intervention that was the same for all members of the treatment group. We were not to interact with the participants in any other ways or in individualized ways.

I worried that the data we generated reflected the responses of human beings when they were treated like faceless numbers by researchers devoid of much of their humanity as a result of following these scripted protocols. The resulting knowledge reflected how human beings behaved when they were not treated as human beings. Considering that about half of a graduate student's time in clinical psychology was devoted to such research, one wondered whether it was time well spent.

MY STORY IV: UNSPOKEN FAMILY AND PROFESSIONAL TENSIONS

I had been practicing and teaching courses related to clinical practice for about 20 years when I came to understand another critical family influence that had affected my career. My father was a pharmacist and had served in the navy in World War II as a pharmacist's mate on an aircraft carrier. His ship was scheduled for the invasion of Japan that was cancelled after the dropping of atomic bombs on Hiroshima and Nagasaki. The sailors on the ship were encouraged to go ashore after the Japanese surrender to view the carnage, and he did. For many years after, he would on occasion scream out in his sleep when dreaming of his wartime experiences. He returned to civilian life to go into business as a part owner of a neighborhood pharmacy. He had been trained in pharmacy in an era when most pharmaceuticals were available without prescription and the trusted local pharmacist was a person who people in the neighborhood went to asking for relief from their various symptoms. Essentially, he was trained to prescribe medication, in many ways on a par with a physician in that regard. Yet he was frustrated that he could not afford to attend medical school and had to settle for a pharmacy degree. Consequently, he freely offered advice to anyone who asked, and his customers usually returned with thanks for his assistance. He was a strong believer in the value of medications that altered mood states and thought nothing of giving his children pills to help them sleep or calm down for an exam. He also freely took them himself and was a stone wall when it came to discussing difficult life experiences such as the war or his childhood. I had a sense that military service in a combat zone was a living nightmare, but only from what was not said.

My mother, however, was a trained social worker who strongly believed in the model of casework in which one tried to understand the social and psychological reasons for a person's behavior and then attempted to talk the situation through to a resolution. If there was a problem in the family, she wanted to try to talk it through as well (except, of course, if it was something she was too frightened to talk about, such as her father's suicide).

The tension in our home because of these competing approaches was palpable, but I never really understood where it originated. In retrospect, it seems now that the fact that my mother turned to me to talk about her concerns, fears, and dark moods when my father was out of the house working 60-hour weeks, or in the home but too exhausted or irritable from work to have much to give, must have upset him. Did my willingness to converse on such topics with her seem like an indictment of his unavailability, inadvertently pointing out his inadequacy, or did it just seem to him an incredible waste of time? I will never know. Regardless, it dawned on me some 40 years later as I was expounding in class one day on the tension in psychology between the medical model in psychiatry and the psychosocial model in clinical psychology that I had been living with that tension my entire life. Little wonder that it was something about which I was passionate, and remain so.

Indeed, for me, the question of whether medications should be the primary treatment for most psychological problems is one of both great social and personal importance. While I was in graduate school, and for the first 10 years after I received my doctorate, I hewed to the mainstream view that relatively mild and moderate psychiatric problems with anxiety, depression, and personality traits such as defiance of authority, shyness, or impulsivity should be dealt with by psychosocial interventions conducted by psychologists, counselors, and social workers. The more severe problems involving psychosis, profound depression, or a complete inability to function in society should be treated by psychiatrists with medication and hospitalization. I did not question that division of labor, nor the pharmaceutical research that supported it, nor the psychological textbooks and journals that published or cited such drug research. There was a kind of peaceful coexistence between psychology and psychiatry in those days. We were not truly brethren in arms, but we were no worse than friendly adversaries, arguing about whether the occasional case was moderate or severe. Generally, I avoided this potential conflict, as I had the one between my social worker mother and pharmacist father.

It was not until the mid-1980s when fluoxetine (Prozac) was introduced that all that began to change, and psychiatry and the pharmaceutical companies began a strategy to redefine all psychological dysfunctions as "biochemical imbalances in the brain" that could be fine-tuned with medications (Kramer, 1993). This research claimed to be based on new evidence that the neurotransmitter serotonin was a bigger culprit in the cause of anxiety and depression than had been thought when the earlier generation of antidepressant medications had been developed. Those medications were presumed to alter both norepinephrine and serotonin levels in the brain. Although they were slow to work and produced many side effects that made some patients discontinue use, many found relief from Prozac, a selective serotonin reuptake inhibitor (SSRI) that often produced a reduction in anxiety that was almost immediate, with minimal immediate unpleasant side effects. It was seen as a miracle drug because it helped mild to moderate symptoms of depression, as well as more serious cases, and patients liked how they felt on the drug much more than on the old-style antidepressants.

However, I was skeptical of such claims on two counts. First, I was seeing that individuals in therapy who were switched to an SSRI antidepressant seemed to quickly lose interest in working on the problems in their relationships that had been the focus of psychotherapy. When I would ask about those interpersonal difficulties, clients would usually respond that nothing had changed in their life, but with the medication it just did not seem to bother them anymore that, for example, their spouse had lost interest in a sexual relationship with them or that their business was heading toward bankruptcy. In other words, they reacted in much the same way people do when abusing drugs. Their life circumstances had not improved; they just seemed oblivious to their problems. In fact, in some instances, clients came into therapy sessions clearly giddy, giggling, and quite intoxicated and reported they had been feeling and acting this way since they started their SSRI. As it turned out, this was another new therapy that was best to receive during its early stages of introduction into the culture. The early claim that 70% of the patients receiving SSRI medications had positive outcomes was exaggerated, and the negative side effects, including significant weight gain and loss of sexual desire, were underestimated (Healy, 2009; Kirsch & Sapirstein, 1998).

In my years at the community mental health center I had not been impressed with the antipsychotic medications in use, which were typically a cocktail of medications for psychosis and depression, with significant side effects. My clients taking them were not able to make much use of the therapeutic relationship. I would later learn that my observations were not unique and that even some psychiatrists had begun to object to the widespread use of high doses of phenothiazine medications (the "antipsychotics") and the greater than reported risk of a disfiguring neurological disorder, tardive dyskinesia, the effects of which could be more socially disabling than psychosis (Cohen, 2010).

The former editor of the prestigious *New England Journal of Medicine*, Professor Marcia Angel of the Harvard School of Public Health, in an unprecedented fashion suggested that an entire generation of scientific findings on psychotropic medications should be discarded as contaminated by the financial interests of the pharmaceutical companies and the psychiatrists whom they employed (Angel, 2005). These companies and their paid psychiatric researchers, she suggested, manipulated the process of conducting randomized clinical trials on antidepressants, antipsychotics, and antianxiety medications through data suppression, selective assignment of patients to treatment or control groups, selective dosing of treatment and control groups, selective use of outcome measures to highlight improvement and hide treatment failures, underreporting of serious side effects, and outright research fraud (Angel, 2005). Prestigious medical school professors were paid large sums of money to have their names inserted into research papers submitted to major prestigious medical and psychiatric journals as lead authors on studies they had neither designed nor executed. This has been generally acknowledged as an accurate critique, and a number of major medical journals (including *The Lancet* and *The New England Journal of Medicine*) have taken steps to insist that authors indicate any financial relationships they have with the companies that manufacture the drugs evaluated in their studies. However, it is unclear how well these new policies are being, or even can be, enforced.

Robert Whitaker's (2005, 2011) investigative journalism gives a clear account of the contemporary history of attempts by the leadership of the American Psychiatric Association to corner the market on the treatment of mental disorders by emphasizing in the diagnostic criteria of mental disorders in the third and fourth editions of the *Diagnostic and Statistical Manual of Mental Disorders* (DSM) those symptoms that improve from drug treatments. In so doing, they contributed to the manipulation of psychiatric research findings and publications by many major pharmaceutical companies to guarantee acceptance of their products. As a result, the number of Americans on antidepressant and antipsychotic medications has skyrocketed, as have the profits of these companies.

The discipline of abnormal psychology is truly as fascinating as most of us expected it to be when we took our first course. Yet, it is currently a field of study in which research on the primary treatment approach (psychoactive medications) is seriously discredited and in which its primary diagnostic system (the *DSM–5*; American Psychiatric Association, 2013) has been rejected by not only over 40,000 psychologists and mental health professionals worldwide (see http://dsm5-reform.com/the-coalition/) but also by the head of research at the National Institute of Mental Health, the U.S. government's primary research center on psychological disorders, Dr. Thomas Insell, who described the *DSM* as scientifically invalid (Horgan, 2013). This is obviously a field undergoing massive upheaval. How does one learn in the face of such confusion?

A PRAGMATIC APPROACH TO ABNORMAL PSYCHOLOGY

In the face of theoretical confusion, professional rivalries, and debates over what constitutes adequate validation of treatment techniques, a return to the philosophy of pragmatism that guided America's first academic psychologist, William James (1907/1975), is an excellent place to start. Pragmatism tells us to put the most trust in the concepts and theories that lead to positive practical outcomes in the real world, as judged by the people most directly affected by those ideas. We are to regard as valid those concepts and theories that produce a tangible difference in our everyday world (Fishman, 1999). Pragmatism is a philosophical approach that favors the judgments of everyday people, not the societal experts. It is much like the democratic approach to choosing a leader or laws to govern a people. Democracy assumes that the people most affected by a leader or laws ought to make these choices, not the people who are at a distance and cannot observe the consequences of the choice. Pragmatism asserts that we find the truth by looking at the impact that ideas and theories have on our everyday existence.

By the same token, the people most affected by our theories of abnormal psychology and clinical practice are the consumers and direct service providers, and they should be considered the best judges of what is good practice. Neither democratic governments nor pragmatic approaches to professional and practical knowledge are perfect methods of choosing who or what to believe; it is only that all other alternatives are worse.

The ideas (theories) that lead us to act in ways that further our practical goals in the world are what we should hold as true. Those ideas resulting in undermining our goals are to be rejected as false. This approach draws our attention to two critical concepts: (a) the practical and (b) goals. Our *goals* are those states of affairs in the world we prefer, value, and think are good for us. The *practical* is about the day-to-day business of living our lives. The beauty of this theory is that no one needs an electron microscope, a $5 million research grant, or supercomputer to tell whether a theory of psychotherapy, or a therapy based on such a theory, is actually making a practical difference in one's ability to accomplish one's own goals. It may take some self-awareness, honesty, careful thought, feedback from significant others, and time, but in the end we are not dependent on any multinational research team, corporation, professional organization, or government agency to answer the question, Is what I am doing working? Am I closer to reaching my goals in how I wish to live my life now than I was before I tried this new approach? Pragmatism encourages the pursuit of local knowledge first and the building of broader generalizations based on actual experience in different locales, rather than on assertions of universal principles of clinical practice (Fishman, 1999).

The concept of "what works" is clearly value-laden, just as *mental health* and *illness* are more implicitly value-laden terms (Fowers, 2005; Miller, 1983, 2004; Tjeltveit, 1999). Pragmatism calls on us to openly acknowledge how moral and ethical values play a part in what we consider "good" or "best practices" to be. A great deal of human suffering that has resulted from dangerous mental health treatments (e.g., frontal lobotomy, eugenic sterilizations, electroconvulsive therapy, antipsychotic medications, aversive conditioning of autistic children) might have been avoided if the technicians, psychologists, and psychiatrists administering these treatments had considered what they were doing within the context of the basic moral framework of humanity, rather than as a scientific treatment (R. Whitaker, 2005).

A pragmatic approach to building a knowledge base in clinical and abnormal psychology is similar to Schön's (1987) generalized model of professional knowledge acquisition that he named "reflective practice," and its origins lie not only in pragmatists of the early 20th century such as William James and John Dewey (Menand, 2001) but also extend back at least 2,400 years to the *Ethics* of Aristotle (McKeon, 1941), who spoke of the difference between theoretical knowledge and *practical wisdom*—knowing what to do and how to do it to accomplish a real-world task or solve a real-world problem. We must not only know how to do things but also have moral values that guide us in knowing whether to do what we know how to do.

Clinical decision making in all of the health professions is a form of practical wisdom (Toulmin, 2003). It requires cognitive information about the nature of a problem, technical skill in how to intervene in a helpful manner, and moral values to guide us in what outcomes of treatment are truly helpful as opposed to expedient or simply profitable to the practitioner. If any of these three components are missing, then practical action fails to be practical wisdom and fails the standard of a pragmatic intervention. Whatever else such a clinical intervention might be—theoretically grounded, spiritually inspired, or empirically validated—it fails to be pragmatic.

A pragmatic approach depends heavily on a community of practitioners sharing their experiences, building a common knowledge base, and refining their theories and practices through reflection on the outcomes of their efforts. This work is best documented through case study research (Fishman, 1999, 2013). This will come as quite a shock to those who have taken even an introductory research methods course in psychology and who have learned that case studies are permitted in the early stages of exploring an area of research (the context of discovery) but not in the later stages where causal scientific claims are being tested (the context of justification). Fishman (1999, 2013) has effectively refuted that argument, though his position is often ignored in the scientific journals. Much of this argument pivots on the usefulness of thinking of human actions as caused in the same sense that chemical or physical reactions are caused. Fishman argued that all human actions in the real world are context-dependent and influenced by multiple, often nonreplicable factors. Consequently, careful comprehensive case studies, often including quantitative measures, are preferable to using methods of empirical validation with control groups and rigid predesigned methods.

In this volume, I follow in the pragmatic tradition of James and Fishman and present abnormal psychology through the knowledge base of clinical practice (clinical case studies) supplemented by empirical survey research related to epidemiology and the functioning of the mental health system, as well as some literature reviews on etiological factors and treatment outcomes.

THE CASE OF PETER: A PRESSURED AND TWISTED BRAIN?

How we think about mental illness and treatment makes an enormous difference in outcome, but unless one has extensive experience in clinical work or personal experience as a consumer, it is hard to see how theories could make that much difference. To illustrate this, the case of Peter is presented. First, the case is described as it would be traditionally in a medical or psychiatric setting leading to a diagnosis and treatment plan. In the retelling I describe Peter as he emerged as a person in psychotherapy. To protect confidentiality, no real names are used and any details of the case that might reasonably be thought to lead to a reader discovering "Peter's" identity have been altered in such a way as to preserve the psychological and social integrity of the case.

Peter in Psychiatric Treatment

Peter is a 21-year-old Caucasian male who dropped out of college after one semester at age 18 years. He recently returned home after 3 years living and working in Texas, where he held positions of increasing responsibility in an environmental lab. He has been living with his parents for 9 months, becoming increasingly reclusive and noncommunicative. He had been fired from several low-paying jobs since his return to the area. His mother brought him to the interview because she is worried about the way he has become withdrawn and noncommunicative. Peter rarely leaves his bedroom, sleeps all day, and spends evenings and nights either watching television or surfing the Internet. He rarely interacts or talks with anyone in the household or with visitors to the house, even relatives he has known his whole life. He does minimal chores when asked.

Several months ago his mother took him to a psychiatrist who diagnosed him with bipolar disorder and placed him on medications usually used to treat depression and thought disorder (psychosis). These included lithium (lithium carbonate, 1,500 mg/day) and olanzapine (5 mg/day). The psychiatrist also referred him to work with a counselor in his office on a weekly basis. Peter discontinued both after a few months. He said the medication slowed his racing thoughts, but he did not "feel like himself" on the drugs and preferred a more natural approach. He is asking for an evaluation as to whether he should resume the medication.

In the first interview, he reported these events and experiences in a halting and disjointed manner and was difficult to follow. He repeatedly checked with the interviewer to see what the interviewer was thinking and seemed wary and defensive, as if expecting to be deemed odd or strange. His speech was peppered with neologisms, and his sentences trailed off into incomplete thoughts. When prompted, he would finish a thought that he had left hanging. He complained that his head seemed pressured and his brain strained or twisted in his skull. He was unable to explain what this meant exactly or what other physical symptoms in his head or neck were associated with this brain state.

Peter reported no motivation to return to the world of work, though he expressed awareness that this was not the way a 21-year-old person should be living. In discussing his life in Texas the year before returning east, he indicated that he had been feeling unusually good during that period. He deeply regrets now that he did not stay. He had been eating healthfully, exercising a good deal in preparation for participation in a half-marathon, and generally thriving. This is the period that his previous psychiatrist saw as indication of a manic prologue to his current depression. Peter described himself as having gone overboard in trying to lose weight and get into shape; he did not know how to sustain this, so he left for home.

When asked the source of his problems, he attributes much of his troubles to his astrological sign or to his inborn introverted personality. Peter's previous psychiatrist told him he had a chemical imbalance in his brain that he will have to learn to live with the rest of his life and that medications would help control the effects of the imbalance.

Peter reports that he has two siblings, a brother 2 years older and a sister 5 years younger. They are both doing well in school and socially. He believes he is the only sibling "not making it." His parents have been married for 30 years and are both hard-working members of the business community who are presently quite successful, though there have been some tough financial times in the past. They have health insurance that covers his treatment. There is no known psychiatric history in the family, though he does not know much about his mother's extended family and describes them as rather "sketchy."

Given Peter's recent history, the psychiatrist reiterated the message he had received from his previous psychiatrist and strongly urged Peter to go back on medication to treat his biochemical imbalance. He pointed out that the side effects he had experienced were common and that they could try a new atypical antipsychotic medication that tended to have fewer side effects than his previous one. Because he had not benefitted from counseling, the psychiatrist suggested that he need not resume that aspect of his treatment so long as he was taking his medications.

Peter in Psychotherapy

My first contact with Peter was over the telephone in a call initiated by his mother, Kathy. She had called to ask for an appointment for Peter, briefly describing him as needing help because he had taken himself off his medication for bipolar disorder and was becoming a recluse, sleeping in his bedroom all day and staying up all night watching television or browsing the Internet. I was struck by the way she talked about him as though he were a young adolescent, despite the fact that he was 21 years of age. One indication of this was the fact that she was prepared to end our telephone discussion without having him talk with me. I have a general policy that I will not make an appointment for someone to come for an initial visit for psychotherapy unless I have a preliminary phone discussion with the person in question, so I asked to speak with Peter, and though he was entirely passive in our discussion of what his mother said, he did not resist the idea of making an appointment, saying, "I guess I have nothing to lose." Peter was faithful in keeping his appointments, though he did on occasion oversleep and arrive late. During the initial sessions he spoke haltingly, often in incomplete sentences, occasionally creating neologisms by combining two words with related meanings into one. His clearest and most lengthy comments were those expressing a great deal of self-loathing for messing up his life, especially about leaving Texas to return to the East.

He could not explain why he had so impulsively left a good job in a city he enjoyed living in to come back without a job or a plan to get one. He wondered whether the psychiatrist who had prescribed the mood stabilizer and antipsychotic medication might have been incorrect to interpret Peter's decision to leave as a sign of mania. Most every session in the first few months ended with a question of whether I thought he would be better off on medication. I took this to mean he wondered whether we were wasting our time, and I reassured him that I thought we were on the right path and that psychotherapy was a slow and at times painful process. I assured him that if he wished to return to the psychiatrist for medication I would support that decision, though it was not something I would have initiated. I further explained that when we make impulsive decisions—like the one he made to leave Texas—there usually is a reason, even if it is not known at the time. By carefully reviewing in therapy the weeks and months preceding his departure, I assured him it was likely we would find out what he was thinking and feeling that led to that decision.

As we proceeded, Peter revealed that he found his mother both overinvolved and controlling and at other times quite distant and emotionally needy. His father, with whom he identified, was described as "like me, introverted and noncommunicative." Dad worked long days, coming home for meals, but rarely conversing with anyone while home. His brother was 2 years older than Peter and led a charmed existence as prince of the family, successful in everything he touched, except relationships with women. His younger sister, 5 years younger than Peter, was the family princess. She was in high school and partying all the time with college boys who were living life in the fast lane. Peter did not use the terms *prince* and *princess* in describing his siblings, but everything he said pointed to those characterizations and what must have been his anger as the lost child in the middle.

Peter struggled in school from the second grade onward, except for in sports, in which he was a great success, though always in his brother's shadow. By eighth grade he was drinking with his brother's friends, and he reported that high school was a blur of alcohol and pot punctuated by athletic success. His teachers seemed to have passed him to keep him playing athletics, despite the fact that he was stoned for many classes and rarely did more than the bare minimum of homework. He went to a college renowned for its athletics, but withdrew after one semester, which he again spent inebriated.

None of these features of his life history were stated directly, and it often took several sessions for bits and pieces of each storyline to emerge. I listened, encouraged self-exploration, and offered mildly interpretive summaries of what I heard ("Seems like your brother and sister can do no wrong in your parents' eyes—that would have upset me growing up as their brother."). He felt disloyal to his family when he said anything negative about anyone but himself. Over the succeeding 6 months the following family context for Peter's "bipolar disorder" emerged.

- Throughout his childhood there had been periods of financial feast and famine as his parents' various investments succeeded wildly or failed miserably.
- In either instance, neither parent was in the house on weekdays before 7:00 p.m. and the children were cared for by a succession of sitters, older cousins, and so forth. When they did arrive home, Mom was irritable and explosive and Dad was withdrawn and uninvolved.

- A few months before he left Texas he had spent time with his parents on a vacation and had been convinced they were headed for a divorce, though they never discussed this with him or the other members of the family.
- His mother had over the phone belittled his career plans in Texas and informed him that if his sister did not straighten out she would be sent to the state institution for delinquent adolescents.
- He had felt guilty being happy in Texas when everyone back home seemed so miserable. He thought he had no right to be happy if they were not.
- He thought now that he had figured out how to be a happy and successful person, he could return to his family and teach them how to live healthy and happy lives, especially his younger sister, who he feared was headed for disaster.
- He was a great admirer of the Dalai Lama and other political activists for their efforts toward social justice and peace, and he felt his family would not approve of such political ideas.

Peter had been taught an intense form of family loyalty in which one was never permitted to question family values or the actions of one's elders, no matter how harmful those actions were to the children. Everyone was supposed to have the same opinions, feelings, and lifestyle or risk being written off as not worthy of membership in the family. Although he seemed to be a lost soul, hiding out from the world in his bedroom, he actually knew what he liked, what kind of life was fulfilling for him, and what made him a happy person. He was trapped in his belief that he only deserved to live that life if his family would join him, and they would have no part of it. But he had never told them why he had really come home or how he felt about their cavalier rejection of his suggestions for a healthier and happier lifestyle. Faced with ostracism and rejection and feeling to blame for his own errors in judgment, he withdrew from the family.

Not unlike his spiritual and political heroes, he was now imprisoned in an act of resistance to the power politics of his family. I shared this interpretation with him in a number of forms, complimenting him on his generosity of spirit, courage in tackling the unspoken issues in the family, perceptiveness, and so forth. I encouraged him to take ownership of his future and not to leave it in the hands of the rest of the family to decide. We began talking about his need to get a job so that he could move out of the house and be on his own again.

As with all discussions with Peter since the first phone call, he tackled new challenges by a mixture of avoidance and then decisive action. He began to work for his mother around the house doing odd jobs and was beginning to check the classified section of the local paper for a different job when he seemed to hit a wall. For several weeks we were just stuck, and then toward the end of one of these lackluster sessions, Peter commented:

> I guess I had better tell you something I promised my brother that I would. I don't know how to say this except just to say it—my father asked my mother for a divorce yesterday, and the poor woman is completely devastated.

This was the clearest and most emotionally open statement he had made about his family situation in the 9 months I had worked with him. He was fully present for the final 15 minutes of the session. His thinking and communication were sharp and quick. He was able to be angry without feeling shame or reticence.

Over the next 6 months, there was a cascade of revelations about the psychological family context in which Peter's problems were imbedded. These were issues that Peter had known about but had never considered relevant to his own difficulties functioning in the world. His father seemed oblivious to the impact his decision to leave was having on the rest of the family, and his mother began drinking heavily alone in her bedroom at night (as she had done periodically in the past). His older brother competed openly with Peter to be Mom's savior and belittled and humiliated Peter whenever Peter threatened his preeminence as prince of the family. His younger sister ended up in drug rehabilitation after nearly losing her life. Other revelations of equally meaningful family secrets cannot be revealed without jeopardizing confidentiality.

As each aspect of the family's pain and conflict emerged, Peter grew stronger and more independent. He found a job in the community and then went back to college, first part-time and then full-time, earning excellent grades. Two years into the therapy he decided to transfer to an out-of-state university, and our work together ended. There was still work to be done, but Peter had emerged from his period of withdrawal and hopelessness and was making a life for himself more independent of his family's conception of who he had to be.

Reflections on Peter's Case

The section of the case study entitled "Peter in Psychiatric Treatment" is based on Peter's report of his prior contacts with a psychiatrist and supplemented by my own experience working with the psychiatrists who practice in my locale and how they tend to discuss their treatment. The description is largely in terms of an *extraspective* account—what Peter said and did during the interview. The theory of the case is physiological or biomedical, presenting Peter with a biological account of why it feels to him that his brain is broken. There is a biochemical imbalance in his brain that is causing his problems, and the medication he will be given will directly alter the biochemicals in his brain, presumably to rebalance them. Peter's brain is described by him and to him in terms that are objectified: "This is what your brain is doing," not "This is what you are doing." Peter's life history to the extent that it is reported (depending on the psychiatrist, the interview would have been between 30 and 40 minutes) is used to provide evidence that his behavior fits a pattern of a diagnosis of bipolar disorder. Because he fits that pattern and that pattern is presumed to be due to a genetic or biochemical process in the brain that is no longer normal (imbalanced), then the treatment with brain altering medications is seen as logical and appropriate. The psychiatrist presents to Peter an explanation of his problem behaviors (impulsive decision making, social withdrawal, incoherent communications) as determined by his brain state and not as something he can control or alter without medication. He is a passive victim in his own life story, and the psychiatrist is a heroic figure who can act logically and rationally to put Peter's life in order.

In the account of the psychotherapy I actually did with Peter (altered only to preserve confidentiality), I approach Peter with the benefit of considerable clinical experience. I had settled on a style of practice that was a combination of humanistic values emphasizing the encouragement of autonomy and personal freedom, a psychodynamic understanding of the importance of early childhood influences that may be unconscious, and the importance of understanding a client's family system. I had learned that it was imperative to provide my clients with both the support they needed to become the person they wanted to be and with sufficient self-understanding so that clients would begin to make sense to themselves and understand why they engaged in the self-defeating actions that sabotaged their own growth. For that understanding I had come to rely on interpersonal and object relations theory as captured in the works of Fromm-Reichmann (1950), Malan (1995), and Karon and VandenBos (1981).

I was generally skeptical of the benefit of psychotropic medications except in circumstances in which no other psychotherapy had been found to be helpful, or in emergencies to return a person's sleep cycle to some semblance of normality or calm an extremely agitated individual. In these emergency situations I expected that medication would not be needed for more than a week or two once the effect of psychotherapy was evident. At the time I worked with Peter there was a great deal of experimental psychopharmacological research supporting the use of medications with bipolar disorder accompanied by thought disorder as the treatment of choice, but for the reasons described earlier, I was not all that convinced of the validity of that research (Kaplan & Sadock, 1989).

I saw Peter as a 21-year-old young man who had been in intense psychological pain and suffering for a year or more and whose pain was an exacerbation of an internal sense of frustration and desperation that he felt for most of his life. He was raised by parents who themselves had difficult lives, who struggled to find financial stability, and whose personal relationship was greatly strained. He was not the only child of this marriage in trouble, but the only one they were willing to acknowledge to the rest of the world as in trouble. Peter had never really participated in his own education, having had some mild learning difficulties in the elementary grades and having engaged in extensive substance abuse from middle school on. He had many good qualities—compassion for others in the family, a sense of loyalty to his parents, an insightful understanding of other people's motivations—that he kept well hidden. He knew he was not living anywhere near his potential, and I sensed in speaking with him even the first hour that he had a vast amount of untapped potential as a human being. I believe he felt my awareness of who he might become and was willing to trust me to help him bring out his inner self. He had submerged his identity his entire life to keep his older brother from being threatened and to keep his parents from feeling burdened by a second child. He resisted asserting his own agency in the world and taking responsibility for himself rather than the other people he cared about who might be threatened by his taking up more of the oxygen in the house. It was a slow and at times frustrating process for both of us but more than worth the effort in the end.

THE WAY FORWARD

In discussing the various aspects of abnormal psychology in the chapters to follow, I pay close attention to how the pragmatic aspects of the psychodynamic, humanistic–existential, and family systems approaches can inform a viable alternative to the dominant bio–cognitive–behavioral view of psychopathology. In focusing on literatures that can offer both short-term symptom relief as well as the possibility of life-transforming psychological treatment, I do not intend to denigrate or disparage bio–behavioral treatments that offer relatively brief contact with providers and relatively quick symptom relief, although they are, generally speaking, less concerned with life-transforming effectiveness.

2

THE SOCIAL, POLITICAL, HISTORICAL, AND PHILOSOPHICAL CONTEXT

My story in Chapter 1 was not just about me and my attempts to survive and make a life for myself but also about three generations of a family of immigrants to the United States trying to survive and thrive in a new country; it was also about several generations of a disparate group of academic philosophers, physiologists, theologians, physicians, pastors, and educators fashioning the new institutions in American society—the academic discipline of psychology and the new profession of applied and clinical psychology. These three stories, as complicated as they may be, are also a part of a much larger story of the history of the late 19th, 20th, and early 21st centuries in Europe and North America. These were years of cataclysmic changes, including two World Wars, the mass murder of tens of millions of civilians in Nazi Germany and Stalinist Russia, and the first use of nuclear weapons by the United States on civilian populations in Japan at Hiroshima and Nagasaki. In the post–World War II period, the United States became the wealthiest nation on earth, fueled by

http://dx.doi.org/10.1037/14693-002
Not So Abnormal Psychology: A Pragmatic View of Mental Illness, by R. B. Miller
Copyright © 2015 by the American Psychological Association. All rights reserved.

a consumer economy, technological change, and globalization of business and culture. In this chapter, I examine the historical, philosophical, political, and economic context in which abnormal psychology developed into a subdiscipline of psychology.

THREE HISTORICAL THEMES: PUNISHMENT, HEALING, AND GLORIFICATION

In writing about the history of psychiatry and psychoanalysis, Ellenberger (1974) looked at the anthropological evidence for how the behaviors we label as *mental illness* have been regarded in non-Western, preindustrialized societies. He found evidence of three overlapping but also distinct cultural responses. The first is to regard the behavior as a violation of acceptable behavior, deserving of punishment. Here we see the individual who is bizarre or dangerous being confined, bound, or beaten to secure submission to the social norms of the group. We also see the Elizabethan Poor Laws of 1601 sending the unemployed who were incapable of working (including those who were "mad") to prisons with petty thieves, paupers, and debtors, where they often perished because of miserable living conditions (Day, 2008).

In the second cultural response, the disturbed individual is seen as ill and in need of healing. The healing may be performed by a lay healer administering herbs or other forms of physical care or by a priestly healer who attempts to drive away the evil spirits. Both these traditions are easily recognizable today. The lay healers have become the naturopaths, psychiatrists (and other physicians), herbalists, and chiropractors of today. The priestly healers have become the subset of religious leaders who do pastoral counseling, counselors and psychotherapists, and occult practitioners (e.g., astrologers, fortune-tellers).

Finally, there is the cultural response of acceptance and glorification, where extreme psychological pain and suffering is respected as providing an opportunity for growth and insight and appreciating more what we have after experiencing a loss or disappointment. According to this view, even hallucinations or delusions are seen as evidence of the possibility of deep personal transformation, sometimes even the possibility of direct communication with the gods. Such a person is in a position to act as an intermediary between the social group and the deity. We see this today in some mainstream religious groups that view claims by a preacher or church member to have spoken directly to the Almighty as proof of their sacred calling, rather than as auditory hallucinations. The experience is seen as authentic—having great meaning and significance—and the question of whether it is "real" or "true" is not even raised.

Ellenberger's (1974) analysis is most useful today as we examine contemporary forms of treatment to see why such treatments might blur into attempts at social control that may rely quite forcefully on the use of physical isolation (such as time-out rooms), the use of punishments as consequences in behavioral management programs at home and school, or the use of forced invasive medical procedures that control behavior (e.g., sterilization; involuntary electroconvulsive therapy; modern day lobotomies, referred to as *cingulotomies*). Involuntary treatment is experienced by patients as a loss of personal freedom and dignity comparable in many ways to incarceration for a crime. Psychiatrists and other mental health workers often reject this claim by patient advocacy groups as unfair or unrealistic, suggesting it is further evidence of psychotic thought processes at work. My view is different: If it looks like punishment, feels like punishment, and smells like punishment, it probably is punishment.

SOCIAL CONTROL OR INDIVIDUAL TREATMENT

As a newly minted PhD in clinical psychology I took a job in one of the recently created community mental health centers resulting from President Kennedy's landmark mental health policy legislative program that was voted into law in 1963 (Joint Commission on Mental Illness and Health, 1961). The goal of this program was to reduce the need for state mental hospitals by treating people in the community first, aiming to prevent psychological problems from requiring hospitalization. To accomplish this goal, these services had to be made affordable to those at low- and middle-income levels who could not afford private psychiatric or psychotherapeutic care.

I had done one of my internship experiences at the mental health center and was hired as a staff psychologist. I was fortunate to be surrounded by a diverse multidisciplinary group of professionals with training and degrees from psychiatry, social work, psychology, mental health counseling, psychiatric nursing, and rehabilitation counseling. In many ways our training overlapped, but in other ways it did not. Some of us were committed to family systems therapy where the whole family was "the patient," others were committed to Freudian psychoanalysis, humanistic (Rogerian) psychology, supportive psychotherapy that focused on daily problem solving to build self-esteem and adaptive skills, and behavior modification/therapy. It was a wonderful, intellectually stimulating environment in which everyone wanted to learn from one another, and no one claimed to have all of the answers for the challenging clients we were responsible for helping. In retrospect, that was probably the most critical element because, in fact, no one had all the answers and no one pretended they did. Consequently, we all just kept learning and growing in our abilities to do good therapy. It was helpful to see multiple perspectives being applied to actual cases and to see that many different approaches are needed when dealing with complex human problems in the diverse individuals encountered in the real world of clinical practice.

It was in the context of these more free and open dialogues about clinical treatment that I began to be more unsettled by the fundamental tension that existed in the role of a clinical psychologist or other mental health professional in the mental health system. On the one hand, as the "experts" on abnormal behavior, we were expected to find a way to predict and control the behavior of our clients. On the other hand, as psychotherapists, we sought to strengthen our clients' ability to deal with reality in a collaborative manner and without threatening them with dire consequences for exhibiting their symptoms. Yet, at staff meetings we would periodically hear that several of our outpatient clients were creating a nuisance downtown, talking to themselves or the hallucinatory voices they were hearing in a manner that was frightening to passersby. The chief of police called to warn the director of the agency to take care of this problem if he wanted the police department's support for our agency's budget at the next United Way board meeting. (If clients were disturbing the peace or becoming violent, we believed that was for the police to handle; we did not think it was the police's place to set the agenda for our therapeutic sessions.) We were instructed by our clinical psychologist supervisor to do everything we could to assert control over these individuals' behavior in public.

This was an eye-opening experience for me. Here we were implementing a radical new national policy on mental health where our goal was to prevent voluntary and involuntary hospitalizations at the state hospital, and the director of this new program was ordering us to give priority to making sure our clients maintained public decorum—whether or not it interfered with building the trust needed for a therapeutic relationship that might truly rectify the problem (i.e., psychosis).

Faced with such a dilemma, I began to question exactly what sort of a profession I had joined. Over the years, that has grown into a larger question about the social role of the other professions and institutions I worked with and in and the role of mental health treatment and "mental illness" in our society, economy, and political institutions. I was well familiar from my days as a student of political philosophy with the age-old question of the trade-off between individual liberty and social order. That discussion soon took on a new meaning for those of us in psychology after B. F. Skinner's (1971) book *Beyond Freedom and Dignity* became a *New York Times* bestseller.

Skinner had invited all educated readers to rethink the role of psychological theory in American society. He maintained that behavioral psychology had proven that human beings as biological organisms have no real free will and are entirely the product of biological forces and environmental conditioning. He further proclaimed that Western democratic ideals of respecting individual freedom and human dignity are based on the illusion of free will, a religious idea that he maintained had been disproven by behavioral psychology. From this, Skinner concluded that we should give the government the authority and power to alter the destructive behavior of individuals by using the reinforcements under its control (the tax code and government benefits) to alter the unhealthy behaviors of its citizens, whether they liked it or not. This was, he claimed, the only way to solve intractable problems such as poverty and environmental pollution. Few students in psychology courses today are exposed to this aspect of Skinner's contribution to experimental psychology, but it is a critical one. There is a slippery slope between a science of behavior that is geared to the prediction and control of behavior to generate the "laws of behavior" and a science of behavior that leads to laws to control the behavior of the citizens of a democracy in ways that reduce a sense of personal individual freedom and dignity.

Granted, if Skinner's argument is correct, that is not much of a loss because our belief that we have personal freedom and a sense of dignity is illusory. Skinner was commendably consistent and followed his view of the science of behavior through to its logical conclusion. He understood philosophy and knew how to fashion a powerful argument. Once one denies the reality and importance of human feelings, emotions, perspectives, and judgments and instead only focuses on publicly observable behaviors and physiological responses, one eventually must reject the reality of human freedom and human dignity and focus instead exclusively on human adaptability and functionality. Skinner also illuminated in an extraordinarily clear fashion something that is usually ignored in the education of psychology students: the close link between psychological theory and practical moral and political philosophies, ideologies, and agendas.

It has always been a central goal of American academic psychology to be of use in smoothing out the rough edges in various social institutions (James, 1892/1983), schools, hospitals, prisons, and so forth. Theories of human behavior and developmental, personality, social, abnormal, and clinical psychology have implicitly sought to have a major impact on not only how we live our lives but also how we think we should live our lives. Unfortunately, this social and political agenda is rarely articulated in the manner in which Skinner did in *Beyond Freedom and Dignity*. In fact, it is often denied, and the "social goods" that are promoted and encouraged by psychological theory and practice are presented as objective facts rather than social values (see R. B. Miller, 2004; Tjeltveit, 1999). We are taught not that human freedom should be limited by behavioral control from above for the public good but that there is no such thing as genuine freedom anyway, and so psychology is not siding with authoritarian government or corporate control, it is just doing the necessary social engineering required to preserve the common good.

Carl Rogers (Evans, 1975) openly objected to Skinner's arguments on social control in a series of debates before psychological conferences. Beginning from the *intraspective* (subjective experience) orientation, Rogers argued that we must conclude that there is an undeniable (though not unlimited) human freedom to choose one's own actions and beliefs. Skinner, starting from the *extraspective* (observable behavior) orientation, argued that we must conclude that our actions are determined by forces beyond our control. This was what the great Enlightenment philosopher Kant (1724–1804) had described as an *antinomy of reason*: two statements that start from valid assumptions, reach logical conclusions, and are both therefore true, but that contradict one another. Kant's (1781/1929) view was that the human condition requires us to accept paradoxes, and this was one of them: We are, in a way central to our being, free to choose and create the direction of our life, and in a way central to our being, determined and controlled by the physical and social forces around us over which we have no control.

Skinner was at least honest and forthright in his applied psychology—he thought we needed to control the behavior of the masses to reduce poverty, crime, and other social ills, and he was not afraid to acknowledge that he was indeed simply trying to control what other human beings wanted to do that he thought was unwise. For Skinner, punishment was punishment (an attempt to suppress a behavior), and social control was social control.

Avenues to Healing: Illness, Disease, and Sickness

The psychiatrist and medical anthropologist Arthur Kleinman (1988) made a set of distinctions in his cross-cultural work that helps to illuminate the debate that Szasz (1960/1984) started as to whether mental illness or disorder is a disease of the nervous system. Kleinman distinguished *illness*, *disease*, and *sickness*, and he did so in a manner that paid particular attention to the social context of suffering. *Illness* is "the innately human experience of symptoms and suffering" (p. 3). It is the commonsense understanding that an individual and her or his family members (and larger culture) have about symptoms and disability, how to think about them, live with them, and what is to be done in response to the problem. The experience of illness is "entirely shaped" by the culture in which we live, though there are local variations in the overall understanding. This is contrasted with what Kleinman termed *disease*. Illnesses are transformed into diseases by practitioners who see the patient's illness through the theoretical lens that was provided to them through their own training. This theory "reconfigures" the illness into a "narrow technical issue" for which they have a technical solution. Even when patients feel their illness is a punishment for their sins, or that they have been inflicted by evil spirits, the Western physician nevertheless focuses on physical symptoms and medical interventions such as surgery or medication without addressing the life circumstances that have contributed to the development of guilt or the necessity of punishment.

Although *disease* is a narrower term than *illness*, Kleinman reserved the term *sickness* for a phenomenon that is much broader than illness—namely, those situations in which social groups or broad cross sections of the population develop common symptoms in response to "macro social forces." Here the patients themselves or their families may identify the onset of some kind of disorder with circumstances of political repression, economic hardship, or "other social conditions that create human misery" (p. 6).

Kleinman used a study of patient narratives (case studies) to demonstrate that, particularly in the case of chronic illnesses, the biomedical model systematically prevents a practitioner from taking seriously the patient's experience of suffering and the interpersonal and social precipitants and consequences of that suffering. He carefully documented what most of us know from our own experience as patients of biomedically trained physicians, that at times the patient's illness may be aggravated by successful, technically correct treatment of their specific diseases. The result is more, not less, human pain, suffering, and misery.

Kleinman's analysis helps us to understand how the language of emotional pain and suffering has all but vanished from the landscape of abnormal and clinical psychology (and other mental health disciplines). As we have adopted the biological model in academic psychology through physiological psychology, behavioral genetics, and neuroscience, and the medical model in professional psychology through the adherence to the *Diagnostic and Statistical Manual of Mental Disorders* (5th ed.; *DSM–5*; American Psychiatric Association, 2013), increased use of psychotropic medications, and empirically validated treatments, we have systematically excluded the consideration of client/patient suffering. The *DSM–5* talks of distress, disturbance, disorder, suicidal and homicidal ideas, and a whole catalogue of symptoms that indicate that a person is indeed suffering, but not the suffering itself. Do we suffer from mental disorders as *DSM–5* proclaims, or has our suffering come to be defined as mental disorders and colonized by the mental health professions as their special province of expertise? The patient's suffering is redefined or seen as equivalent to "nothing but" the symptoms and diagnoses of *DSM–5*. We psychologists have emulated psychiatry so well that we have all too often similarly succeeded in abandoning our clients to their suffering.

Robinson (1995) noted in his exhaustive intellectual history of psychological theories and conjoining research programs that since the Ancient Greeks, the preference for explanations of the mind that reduce the mind to a physical or material substance coincides with civilizations that are experiencing great wealth and prosperity, whereas theories in which the mind or subjectivity is seen as having existence in its own right tend to be in ascendance in civilizations that have experienced decline and devastation.

Psychological Suffering

In the analysis presented in the last section, the everyday sense of the term *suffering* has been taken for granted. Given the powerful implications of Kleinman's analysis, it makes sense to follow Goldfried (1995) and attempt to use the common, everyday, pretheoretical language as a means of bridging the divide in abnormal psychology between the scientists and practitioners. The term *suffering* is defined in the *Oxford English Dictionary* (Suffer, 2014) as "the bearing or undergoing of pain, distress, or tribulation." If we go further and look at the meaning of the verb *to suffer*, we find further support for a social, even moral, understanding of suffering. To suffer means (a) to undergo or endure "something painful, distressing, or injurious . . . inflicted or imposed upon one; to submit with pain, distress, or grief" or (b) "to go or pass through, be subjected to, undergo, experience . . . something evil or painful." The examples given of experiences that one may suffer include "pain, death, punishment, judgment; hardship, disaster; grief, sorrow, care . . . wrong, injury, loss, shame, disgrace."

We see immediately that the sense of physical pain, harm, or death is the first or most common meaning but that it is quickly followed by reference to emotional pain, loss, difficult experiences, and the pain of having been injured or injuring others in interpersonal relationships. This is important to note because in the biomedical model the patient's suffering is interpreted entirely as physical pain, which is then treated in terms of its physiological components or cause, and so the meaning of suffering is reduced from a multidimensional to a one-dimensional construct. Unless the concept of pain includes the emotional pain of guilt, shame, disgrace, jealousy, vengeance, humiliation, betrayal, abandonment, terror, and insecurity generated in interpersonal and social relationships, it is a great linguistic and personal disservice to patients to treat their suffering as simply the physical sensations and conditions of the body.

Kleinman's analysis is consistent with long traditions within philosophy, humanistic psychology, and sociocultural psychiatry that consider the problem of human suffering as a moral problem (see R. B. Miller, 2004, for further discussion). Psychological suffering occurs in the context of what human beings do to one another, whether in our relationships we are caring and compassionate or cruel and dismissive, honest and forthright or devious and manipulative, honor our commitments and promises or betray others trust. In short, psychological suffering is about whether in search of the good life for ourselves we are good to one another.

Epidemiology of Psychological Suffering

Our contemporary, biomedical disease model of psychological suffering is embodied in *DSM–5*. The diagnostic categories of the previous editions of the *DSM* have been used in most all research in psychiatry, clinical psychology, and related mental health disciplines for over 60 years. Though there is some indication this may be changing (see the *International Classification of Diseases* discussion in Chapter 3), for now any attempt to discuss the extent of the pervasiveness of the psychological problems to be covered in the study of abnormal psychology must begin (though not end) with research using these categories.

It is often said that the goal of a good scientific theory is to "carve nature at its joints." When this is accomplished one has a better chance of generating a powerful theory that permits clear operational definitions, precise measurements, powerful predictions, and new discoveries. Such a theory, by focusing our attention on the critical meaningful patterns in the buzzing confusion around us, leads to clarity of thought and decisive pragmatic results. Implementing the theory produces a change in the world around us that is beneficial to those concerned. The chemical table of elements is the standard example of such a theory. Its classification system is powerful. It permits an explanation of many mysterious phenomena with a limited set of explanatory principles and has led to enormous technological changes with major impacts on how life has been lived in the 20th and 21st centuries.

Hoping for similar results, the American Psychiatric Association has promoted the *DSM* as the basic nomenclature and system of categorization for psychological and psychiatric problems. In so doing, the suffering of human existence has been transformed into a set of medical disorders and the astounding conclusion that about half of all adults living in the United States will at some time in their lifetime experience at least one significant mental disorder (Kessler, Berglund, et al., 2005). The most common of these are anxiety disorders (29%), impulse control disorders (25%), mood disorders (21%), and substance abuse or dependence (15%; these numbers add up to more than 50% because the diagnoses are not for the most part mutually exclusive, and thus individuals in the survey may have more than one mental disorder).

When interviewees in these surveys were asked only about the most recent 12-month period, the rates are not as high (Kessler, Chiu, Demler, & Walters, 2005). In the previous year, 26% of the participants met the criteria for at least one mental disorder; the most common categories were anxiety disorders (18%), mood disorders (9.5%), and impulse control disorders (9%). In a single year, more than one in 20 Americans (6%) experienced a severe disorder including a suicide attempt, psychosis, serious violence, or an inability to function in one's work or home environment. Only 41% of those with a mental disorder sought treatment in the previous year; however, the most common source of help was from a general medical provider (23%). Help was sought about as often from an alternative health care professional or spiritual adviser (15%) as from psychiatrists (12%) and psychologists, social workers, or other mental health professionals (16%; P. S. Wang et al., 2005). The overall rates of mental illness in the United States have remained constant between 1991–1992 and 2001–2003. Another government study (Substance Abuse and Mental Health Services Administration, 2009) found that in the most powerful and wealthy nation in the world over one million individuals attempted suicide in a 1-year period. The number who actually made plans to do so was twice as great (2.2 million), and the number of completed suicides was estimated at about 30,000 individuals. In a given year, 60% of the individuals with a diagnosable mental disorder are not in treatment.

The Mental Health System: Treatments and Providers

Clearly, there is desperate need for mental health treatment. But what kind of mental health services are available for those people in the United States experiencing unbearable levels of psychological suffering? When mental health treatment is discussed in introductions in the mainstream literature of psychology, psychiatry, social work, and counseling, there is a tendency to downplay the scientist–practitioner divide or treat it as a thing of the past. Instead, various "integrative" approaches are offered, the most common among these being the biopsychosocial (Engel, 1977) and the diathesis–stress (Meehl, 1962; Zubin & Spring, 1977) models. Each of these models postulates a person's physiological vulnerability (the *bio* or *diathesis* component) to developing disturbing behaviors that is triggered or exacerbated by social factors such as poverty or violence (the *social* or *stress* component), as well as psychological factors within the individual such as beliefs, perceptions, emotional reactivity, or personal history (the *psycho* or *stress* component). However, in the contemporary world of mental health practice these integrative theoretical models have become, in effect, just other means of marketing a biological approach that heavily favors medical interventions over psychological and social therapies (Ghaemi, 2009).

Perhaps the clearest and most concrete way to demonstrate the shrinking role of psychosocial/stress treatment is in terms of health care expenditures related to mental health and substance abuse problems. The latest year for which there is consistent data is 2009, a year when the gross domestic product

(GDP) of the U.S. economy was $14.5 trillion. Of that amount, all health care spending in the United States was about $2.3 trillion (or 16% of GDP). Expenditure on mental health and drug abuse services of all kinds (in hospital, outpatient, medications, counseling, and psychotherapy) was $172 billion (or about 1% of GDP). Mental health and substance abuse spending is about $7 of every $100 spent on total health care. In 1986, mental health and substance abuse care amounted to $9 of every $100 spent on health care in the United States. Mental health and substance abuse care as a percentage of GDP has remained at about 1% since 1986, whereas the percentage of GDP devoted to health care has climbed from 10% to 17% of GDP. This clearly indicates that as our investment in physical health care has intensified dramatically, our commitment to mental health care has remained stagnant (Rampell, 2013).

However, psychotropic drugs constituted 7% of mental health treatment costs in 1986, 23% in 2003 ($23 billion), and 28% ($42 billion) in 2009. This amounts to a quadrupling of the role of medications in the treatment of psychiatric and psychological problems since 1986. Because the total spending on mental health care has dropped from 9% to 7% of GDP, that means there has been about a 20% drop in expenditures on the psychosocial aspects of treatment within the biopsychosocial model. Antidepressants and antipsychotics together accounted for 66% of spending on medications, whereas attention-deficit/hyperactivity disorder (ADHD) medications constituted another 14%. Equally surprising is that Medicaid's (the state-sponsored health care for low income persons) share of all mental health treatment reimbursement increased from 16% in 1986 to 27% in 2009. Public payers of all kinds (e.g., Medicare—health care insurance for elderly and disabled people, sponsored by the federal government; Medicaid state government budgets; the Veterans Administration) pay for 60% of all mental health services (Levit et al., 2013). Because government has become the predominant payer for mental health services, we can see that the biomedical model has been adopted by not only private health insurance and managed-care companies as a preferred treatment but also by many levels of government as well.

As for providers, in 2012, the following data were reported in terms of manpower and salaries (U.S. Department of Labor, 2012). Excluding academic clinical psychologists, there were about 103,000 practicing (mostly doctoral) psychologists, with a median income of about $77,000. There were over 230,000 professional mental health and substance abuse counselors, with a median income of $42,000 (marriage and family counselors' median income was somewhat higher: $49,000). Rehabilitation counselors numbered an additional 104,000 providers, with a median income of $37,000. There were 109,000 clinical social workers, with a median salary of $43,000. In all, there are nearly 550,000 nonmedical professionally trained mental health providers. And yet, many people are shocked to learn that in 2012 there were only 24,000 psychiatrists in the United States and that their median income was $177,000. We see here the economic impact of the success of the biomedical model on the personal incomes of its practitioners. Their average incomes are more than double those of doctoral-trained psychologists and more than 4 times the incomes of mental health professionals trained at the master's level.

The Consumer's Perspective

In my academic and clinical experience, many students, consumers, and professionals in training find the range of psychiatric and psychological disorders and diagnoses, treatments, and professions offering services confusing or disturbing. Often they assume they are just not smart or wise enough to figure out what must be obvious to everyone else. Nothing could be further from the truth. As one attempts to learn about what is variously referred to as abnormal psychology, psychopathology, psychiatric diagnosis, clinical treatment planning, or options, one encounters a perplexing array of theories, advice, and experts offering conflicting advice and direction to those who are need of assistance, often ignoring or disparaging other points of view. Psychologists are generally licensed with a doctoral degree (PhD, PsyD, or EdD), though in about 10 states those with a master's degree in psychology (MA or MS) may be granted a full or limited licensed as either a psychologist or psychological assistant of some kind. Clinical social workers are generally licensed for practice with a master's degree (MSW), as are mental health, marriage and family, and rehabilitation counselors (MS or MEd). Psychiatric nurses (MSRN) are licensed with a master's degree and psychiatric nurse practitioners with a master's (MS) or doctoral degree (PhD). Psychiatrists must graduate from medical school (MD degree) and complete a 3-year hospital residency. When faced with this alphabet soup of degrees representing diverse kinds of professional training, it may seem as though this is just like any other area of professional expertise, difficult for the layperson or new student to comprehend.

Now, it is true that life looks simpler from afar. But when the people turning to the mental health care system for assistance are already overwhelmed, confused, and often in life-threatening crises, such a cavalier realism has a hollow ring. So many of our loved ones and close friends turn to the mental health professions for help and in turn receive a confusing array of diagnoses, powerful medications, and traditional or new-age psychotherapies, with extremely varied results. This state of affairs is as much a part of the mental health problem in the United States as depression; substance abuse; traumas of child, sexual, and spouse abuse; autism; schizophrenia; ADHD; and all the rest. We have allowed our theorists and researchers to present ideology as theory, conjectures as facts, assumptions as conclusions, and illusions as reality. Next I catalogue five such illusions.

ILLUSION 1: "MENTAL DISORDERS" CAN BE OBJECTIVELY DEFINED

As noted in Chapter 1, attempts to define terms such as *abnormal behavior* have led to conflicting and confusing results (Wakefield, 1992). The simplest criterion, that a behavior is abnormal when it is statistically rare, fails miserably, most obviously because the epidemiological research cited previously shows that many of these disorders are in fact quite common. Moreover, many rare behaviors can actually be desirable, for example being a charismatic personality. There is no a single criterion that properly classifies as "abnormal" or "disordered" all of the symptoms or interpersonal behaviors that are typically diagnosed or treated by the mental health professions. Furthermore, there is not a single *DSM–5* mental disorder that can be diagnosed in clinical practice (as opposed to research studies) by a physical or physiological test. We must conclude that there is therefore no clear definition of these phenomena, and no clear criteria. Our language is imprecise, ambiguous, culturally bound, and lacking often in objective referents, because the phenomena are essentially subjective and the language being used by both patients and providers is often metaphorical.

This is brought home on an everyday level by the confusing array of diagnoses the same patient will receive from different providers as he or she moves through the mental health care system. It is not uncommon for individuals to receive four or five overlapping and even contradictory diagnoses. For example, a grade school child may over a period of several years accumulate a series of diagnoses such as attachment disorder, oppositional defiant disorder, ADHD, bipolar disorder, and learning disability, while eventually being simultaneously treated with three or four powerful, mind-altering prescription medications. Concurrently, the child's parent(s) will have received suggestions, feedback, and corrective advice from an array of teachers, special educators, school psychologists, pediatricians, child psychiatrists, child counselors or psychotherapists, clinical psychologists, or school social workers who are rarely coordinated in their approaches.

ILLUSION 2: MEASUREMENT IS THE KEY TO PROBLEM SOLVING

Not everything important in human existence is tangible, observable, and measureable. The great British mathematician, Alfred Whitehead (1925, p. 64), referred to the contrary belief as "the fallacy of misplaced concreteness."

We struggle to isolate, express, and communicate much of what is felt at a profound and deep level. This is true in both our moments of great joy and great sorrow, exhilaration and terror, compassion and rage, love and hate. What most matters to us is often elusive, complex, and mysterious. When at a deep level we are wounded, ripped apart, raw, vulnerable, confused, and disoriented, we flail around seeking comfort or answers to our pain and suffering. In such times we feel as though our life is, or may be, over. We teeter on the edge of losing our sense of being a coherent self or have become alienated from those who we have loved or who have loved us. We are isolated and alone.

In such an overwhelming state of being, attempts to be analytical yield many parallel universes of truth. A person in such state appears physically unhealthy—sleep, eating, sexual drive, energy, and strength are all adversely affected. Cognitive functioning is disrupted by poor memory, inattention, difficulty communicating, and diminished problem solving. Emotions are volatile and unpredictable, and relationships are frayed and conflicted. The ability to perform social functions such as working or schooling is derailed, and participation in a social network often severely curtailed.

In such circumstances, most any reasonable attempt at defining the problem (i.e., a diagnosis or problem formulation) is both partially true and highly misleading. The obvious reason is that the description is incomplete, but more important, it is misleading because in times of despair, panic, rage, and so forth, we are simultaneously struggling to hold things together, fearful that we might be losing our minds, attempting to reassure ourselves as well as others who may be concerned about our well-being or competency to perform our social roles, and surprised or thrown by the thoughts and feelings that emerge into our consciousness uninvited and unwelcome. In short, we are too overwhelmed or too defended to know what is fully happening or to understand what the problem really is.

Neither the scientific nor practitioner theories of abnormal psychology fully take into account the important role of the chaos, complexity, and confusion experienced by the individual or the significant others who accompany the patient/client for help. Often in this state of crisis, there are dimensions that do not fit neatly into any strictly psychological theory, complexities of a spiritual, moral, legal, and cultural or historical nature. The circumstances that trigger the sense of being overwhelmed may include being embroiled in social, political, or economic turmoil, combat, violent assault, sudden onset terminal disease, litigation or prosecution, and so forth.

A person in crisis is suffering simultaneously at all of these levels (physiological arousal, irrational emotions, sense of self, family stress, cognitive distortions, behavioral patterns, and other social problems), and so help that is offered in any one of these areas will be somewhat beneficial, at least over the short run of several weeks or months. Thus, for those in the helping professions who subscribe to narrowly defined treatment approaches, evidence can be found for effectiveness of each approach (Luborsky et al., 2002; Stiles, Barkham, Twigg, Mellor-Clark, & Cooper, 2006). This is especially true if the specific treatment is accompanied by a supportive, respectful, and consistent relationship that lessens the feelings of social isolation and provides hope and a sense that human beings do survive what seem at the time to be impossible circumstances.

ILLUSION 3: THE GENERAL QUALITY OF MENTAL HEALTH CARE IS ALWAYS IMPROVING

What generally happens next once a person in such a predicament enters the managed care or public health care system is that she or he is told (a) "You have a mental disorder/mental illness, (b) which is caused by a chemical imbalance in your brain (c) and is probably genetically transmitted, and (d) treatment requires you to be on a substantial dose of mood stabilizing antidepressant or antipsychotic medication for at least several years, perhaps for life." Psychiatrists claim, and indeed my experience confirms, that for some significant minority of patients this message comes as a great relief: "Then it is not my fault for feeling this bad or doing these bad things, and the medication is going to fix things and make it better for me." We conceive of painful emotional and stressful periods of our lives as illnesses that can be fixed by medication, a natural extension of the medical setting in which this explanation and treatment are delivered. It turns psychiatry into just another branch of medicine, a link that many psychiatrists have always longed for and that the National Institute of Mental Health (NIMH) has been promoting in public service announcements for decades (Albee & Joffe, 2004).

Now, if the only choice is between feeling to blame for intense emotional pain and its consequences and being told one has a defective brain that can be fixed, it is not hard to choose the biomedical model. If it were really that simple, and the scientific claim true, who could argue? But it is not that simple, and the status of the scientific evidence for the claim is equivocal. The relief of "it is not my fault" is often short lived. As the reality sets in, one is often left with the sense one is a defective person, and that this defect may be inherited by one's children and grandchildren. Furthermore, suggesting that pills will fix the problems or are the centerpiece of any effort to fix the problems communicates that one is not really responsible for doing anything different to improve one's psychological state (except, of course, take the pills). It introduces a kind of fatalism about psychological pain that is destructive and likely to feed the downward spiral one is attempting to reverse. In worst-case scenarios, I have seen patients and students who regard their diagnoses of bipolar, schizophrenic, or ADHD disorders as a free pass to engage in any actions they wish without believing themselves accountable because they have "got" this disorder, and their brain makes them act this way (Valenstein, 1998).

Damaging as it is, this lack of responsibility also means that the conditions that contributed to the problem in the first place fall off the radar. If a married woman is depressed and medication is the treatment, any urgency about addressing the marital problems and seeing what can be done to resolve them is often lost. Similarly, if a middle-aged, male, middle-level manager in a large corporation is depressed and then medicated, the personal toll of an unhealthy work environment affecting hundreds, if not thousands, of others is lost from view. If the child who is not doing well in school is medicated for ADHD, the anxiety of living with parents who have unresolved marital problems and leaving for school each day wondering if both parents will still be there when one returns is lost as well. If the adolescent is diagnosed and medicated for a schizophrenic disorder, no one need look at his fragile sense of self that has been undermined by years of family and sibling conflict and hostility and marginal participation in school. If the child is diagnosed with "conduct disorder" after years of living in a crime- and drug-infested neighborhood with deteriorated schools and burned-out teachers, we as a society do not have to ask ourselves what the psychological cost of either poverty or relative economic deprivation might be. Perhaps this is why we have been willing to accept the relatively low rates of successful treatment with the typical drugs prescribed, often little better than the results with placebo controls in long-term studies and with much higher rates of serious side effects than typically reported by the manufacturers or told to the patients before they start the medication. Finally, as many psychopharmacologists will admit, the chemical imbalance in the brain is a hypothesis and not a confirmed finding in any of the disorders in question (Healy, 2009).

There is something deeply troubling about the way the 100-billion-dollar private and public mental health care system is organized in the United States today. We now have "epidemics" (Whitaker, 2011) of psychiatric disorders that did not exist (e.g., social anxiety disorder or bipolar disorder in children), or barely existed (childhood autism or ADHD), 25 years ago and an avalanche of psychiatric pharmaceuticals (estimated expenditures at $42 billion per year) so pervasively prescribed by general practitioners and pediatricians that they are now showing up in the groundwater and water systems of major metropolitan areas (Calisto & Esteves, 2009). Drugs are increasingly marketed to populations that cannot or do not decide for themselves whether to take the medications (children, elderly people in nursing homes, and those ordered to by state mental health and correctional authorities), which not surprisingly have profound metabolic side effects that reduce life expectancy by 20 or more years (Lieberman et al., 2005). It is a system of care that frequently is far more destructive ("crazier," if you will) than the "crazy" people it purports to help.

By receiving a psychiatric diagnosis or prescription for a psychoactive pharmaceutical or by entering one type or another of counseling or psychotherapy, one is likely to enter a world where terms are ambiguous and slippery, theories faddish, science shoddy and often corrupt, competing professions undercut each other's legitimacy, and the pursuit of power and profit easily masquerade as pseudo-compassionate concern. Considering that this is an arena that consumers only enter when they are low points in their lives and at moments of greatest vulnerability, the disparity between what is promised and what is actually offered is at the very least frightening and at worst a national tragedy affecting millions of Americans a year. "Buyer beware" is insufficient, though warranted, preliminary counsel. The "buyers" here are a diverse group who may not see themselves as buyers. These buyers of a failing system of care include psychiatric patients, family practice and pediatrics patients, counseling and psychotherapy clients, state hospital and private psychiatric hospital patients, undergraduate students taking general and abnormal psychology, graduate students in the mental health professions, and medical, pharmacy, and nursing students and residents. Much of the "product" that all these groups are receiving (viz., mental health services and a way of thinking about those services) is broken and defective, and those selling this product either know it is defective, or ought to know.

ILLUSION 4: THE WAY TO IMPROVE MENTAL HEALTH CARE IS THROUGH MORE AND BETTER SCIENTIFIC RESEARCH

For purposes of scientific analysis, we can separate human action and behavior into physiological, cognitive–behavioral, conscious and unconscious, and emotional or interpersonal elements and attempt to isolate and identify specific causal relationships among these factors. In the real world of human relationships and clinical interventions, however, such an approach to the problems of human emotional pain and suffering generally falls far short. The theories and data derived from them typically conflict. The controlled research environment in which the studies are conducted generally differs from the settings in which nonresearch clinicians practice, and the populations who volunteer for such studies are often different from actual clients in clinical practice. Study results show the average gain for clients treated by a variety of clinicians, and there is no way to know how these research clinicians compare with the clinician who might be attempting to use the results in the community. The most technically sophisticated research is often the least applicable to everyday life. It is useful and necessary background knowledge, but it is an insufficient knowledge base for being truly helpful to real patients/clients in real clinical situations (Dattilio, Edwards, & Fishman, 2010).

The difficulties encountered when one tries to evaluate a clinical practice as it is conducted amid the complexity of real-life situations are exemplified in the two cases discussed in Chapter 4 involving humanistic play therapy. The play therapist (also the cotherapist in the case at the end of this chapter) has practiced play therapy since the mid 1970s. She has worked with low-income children in schools and at a community mental health center and, for the last 30 years in private practice, with children from widely disparate cultures and backgrounds. Although no one is successful with all their cases, her practice is sustained by word-of-mouth referrals from parents and human services professionals who hear from those parents how much their children have improved while taking minimal or no medications.

Yet, the scientific research literature on psychological treatments of children clearly stated in the mid 1970s that there was no empirical evidence that humanistic play therapy was effective (Barrett, Hampe, & Miller, 1978), whereas behavioral approaches were supported by empirical evidence. About 10 years later, a literature review using the more advanced statistical methods of meta-analysis (Casey & Berman, 1985) looked at a larger body of work and concluded that both humanistic play therapy and behavioral techniques were effective, but only if both methods were studied using outcome measures with the same degree of specificity. If behavioral outcome measures similar to those used during behavioral therapy to measure symptom change are used also as outcome measures (as they typically are in behavior modification studies), the behavioral approaches appear superior, as they did in Barrett et al., 1978. Weisz, Weiss, Alicke, and Klotz (1987) agreed with Casey and Berman that both forms of child therapy are clearly effective, though they argue that their meta-analysis of the data supports the view that the behavioral treatments consistently produce better results. Ten years later, Weisz, Weiss, Han, Granger, and Morton (1995), looking at the same question with even more sophisticated statistical analyses, concluded that both humanistic and behavioral approaches are effective; however, the cognitive–behavioral approach seemed more effective with aggressive and hyperactive children, whereas both were equally effective in working with children who seemed overcontrolled and fearful. Recently, Weisz (2014) suggested that despite overwhelming research support for the empirical efficacy of childhood treatments, especially the far more frequently studied cognitive behavior therapy approaches, we have little or no idea how these empirically validated treatments fare in the real world of community clinics. Weisz is now arguing for the development of a whole new research paradigm to demonstrate how these studies translate into the real world of clinical practice. He acknowledges that we are now only in our infancy of knowing how to do this. It is astounding that the research literature is still claiming that there is no way to know whether play therapy works, 40 years after it was clear to me and everyone else who knows the work of this play therapist that it can work exceptionally well.

The fundamental assumption that science is a unitary concept and that a scientific approach to psychology must look like a scientific approach to biology is only one of the possible assumptions on which one might construct psychology, and it is not necessarily the most sagacious. The historian and philosopher of science Stephen Toulmin (2003) argued persuasively that scientific rationality is not identical to reasonableness and that social sciences must be guided by human reason; scientific rationality should only be applied when it is reasonable to do so. For Toulmin, scientific rationality is the attempt to find universal principles of explanation similar to the laws of physics. Human reason, however, attempts to solve local problems that may never appear again in exactly the same form and must be solved by heuristics (practical rules of thumb) rather than universal principles. Human reason does not exclude moral principles or human emotions in deciding a course of action. Pragmatism is a human reason approach par excellence.

It is popular today for research psychologists to decry "pop psychology" as "pseudoscience" (Lilienfeld, Lynn, & Lohr, 2004). In academic psychology this is equivalent to labeling an idea as a heresy that corrupts the rightful influence of scientific authority in our culture. Yet, if Toulmin (2003) is correct, and he may well be, then much if not all of the "legitimate scientific work" in abnormal and clinical psychology and psychiatry is itself pseudoscience, in that it applies the wrong scientific method to studying human interactional processes.

Furthermore, most of what passes for scientific research today in applied psychology and related disciplines is essentially various attempts at human behavioral engineering, testing whether it is possible to bring various disturbing behaviors under the control of recognized and authorized professionals. Rather than exploring fundamental questions about the nature of the mind and behavior, this is research designed to serve the ends of the major institutions in society that pay for the research to be done and wish to be more effective in controlling our behavior—schools, corporations, the military, government agencies, health care systems, and so forth. Pharmaceutical company scandals have highlighted this for all of us to see in recent years (Angel, 2005; Healy, 2004). Dr. Steven Hyman, former director of NIMH, has acknowledged that the search for new drugs that alter brain chemistry as a treatment for mental disorders has ground to a halt because of increased accountability for unadvertised side effects, misleading advertising concerning positive main effects, and a resulting decline in profitability (Horgan, 2013).

Technology has transformed human existence in many areas, and its power has been attributed to, and has greatly enhanced, the rhetorical power of science. Although we are quite sophisticated about the potential downsides of technology (e.g., ecological disaster, nuclear weapons, loss of privacy), few people are willing to be seen as critical of science itself. Science is believed to be the supreme evidence of human intelligence, and to dispute the role of science as the final arbiter of truth is seen as folly. In the mind of the educated person, science has replaced Christianity as the "one true faith" of our culture, and not without reason. But we must learn to differentiate the intellectual power, logic, and elegance of scientific thought from the rhetoric of science that is used by advocates of various technologies, whether these be a nuclear, electronic, robotic, or behavioral. At the same time, real help is available from ethical practitioners in all of the mental health professions, and it is often highly effective in relieving symptoms and even transforming lives (Malan & Della Selva, 2006). These practitioners recognize the importance of science as one source of knowledge they need to be of service to consumers/clients. They also recognize that science without a moral perspective—without basic human decency—is fraught with danger. The problem is that for clients, it is often difficult to tell in advance what sort of practitioner you have encountered. It is bad form today for clinicians to say that they practice anything other than evidence-based medicine or psychology. Some of the people who say this really believe it, whereas others consider it a kind of password to legitimacy, and move on.

ILLUSION 5: MORAL VALUES HAVE NO PLACE IN MENTAL HEALTH DIAGNOSIS, TREATMENT, OR RESEARCH

A corollary to the assumption that psychology is a natural science is that as such it is a value-free enterprise. Good scientists seek the truth, report their findings, and leave their personal moral or political values aside while functioning as scientists. When researchers or practitioners fail to do this, their work is no longer considered to be valid science and is discredited. The natural sciences aspire to see the world as it is, uninfluenced by how we wish it to be. Changing the world to be more the way we would like it to be involves combining knowledge of how the world is structured scientifically with our dreams of how it might be. In the natural sciences, scientific theory and fact give way to technology as the enterprise of pure science shifts to applications of scientific understanding.

Theories of mental health or illness and prevention or treatment programs based on these theories are entirely concerned with changing the world to make it less "mentally ill" and healthier. As in medicine, education, pastoral care and engineering, our understanding of the world is only the first step in deciding how it should be. Here, our moral, aesthetic, and social and political values must be integrated with our knowledge of the way the world is. Technology of any kind is therefore not value free.

However, abnormal psychology, psychopathology, and psychiatric diagnosis have a special problem in this regard because the problems for which patients and clients seek help are often their own moral dilemmas and debacles. Therapists and counselors are the secular equivalent of the local church pastor. Shame, guilt, and fear of social ostracism are the coin of the realm. Inevitably, these bring us into the realm of moral and ethical values. Mental health and mental illness are entirely in the realm of values—how people wish to live their lives and behave, how they wish others to treat them, and how we wish our clients or patients to think, feel, or behave. As disciplines, professions, and important influences on popular culture, psychology and psychiatry have not come to terms with how the infusion of moral values limits the applicability of natural science theorizing and research methods to the knowledge bases of their professions. These fields are applied science at best, and the basic science is so far removed from the applications that it often does not even make sense to use scientific research methods to study the outcome (Fishman, 1999). The power to validate judgments and perception and decide whose behavior is deemed rational and whose irrational or "mad" brings mental health professionals into potential conflict with other professionals who have also been delegated responsibility for managing or controlling various segments of the population (e.g., doctors, teachers, police officers, prison officials, military officers, insurance company and managed care administrators).

There are also times when questions of public policy and political debate directly affect mental health programs and treatment. Eugenics was an international movement of the 1920s and 1930s supported by the political and financial elites to prevent population growth among those members of the lower classes who threatened the way of life of the elites: indigent minorities, petty thieves and prostitutes, delinquents, the mentally retarded and mentally ill, addicts, and so forth. The threat was either direct in the case of delinquents, thieves, and addicts, or indirect in the public monies that would need to be raised by taxes on the elites to educate or support the groups in question: the mentally retarded and mentally ill. The solution of the eugenics movement was to prevent these groups from having children and passing along their supposedly defective genes to the next generation, either by sterilization or institutionalization in settings where they could not procreate (R. Whitaker, 2005).

Hitler was known to admire Henry Ford's support of the eugenics movement in the United States, and when Hitler decided to go the United States one better by killing "life unfit for life," he began with mentally disabled children and then moved on to mentally disabled adults before attempting the mass killings of ethnic and religious minorities. The whole extermination program was built on the concept of public health and hygiene, cleansing the country of defective forms of life; the medical community (considered the most scientifically advanced in the world at that time) provided ideological justification for the killings and shared administrative responsibility for running the death camps (Lifton, 1988). The first physicians to be enlisted into the genocidal program were German psychiatrists who administered the programs in which the mentally disabled and ill children and adults were killed by lethal injections at psychiatric hospitals and treatment facilities.

During this same time, period sterilizations, lobotomies, and massive doses of electroconvulsive shock treatments were used on institutionalized mental patients in the United States to achieve the goals of eugenics (R. Whitaker, 2005). These programs were only stopped after World War II when the public was awakened to the similarities between the Nazi death camps and the psychiatric treatment programs in U.S. state hospitals. On a much more positive note, John F. Kennedy, whose own family had experienced the tragedy of the modern psychiatric "treatment" of the day in the care provided to one of his siblings who remained incapacitated her entire life, made the development of a national program of community mental health centers one of his political priorities. These programs offered a shift away from hospital and medical care and toward community programs that offered psychological and social programs of care (Joint Commission on Mental Illness and Health, 1961).

These programs struggled to survive during subsequent Republican administrations. Presidents Nixon and Reagan tried to eliminate them entirely, and President G. H. W. Bush[1] declared the 1990s as the decade of the brain, shifting research away from psychological and social causes of psychiatric disorders and toward medicine, genetics, neuroscience, and psychopharmacology (Steinmetz, 2013). President Bush left the White House after one term and joined the board of Eli Lilly, the manufacturer of the first popular selective serotonin reuptake inhibitor drug for treatment of depression, Prozac (M. Levine, Perkins, & Perkins, 2005). Whether due to the powerful pharmaceutical company lobbying or the success of their joint campaign with the American Psychiatric Association to convince us all that our suffering is due to "chemical imbalances" in our brains, even Democratic administrations have allowed the health care system and NIMH to give priority to the biomedical viewpoint. It seems that anyone who challenges it in Washington is deemed antiscience and placed into the same category as those who reject scientific evidence regarding evolution or the evidence of human contributions to global warming.

There is, of course, much more to the politics of mental health than presidential initiatives, including the uses of psychiatry and psychology in the Defense Department and the Veterans Administration and the lobbying of Congress by professional organizations such as the American Psychological

---

[1]Bush's father, Senator Prescott Bush, was an important advocate for eugenics prior to World War II. Although it would be wrong to blame the son for his father's views, there is an undeniable symmetry in that prominent politicians today continue to operate on behalf of corporate interests profiting from research that dehumanizes those who suffer from mental illness.

Association, American Medical Association, American Hospital Association, National Association of Social Workers, National Education Association, and various extremely powerful pharmaceutical companies. Some of these topics are discussed in later chapters, but suffice it to say for now that when an interaction with a mental health services provider appears to make no sense and to seem counterproductive, the reasons can sometimes be found in the political and economic forces that have shaped the system. The funding available for treatments, the definitions of "best practice" treatments by government or pharmaceutical company sponsored research, the kinds of training of providers that the government has supported through grants to higher education or directly to students—all eventually have an impact on what transpires in hundreds of thousands of individual clinical mental health interviews taking place every day in the United States.

Occasionally in a society, the political role of public mental health treatment is so blatant that no one can deny it (though critics may claim it is an unusual aberration). Such was the use of psychiatric treatment during the decades just before the collapse of the Soviet Union. Scientists and writers who had been arrested for opposing the control of the state over personal liberties were sent to mental hospitals on the grounds that their opposition to communism showed that they were no longer thinking rationally (i.e., psychotic). They were then treated with massive doses of antipsychotic neuroleptic medications that left them unable to do more than sit in a chair, drooling. As a form of political repression, their relatives and friends were permitted to occasionally visit them to see the consequences of political opposition to the state (Bonnie, 2002).

VALUES FOR AN ABNORMAL PSYCHOLOGY WITHOUT ILLUSIONS

In this volume I aim to avoid as much as possible a "concealed values" approach to abnormal psychology. To that end, I will at the outset declare the value basis of my own approach to the discipline:

- Psychological knowledge should be developed for the purposes of bettering the human condition for all people, regardless of social class, race, religion, gender, sexual orientation, and nationality.
- Psychological discourse should be open to all participants who engage in dialogue and discussion in a manner respectful of the other participants, whether or not those participants are in agreement with the ideas being proposed.
- All plausible theories and ideas should be examined and debated in a reasoned manner. Passionate and compassionate concerns

are not incompatible with reason, only with a hyperrationality that is overly objectifying of human experience.

- Advocates of alternative epistemologies (routes to knowledge) are welcomed into the dialogue so long as they identify the basis of their claims and their reasons for trusting such a basis.
- Participants are free to question theory, evidence, data, and the underlying values implicit in the ideas being proposed.
- Biological, psychological, social, political, economic, and spiritual factors all affect the human beings who seek treatment in the mental health system. Abnormal psychology would be foolish to ignore the importance of any of these forces in our lives.

CASE STUDY: A LIFE-SAVING NONDIAGNOSIS BY A COUPLE'S THERAPY TEAM

Early in my career I worked in the outpatient service of a community mental health center in northern New England and did couple's therapy with a cotherapist. I had recently completed my doctorate in clinical psychology from a program that was strongly behavioral in orientation but in which many of the clinical supervisors in the community internship placements were psychodynamic, interpersonal, or humanistic. My cotherapist for this case was a highly skilled person with a BSW, who had about five years of clinical experience. Her casework training was supplemented by a strong interest in humanistic psychotherapy. Our outpatient service was equally eclectic; we had individuals with PsyD, PhD, MSW, BSW, MSRN, and MA rehabilitation counseling degrees all working together as clinical peers. We offered individual, couples, family, and group therapy, as well as school and correctional center consultation.

We were free to choose cotherapists for work with couples and families on the basis of our ease of working together and schedules. In this context we saw a young attractive couple in their late 20s who had three children in elementary school. They were worried about keeping their marriage together because they had married during their freshman year of college. She had dropped out of school to have their first child, whereas he had finished college. He had a good early career job in the business community, and she stayed at home with the kids. They were self-referred and seen on a sliding-fee scale.

They had the fairly typical problems of young couples (budgeting on limited resources, adapting to in-laws on both sides of the family, being overwhelmed at times with three children under 10 years, and most significantly to us, an almost utter incapacity to talk with each other about their problems). She had initiated the contact with the agency. Also quite typical, the communication difficulty took the form of the female partner trying to discuss family or relationship issues with the male partner, who would listen briefly and then withdraw from the conversation. This could also be observed in the sessions as well. He was responsible and hardworking at work and home, but he could not deal with interpersonal conflict or his wife's emotional distress. The most difficult issue for them to discuss was her strong dependency on her parents and his feeling that they were intruding into the marital relationship. We worked on making the sessions a safe place for the wife to express her frustrations and for the husband to be able to hear them without running away by giving them each support for how difficult their separate responsibilities had been since the first unplanned pregnancy. We were fortunate so early in our careers to have a case where both members of the couple were highly motivated to work on their problems and where learning to communicate more effectively was sufficient to ease their burden. We modeled empathic listening and nonaccusatory expression of feelings.

We saw the couple once per week for about six months and then once every 2 weeks for another 3 months, after which they terminated. We each had weekly supervision with the outpatient director, where the case was occasionally reviewed, and we also presented it to the outpatient case conference for discussion on several occasions. This was how all either very successful or very difficult cases were handled. Generally this case was regarded as successful because both husband and wife reported that the level of conflict in the marriage was quite reduced and felt ready to end counseling.

About six months later, my cotherapist received a tearful call from the wife saying that she was in the hospital, having had an emergency appendectomy. The surgery was successful in that the appendix had not burst, but she was experiencing an abnormal degree of postoperative pain. She reported that her surgeon could find nothing abnormal in her postoperative recovery other than the pain. He had become convinced it was a result of emotional issues and referred her for a psychiatric consult with the psychiatry service of the hospital. She refused and asked instead that we do the consultation. She was scared and distrustful of the hospital staff because of the way they were dealing with her pain. The surgeon involved was a senior member of his department and was known to be intimidating. She found him insensitive, arrogant, and hostile. In fact, my cotherapist had once been treated by him and she had sworn never to allow him anywhere near her again. The hospital had a reputation for discouraging consults by community practitioners, especially from mental health workers. Neither of us felt prepared to tackle the health care establishment or this particular physician alone, so we decided to do the consult as a team and see the couple in the hospital together. We made an appointment for the next day because of the urgency of her pain, and on arrival reviewed her chart, which confirmed that her only complaint or symptom was pain in the area of her incision. The physician's notes indicated that he thought the pain was "hysterical" and there was no physical basis for it. On the basis of our prior contact with her, the wife did not at all fit the classic picture of hysterical pain. She was open and direct with her feelings, not afraid of anger or sexual urges, and showed no signs of *la belle indifference*. In fact, she seemed frightened, quite sad, and alone.

Her sense of isolation was extreme. First, she had intense pain and, second, because the surgeon had diagnosed the pain as psychogenic, none of the nurses or physicians wanted to attend to her pain. She felt like a leper— shunned and isolated. We had never in the year of couple's work seen her so distressed. We spent an hour with the couple. The husband felt that there was something wrong from the surgery; he had never seen his wife in such a state. Their communication was excellent, and they described the last 6 months of their marriage as going well prior to her illness. There were no other recent stresses on the family reported by either one. At the completion of the consultation session we concurred with one another and with the clients that it was not likely to be psychogenic pain, and she could always seek another surgical opinion. She was afraid to tell her surgeon herself, and we assured her that we would note in her chart that we did not think the pain psychogenic, which we did.

She called us 2 weeks later to report that she had signed herself out of the hospital and had sought a second surgical opinion from a competent, but not nearly as powerful, member of the medical profession, who worked out of a small community hospital. After examining her, he immediately scheduled her for surgery and removed from her abdomen a surgical sponge that had been left behind in the previous surgery. It had become a source of internal infection. She was on the mend, and we never received another call from her or her husband.

This case illustrates the vested interest that people other than the patient may have in their psychiatric diagnosis and the danger to the patient in accepting such a diagnosis. Had the woman in this couple accepted that she was just a "hysterical" female with psychogenic pain, the infection in her abdomen would have remained undiagnosed for much longer and the second surgery delayed to the point where the infection might have become life-threatening. So long as the patient could be seen as a psychiatric case, her perspective on her condition could be invalidated by the rest of the health care team and the possibility that the physical care she had received in the first surgery was at fault avoided or denied. Whether the surgeon was aware of his misuse of the diagnosis is impossible to know. Mistakes are made by generally well-meaning and competent individuals in all walks of life and all professions. That is why we must be informed and vigilant consumers of products and services.

Psychiatric diagnoses, as they are typically used, are essentially and inherently harmful to personal well-being. This is why Carl Rogers and many of his followers refused to use them at all and why an international movement led by the Society for Humanistic Psychology is calling for the replacement of *DSM–5*. Psychiatric diagnoses today are forms of invalidating the experience of patients that they are being harmed or hurt in their interactions with the world—that is to say, the diagnoses are used to invalidate their suffering. There is much discussion in the psychiatric literature of efforts to counteract the stigmatizing aspects of mental illness or diagnoses (Corrigan, Morris, Michaels, Rafacz, & Rüsch, 2012; Parcesepe & Cabassa, 2013). This is quite ironic because it is the language of mental illness and diagnosis itself that takes a sickness that is communal and turns it into an illness or disease that is seen as an individual affliction.

3

THEORETICAL MODELS OF ABNORMAL PSYCHOLOGY: APPROACHES TO DIAGNOSIS, ASSESSMENT, AND DEVELOPMENT

We are pervasively vulnerable to the scourge of unintended consequences whenever we attempt to intervene in other people's lives to reduce their psychological suffering. There is no shortage of failed treatments that can be used to portray the illusory benefits of any particular treatment. Every profession and every theory has at least some proponents who are poorly trained, incompetent, or even fraudulent in how they practice mental health diagnosis and treatment. We must compare theories and professions at their best and attempt to gauge how likely it is for these best practices to actually prevail. There is considerable evidence in psychotherapy and medical literature of the power of the personal relationship between patient and healer (Bohart & Watson, 2011, p. 253). The person of the healer is a major contributor to the success of any formal treatment in psychology and psychiatry. Whether one refers to this as a provider or a placebo variable, the results are very real. Precisely who is presenting the medication, support, interpretation, intervention, and so forth, is a critical factor in symptom reduction. The personal characteristics and

http://dx.doi.org/10.1037/14693-003
Not So Abnormal Psychology: A Pragmatic View of Mental Illness, by R. B. Miller

qualities of the therapist may be more powerful than any specific technique, medication, or insights offered.

Equally important is the person of the patient/client and not just the symptom or problem the patient/client is experiencing (Bohart & Watson, 2011, p. 252). Does the person who is suffering maintain some sense of personal responsibility for recovering from their problems? How motivated is he or she to recover? Is she or he searching for answers and trying to clarify the problem, or instead waiting for a magic bullet or magic therapist to solve all problems?

There are essentially five different theoretical models of how to understand psychological suffering and what can be done to reduce it: biomedical, psychodynamic, humanistic–existential, cognitive–behavioral, and social and family systems. We have explicitly or implicitly encountered elements of each of these in Chapters 1 and 2; one cannot avoid them wherever one discusses the topic of abnormal psychology. Each of these models was developed in particular treatment settings and with specific populations. When applied without modifications to populations or in contexts distant from those in which they were developed, success is less likely.

Although theorists are rarely conciliatory toward theories other than their own, in practice, highly experienced and conscientious practitioners often are molded by their successes and failures with clients/patients into being more eclectic than doctrinaire about their theory and approach. Patients/clients teach us what works and what does not, if we only pay attention to what they tell us, as "reflective practitioners" or pragmatists should do. Nevertheless, it is important for those beginning the study of abnormal psychology to have a grasp of the fundamentally divergent theories that have contributed to the evolution of the discipline.

THE BIOMEDICAL MODEL

The biomedical model in abnormal psychology is most associated with the profession of psychiatry. It is sometimes also referred to simply as the *medical model*, even though many nonmedical personnel working in health care systems directed by physicians have adopted it. The biomedical model uses the physiology of the human body as a basis for thinking about abnormal psychology. It reminds us that a person who is having problems in living (functioning in society, relationships, and work) is not only a psychological and social being but also a human body. We know we cannot separate mind and body, that a high fever or a mind-altering substance can alter our consciousness and bring on hallucinatory experiences, that prolonged illness can be associated with feelings of hopelessness and depression, and that head injuries can produce difficulties concentrating and irritability. (Positive feelings associated with physical characteristics such as appearance, height, weight, racial characteristics, physical abilities, or talents work similarly.) These are all physical aspects of who we are that can have a powerful impact on our self-image and identity as a person. This self-image has been shaped by our experience of living in one's body in this world, and as we mature into adolescence and young adulthood, it begins to have an independent influence on our sense of well-being, happiness, and ability to adapt and feel competent in the world we inhabit.

Adherents to the biomedical models of psychology and psychiatry go beyond just studying and emphasizing the integration of mind and body, however. They claim that in addition to these sorts of biological influences on mental states and behavior, there are differences in brain functioning that in themselves can explain psychiatric disorders. They wish to claim that most of the central topics studied in abnormal psychology, such as anxiety, mood, psychotic experiences and behavior, attention-deficit/hyperactivity, personality patterns, and pervasive developmental disorders, are in themselves evidence of unseen biological disorders. In other words, the stresses of life, health, relationships, and other intense environmental stressors, such as combat or natural disasters, will only produce psychological symptoms in persons who have a predisposing brain disorder or dysfunction. At the risk of some oversimplification, the biological view is that people with normal brains and nervous systems cope with and adapt to whatever stresses are presented, and people who do not cope and adapt effectively (people who are thrown by stress) must therefore have abnormal brains and nervous systems.

There are four areas of biomedical research that have shaped this approach, beginning in the mid-20th century. First was an increased knowledge of the chemical aspects of nerve transmission at the synapse. Second was the growing sophistication in the research on the possibility of the genetic transmission of psychiatric disorders. Third was the blossoming of pharmaceutical research in the 1960s on specific new drugs for depression and schizophrenia, the so-called antidepressant and antipsychotic medications. Finally, in the last 2 decades there has been an emergence of brain imaging techniques such as computerized axial tomography (CAT) and positron-emission tomography (PET) scans, as well as magnetic resonance imaging (MRI) and functional magnetic resonance imaging (fMRI) studies (Eppel, 2013). Specific studies in these four areas are cited when discussing specific disorders in later chapters.

Though in each historical era the evidence produced in support of the biomedical view of individual differences in coping with life's joys and sorrows has changed with the times, the basic theory of materialism of the mind has been with us since at least the ancient Greeks. For Hippocrates, the physiological factor was the hypothesized four humors of the body (black bile, yellow bile, blood, phlegm). Today, despite the more advanced technologies brought to bear on the subject through brain imaging and molecular analysis of neurons and their networks, we seek answers to the same questions as the ancient Greeks: Is human existence a fundamentally material process, or is there something more to life and what it means to be a person? Generations of philosophers over the past 2,500 years have attempted to provide a definitive answer to this question, and each generation of psychiatrists and psychologists for the last 150 years (since the birth of psychiatry in the mid 1800s at German medical schools) has attempted to answer the question for abnormal psychology.

The credibility of neuroscience research related to psychiatry has recently been given low marks by the top team of statisticians in Western medicine (Button et al., 2013). Yet, this is the predominant model for understanding abnormal psychology in most areas of the mental health system. How do we explain such a stark anomaly in which an unsupported theory dominates the public mind and public services? One must turn to the history of the discipline to find a possible answer. The medical model in mental health was originally developed in the mid 19th century in large understaffed state hospitals with poor and indigent immigrant populations whose problems were seen as so extreme that they were considered to be unable to function in society; these people had often been abandoned by their families. Medical treatments that tended to subdue such patients and make them submissive seem harsh and even cruel when examined from outside the era or context in which they were developed. The medical model has fulfilled a key goal of those who govern society: to maintain social control over those who disrupt the families, school, workplaces, and the public order, when those disruptions do not rise to a level that activates the criminal justice system and results in placing people in prisons rather than hospitals (Jansz & van Drunen, 2004).

Psychiatric Diagnosis According to the Biomedical Model: DSM–5

Assessment and *diagnosis* are the general terms given by psychologists (assessment) and the medical community (diagnosis) to the process through which mental health professionals decide what problem, if any, the patient is experiencing and the appropriate treatment that should be therefore recommended. According to the work of Kleinman (1988; discussed in the previous chapter), such an assessment or diagnosis by a health or mental health professional depends on having a conceptual or theoretical framework from which to view the problem. Otherwise, one is using the lay concept of *illness* rather than the technical concepts of a *disease* or *disorder*. In psychology and the mental health professions, the consequences of a diagnosis may vary from referral for psychotherapy, medication, hospitalization (voluntary or involuntary), incarceration, rehabilitation, special education services, and disability compensation, to no treatment at all. In each instance, there is potential for great good to result if the assessment is done in a comprehensive and informed fashion and great harm if it is not. Many of these contexts are "high-stakes" assessments with significant life and financial implications.

The psychiatry profession began to dominate the mental health field in the area of diagnosis and assessment through the publication of the American Psychiatric Association's first edition of the now well-known *Diagnostic and Statistical Manual of Mental Disorders* (DSM) in 1952. It was widely adopted by government, insurance companies, and other emerging mental health professions (clinical psychology, clinical social work, rehabilitation counseling, and clinical mental health counseling). The fifth edition of the *DSM* (*DSM–5*; American Psychiatric Association, 2013) is authored by the Committee on Diagnosis and Nomenclature of the American Psychiatric Association (not the other larger APA, the American Psychological Association). It has grown from a modest document involving about 75 diagnostic entities in *DSM–II* (American Psychiatric Association, 1968) to an imposing tome of about 490 diagnostic codes in *DSM–5*. Its publication is authorized by a vote of the members of the American Psychiatric Association.

In spite of enduring questions concerning scientific validity, *DSM–III* (American Psychiatric Association, 1980), *DSM–IV* (American Psychiatric Association, 1994), and *DSM–5* have all attempted to guide the reader toward the belief that psychological problems are really biological disorders; all were presented as compendia of psychiatric knowledge about not only diagnosis but also prognosis (likely future progress) and etiology (causes of disorders). This was done in three ways: first by including many neurological conditions that may produce secondary cognitive or emotional symptoms (e.g., Alzheimer's disease, brain tumors, infections of the brain, poisoning of the brain), second by the order of presentation of the disorders, and third by highly selective claims of what research has demonstrated about the causes of the problems. The disorders that seem most likely to have a clear biological origin are presented first in *DSM–5*; only evidence for biological causal factors are mentioned in the text, ignoring evidence for psychosocial causation. Intellectual disability (formerly mental retardation) is the first disorder in *DSM–5*, and although it admits that the rate in the population is about 1% and that severe mental retardation (usually associated with biological causes) is .06% in the population, it only mentions biological factors creating risk of the disorder as a whole, despite the reality (discussed in Chapter 4) that there is no known biological etiology for intellectual disability in over 90% of those who receive the diagnosis (Moeschler, Shevell, & the Committee on Genetics, 2006).

The *DSM*s have all been intended for use within a psychiatric context, where it is understood that the diagnosis is based on the results of a clinical interview in which one both observes the behavior of patients and converses with them about their problem. Essentially, the clinical interview produces a self-report by the psychiatrist as to what she or he observed and a self-report of the patient as recounted by the psychiatrist. In an attempt to offset the essentially subjective nature of both psychological problems and our judgments about such problems in other people, the authors of *DSM–III*, *DSM–IV*, and *DSM–5* have over the years worked to make the descriptions and criteria for the primary diagnoses used in the field more behavioral and therefore somewhat more reliable. (*Reliability* refers to the odds that two clinicians evaluating the same patient/client will reach the same diagnosis.) They have done this by formulating lists of specific behavioral criteria for each diagnosis, including the frequency and duration of the behaviors in question. These criteria have been turned into behavioral screening checklists given online or in doctors' offices; these are often used in busy primary care offices as a basis for diagnosis after a brief 10-minute discussion rather than a full clinical interview, as was originally intended.

Adding to the confusion is the existence of what are referred to as *V codes* in *DSM–5*, which indicate circumstances that are not disorders but may be the focus of treatment. The 135 V codes that constitute 29% of all the diagnostic entities in the expanded *DSM–5* are not disorders but may require treatment. These 135 codes are each described in a few sentences with no criteria listed and constitute less than 2% of the descriptive content of *DSM–5*.

The whole purpose of any diagnostic system or nomenclature is to identify the problem requiring treatment to maximize the effectiveness of treatment. These V codes identify problems in living, such as parent–child, marital, or work environment conflict, that are sufficiently upsetting that professional assistance is sought from a mental health professional. Because these are relationship problems involving two or more people, the V codes cannot even be theorized to be within the brain of any one person. Perhaps this is why the V codes are not considered actual disorders by the *DSM–5* committee.

The Need for a Common Language and Criteria for Research

Even today, in both assessment and diagnosis there exists a tension between the needs of a managerial or administrative psychology that helps to compile data on the success or failure of large bureaucracies in terms of the care of "human resources" (i.e., large groups of human beings) and the needs of clinicians for a useful conceptual framework for thinking about the needs of individual patients/clients and for identifying the similarities and differences across patients/clients that might affect the success of treatment. Large-scale epidemiological studies conducted to survey the extent and seriousness of various psychological problems (or as per the *DSM–5*, "mental disorders" surveys mentioned in Chapter 4) in a population or region of a country do require a standardized language (i.e., a diagnostic "nomenclature") of some kind. In addition, the incorporation of reference to psychiatric disorders into various governmental statutes (e.g., governing the insanity defense, civil commitment, disability determinations involving compensation, coverage of treatment costs by health insurance, federal funding for school children with learning and/or emotional disabilities, or whether an individual is allowed to return to their job) means that without some uniform method of defining problems and assessing individuals for those problems, these laws and regulations cannot be implemented in a fair manner. There is a need for a pragmatic system that can make these assessments for institutional purposes without also limiting the understanding of the problems assessed once the point of classification has been passed and the need for treatment has commenced.

One important use of *DSM–5* is in what is referred to in public health as the field of *epidemiology*—the distribution across a population of specific health problems. Epidemiologists look for clues to the causes of illnesses by finding concentrations of an illness in specific physical or social environments (e.g., locale, climate, nutrition, age, gender, race, occupation, socioeconomic class). The National Institute of Mental Health surveys of *DSM–IV* disorders cited in Chapter 1 are a good example of this. When dealing with public policy and the lives of millions of people, it certainly is necessary to have some agreement on the terms we use to communicate about problems and to allow data to be amassed. Such a system requires some way of standardizing definitions and criteria for applying such terms to individuals.

The need for comprehensive epidemiological data exists not only in the world of mental health and illness but also in all of medicine worldwide. In 1948, the World Health Organization (WHO) was formed to coordinate the monitoring and treatment of health problems that transcended national borders (originally the identification and containment of infectious disease epidemics, the development of vaccines, and other public health problems). Such efforts required a system for classifying and reporting the prevalence in each country of various diseases, injuries, and disabilities, and WHO adopted a system that had been evolving since the early 1900s, the International List of the Causes of Death.

In 1948, WHO published *ICD–6*, the *Manual of the International Statistical Classification of Diseases, Injuries, and Causes of Death*. More recent editions were renamed the *International Statistical Classification of Diseases and Related Health Problems*, and the current edition is *ICD–10*, published in 1992 (Cooper, 2014, p. 2007). WHO is currently working on a radical revision, *ICD–11*, scheduled for publication in 2017. For the first time it will include not only a list of diseases and health conditions but also the best international data on the causes and treatment of these conditions. It is being prepared with international input from a multitude of practitioners and scholars who will be given opportunities to suggest and debate revisions on an open WHO website (http://www.who.int/

classifications/icd/revision/icd11faq/en/). The final product will be published by WHO and will be free and open to the public in an online format. No one can say at this time what the impact of such a major international effort will be, except that it seems likely that it will further reduce the dominant effect of *DSM–5* on international education in psychiatry and clinical psychology.

The American Psychiatric Association has been distancing itself from the *ICD* since the late 1960s, when it ceased participating in its development (Cooper, 2014, p. 209). In 1992, WHO published *ICD–10*, a much more detailed disease classification system than its predecessor (though much less comprehensive in terms of causation and treatment than that planned for *ICD–11*). Since 1992, the various segments of the private health care industry in the United States (hospitals and insurance companies) have refused to adopt *ICD–10*. However, public health officials have generally supported the shift to *ICD–10*, and in 2009 the U.S. Department of Health and Human Services, using its authority under the 1996 Health Insurance Portability and Accountability Act (HIPPA; 1996), issued a new regulation mandating the use of *ICD–10* by all segments of the health care industry. This changeover was supposed to be effected in 2012 but has been postponed by Congress twice. It is now scheduled for implementation in 2015. It seems that the worthy public health, administrative, and epidemiological functions of *DSM–5* may well be made redundant by WHO's efforts to continually improve the *ICD*.

PSYCHODYNAMIC THEORY

The psychodynamic approach offers another model for conceptualizing mental illness. *Psychodynamic* is an all-inclusive term for those theories that derive from Sigmund Freud's (1856–1939) original theory of psychoanalysis. These include classical psychoanalysis, psychoanalytic psychotherapy, ego psychology, object relations theory, self-psychology, and neo-Freudian and interpersonal (Sullivanian) or contemporary psychoanalytic theory. What these theories all share is an acceptance of at least three central features of Freud's (1920/1966) original theory: (a) the concept of unconscious mental conflicts, often from childhood, involving impulses, wishes, and intense feelings directed at key family members; (b) the existence of defense mechanisms, which are at least partially unconscious, that protect us from an awareness of these conflicts and fuel a resistance to understanding the conflicts; and (c) the power of a therapeutic relationship to reveal and resolve these conflicts through the process of transference. *Transference* occurs when the patient/client reexperiences emotional childhood conflicts in the therapeutic relationship where these can now be examined and understood rather than remain unconsciously controlling the client/patient.

As a practicing neurologist in Vienna in the late 1880s, Freud saw female patients with symptoms of neurasthenia and hysteria, the predominant patient groups seen by neurologists at that time. (Psychiatry was then seen as an exclusively inpatient hospital-based profession, often in mental hospitals or asylums.) These were conditions with vague, diffuse, physical symptoms without physical explanation. *Neurasthenia* was accompanied by excessive worry, fatigue, weakness of one's limbs, difficulty concentrating, and lack of motivation. *Hysteria* had more dramatic symptoms involving a disruption in the functioning of the senses or voluntary control of bodily movements. (See Chapter 6 for a more detailed discussion.)

During his medical training, Freud traveled to Paris to study with the famous French neurologist, Charcot. Charcot was known for alleviating dramatic symptoms of hysteria with hypnotic suggestion and also for being able to induce with hypnosis the return of such symptoms in his patients. Charcot also demonstrated that patients often had little recollection of what transpired during the hypnotic session, even though they seemed fully conscious during the procedure. Hysteria at that time was more akin to what we would diagnose as borderline personality today. In addition to the somatic symptoms there were also brief psychotic episodes, mood swings, and so forth. Freud took this controversial treatment back to Vienna, translated Charcot's papers into German, and built his practice around the use of hypnosis. Other neurologists of his day prescribed to their patients periods of rest at various health spas in the mountains of Austria, where they would soak in natural hot springs.

During this period Freud consulted regularly with an older physician, also a neurologist in Vienna, Dr. Joseph Breuer. Breuer also was using hypnosis, and he and Freud wrote early papers together on the treatment of hysteria with hypnosis. Over time Freud became frustrated with the rate of relapse in patients with hysteria treated by hypnosis. Freud and Breuer both credit one of Breuer's patients, Frau Anna O., with the initial discovery of the need to talk about emotional conflicts that were present at the time of the first emergence of the symptoms of hysteria. When Freud began encouraging his patients in hypnosis to follow this procedure, he found that his treatments had a more lasting effect. Eventually, he stopped using the hypnotic trance state completely and replaced it entirely with the "talking cure." It is from these thousands of hours of listening to the life stories of his patients that he fashioned the theory of what he came to call *psychoanalysis*.

Freud maintained that psychoanalysis was three theories in one. First, it was a theory of the human mind that, unlike other psychological theories, gave a priority to the understanding of the irrational actions of human beings through an analysis of unconscious mental contents and processes primarily of an aggressive or sexual nature. Second, it was a theory of treatment for symptoms related to anxiety (e.g., irrational emotions, worries, thoughts) that he claimed was more successful than other known treatments of his day. Third, it was a formal research method that permits a window into the unconscious by the analysis of *parapraxes* ("Freudian slips"), dreams, and symptoms. He believed that his careful observation of patients talking about their lives for 6 hours per week over 1 to 2 years was like a microscope in the biology labs he had worked in as a medical student, revealing previously unobservable features of the processes of human development.

He called his theory a *psychosexual theory of development*. It is easy to misunderstand the term *psychosexual*. Many casual students of psychoanalysis assume that this means that Freud believed that children wanted to have sexual experiences and relationships similar to those previously thought to begin in adolescence. Although Freud did note that children might have such thoughts or wishes that are briefly conscious, especially if seduced by adolescents or adults into such experiences, his real focus was on the universal desire to seek pleasure and avoid pain, a standard psychological principle he had taken from the British philosopher J. S. Mill's utilitarian theory of ethics. For young children, pleasure and pain seem to center on nursing and eating in the first year of life (the *oral phase*); toilet training, which in Victorian times was typically begun before the age of 2 (thus labeled the *anal period* in the second year of life); and the increased desire for physical closeness with, and adoration from, one parent or caregiver, often the parent of the opposite sex (the famous oedipal period between ages 3 and 6; Freud, 1905).

This was a bold psychological proposal, and though it has been much amended and revised, the tradition Freud began with his theory of psychosexual stages evolved into an important search for the subtle and detailed interpersonal and intrapsychic processes by which individual personality characteristics develop. His daughter, Anna Freud (1946), explored the development of ego or adaptive functions, namely, how our thinking, problem solving, and management of our own emotional states are influenced by early life experiences. The mid-20th century object relations thinkers in the United Kingdom (Donald Winnicott, 1896–1971; Ronald Fairbairn, 1889–1964; Melanie Klein, 1882–1960) emphasized the development of interpersonal relationships and how these relationships affect the way we think about ourselves, other people, and the world at large. Another group sought to integrate psychoanalytic developmental theory with the growing fields of sociology and anthropology (Erik Erikson, 1902–1994; Karen Horney, 1885–1952; Erich Fromm, 1900–1980; Harry Stack Sullivan, 1892–1949). In each of these shifts, the range of psychological functions (and stages of life) being viewed through a developmental lens and the range of potential important influences on human development were broadened. Taken together, these theories provide a guide to life-span development along a number of psychosocial lines of development: the sense of self, awareness of others, tolerance of ambivalence and conflict, competitive relationships, use of defense mechanisms, problem-solving skills. Adding to Freud's model of the mind developing in response to experiences of pleasure and pain in the body, psychoanalysis now had a much more nuanced theory that included the importance of attachment processes based on the need for nurturance, the emerging sense of self (and related concepts of identity, self-love, and worth), emotional experience, mood, frustration tolerance, and cooperative versus combative relationships with others.

Psychodynamic Defense Mechanisms

One of the key obstacles to appreciating psychoanalytic developmental psychology is that we usually cannot remember much of the first 5 years of our lives that Freud designated as so critical to understanding our unconscious conflicts. Of course, once these conflicts are unconscious, we also have no awareness of them in the present. How often in trying to help someone who is struggling do we have conversations that begin with "What's the matter?" "What has happened to make you feel this way?" "Tell me why you are having these problems or feeling this way," leading to the responses, "I don't know," or "Nothing has happened" or a simple noncommunicative shrug. It is no wonder, then, that the search for reasons and meaning is cut short and other explanations of physiological causes or skill deficits are sought. It is really only those observers or practitioners who understand the role of psychological and behavioral defense mechanisms who are in a position to stay engaged with the patient/client in a manner that permits the meaning of the problem to emerge. Defense mechanisms are the reason we need the logic of the psyche (a psychology) rather than just the logic of rational intelligence to solve the problems that have been classified as falling within the province of "abnormal psychology."

Though his bold and often speculative theories concerning the unconscious made him a highly controversial figure in the history of psychology, psychiatry, and psychotherapy, Freud's identification and elaboration of the role of defense mechanisms in the empirical clinical phenomena that he encountered in everyday practice is perhaps his most widely accepted idea. For Freud (1920/1966), the goal of therapy was to reclaim the parts of oneself and one's past history that have been shut out of awareness through the use of the various psychological defense mechanisms. What this means is that we often do not know ourselves as well as we need to to make the decisions that will guide our lives effectively. Freud (1920/1966, p. 124), who often used the analyses of his patients' dreams to aid in understanding their symptomology, had an enigmatic way of expressing this: "The dreamer does know what his dream means: *only he does not know that he knows it and for that reason thinks he does not know it.*" Thus, we make plans we that we cannot follow through with, enter into relationships that are unfulfilling, take jobs that are boring, and so forth. What is missing is an awareness of how we are going to really feel in situations until we get there; in some cases there is such a blocking of internal self-awareness that it extends to not knowing what we think or feel even in the present moment. To not know parts of our own experience that are too terrifying, we must also shut out information about the world we live in that might touch on those parts of ourselves. In so doing, we create important gaps in our knowledge and understanding of the world in which we live and must survive, including aspects of the people with whom we interact or may depend on for our survival.

How could it be that we act against our own survival needs? To explain this, Freud again turned to a developmental perspective. We are equipped with automatic and often unconscious psychological defenses against deeply disturbing emotional responses to the traumatic experiences of our childhood (and less often, adult lives). These defenses protect us from the worst part of such experiences—for example, the sense that we are about to die at the hand of someone we thought loved us or that some-one that we love and depend on is abandoning us. The mind insists, "This isn't happening," "This can't be happening," or "This can't be happening to me." Although these powerful defenses allow us to survive the worst that life can throw at us, they do not come without a price. The emotional arousal that is being suppressed at these times is converted to a less intense but more generalized sense of free-floating fear, sadness, or bitterness. We do not know (because we do not want to) where it (the past trauma) is coming from or what we can do to feel better, so we just live with it. As a child with little control over the circumstances of our lives, defense mechanisms are survival mechanisms. It would be pure torture to live with such thoughts in consciousness day and night. The defense mechanisms become a barrier to growth when we are older and have much more potential for self-determination, but we fail to exercise that freedom because we are handcuffed by our defenses.

Freud and his daughter, Anna Freud, identified a variety of specific defense mechanisms. In addition to *denial* (the forgetting of a specific event or feeling), he identified the pushing out of awareness of entire inner conflicts and labeled it *repression*. *Projection* occurs when we see our conflicts as belonging to other people ("I'm not angry, you are"). *Reaction formation* occurs when we exaggerate the opposite feeling or judgment to the one we are actually experiencing (saying, "I love that present you got me—thank you so much" and then returning it to the store). *Displacement* occurs when one expresses feelings in the present that were triggered previously (I am mad at my boss, do not express it, and then come home and kick my cat).

Freud also identified healthy defenses that help us diffuse some of our anxiety without creating more problems for ourselves. In creative expression in the arts he thought we *sublimated* our unconscious conflicts over anger and sexuality; likewise in the use of humor. Other defenses are discussed throughout this volume when they come into play with specific problems in living.

Psychodynamic Diagnosis

Freud also relied on the clinical interview, particularly the critical issue of what the individual was doing, thinking, and feeling at the time the neurasthenic or hysterical symptoms were first experienced. Here he would look for conflicted relationships with persons for whom one felt intense ambivalent emotions (e.g., love and jealousy or love and hate). He also set the tradition for psychodynamic assessment of taking a thorough life history, focusing as much as possible on the circumstances of a person's life during early childhood and in memories or dreams that demonstrate intense emotions from those years. Separations from parents, parental marital conflict, deaths or serious illnesses in the family, birth of a new sibling, frequent moves to new housing, and physical or emotional trauma to the child or a family member are examples of family history adults may know about even though they may not remember experiencing such events themselves.

In addition to this informal self-report information, psychoanalytic psychologists carefully observe the way the client enters into the therapeutic relationship for important clues about the way the client feels about himself in relation to other people (in this case, the psychologist). These observations may be of interpersonal style that the client is aware of or may be *transference reactions*, where the client distorts the psychologist's communications. These may be an indication of the client's patterns of interaction with family members early in life. A second source of observation is the psychologist's awareness of her or his own emotional reactions to the client that are distinct from the therapist's usual response to clients of the same age, gender, and background. Referred to as *countertransference*, this may simply be a reflection of unusual stress in the psychoanalyst's life or the residue of unresolved transferences from the therapist's own past. However, these reactions to the client may be a clue to how the client typically affects other people, in which case it is important information about the client. It is important for psychoanalytically trained psychologists to have worked on their own early family relationships to be able to understand the client more fully. Assessment of both transference and countertransference in the interview was introduced by Freud and his followers and remains a unique feature of that type of training in psychology.

Psychoanalysts distinguish in their assessments between neurosis, psychosis, and character or personality disorders. *Neurosis* was the focus of Freud's work and is defined by the presence of intense conscious and unconscious anxiety that appears seemingly out of the blue in adulthood (childhood cases are also possible). He identified two diagnoses within psychoanalysis: hysterical neurosis and obsessive–compulsive neurosis. Although neuroses appear to start at a particular point, character disorders are personality traits that serve as defenses against anxiety. Personality traits such as excessive dependency on others, avoidance of challenges, a need to dominate others, or a need to be the constant center of attention are seen as ways of forestalling the reexperiencing of underlying conflicts from early childhood. These patterns of thinking, feeling, and relating to others emerge in adolescence and are solidified in young adulthood. In *psychosis*, defenses have failed to protect the individual from overwhelming terror and conflict to the extent that the individual's sense of a coherent self becomes disorganized. *Hysterical neurosis* consists of intense, sometimes flamboyant emotional symptoms or their physical derivatives (e.g., fainting, pseudoseizures), whereas *obsessive–compulsive anxiety* involves intrusive thoughts and rituals aimed to ward them off. Psychosis was not treated by Freud, though he saw some application of his theory to explain the meaning of hallucinations and delusions as symbolic of unconscious conflicts similar to dreams. These suggestions have led some psychoanalysts to work with this population (see Chapter 8). One of the earliest female psychoanalysts, Karen Horney, developed an excellent conceptual framework for understanding personality disorders that we will encounter in Chapter 7 of the present volume.

In the first half of the 20th century, two formal means of assessing unconscious conflicts were proposed: the Rorschach Inkblot Test (Exner, 1993; Rorschach, 1921/1942) and the Thematic Apperception Test (Murray, 1943). Prior to World War II, when psychological practice was restricted primarily to assessment, these tests were commonly given by psychologists. Multiple ambiguous pictures or forms are presented to the client and she or he is asked to describe what he or she sees in the picture or to tell a story about it. Because the same set of cards is used by each person administering the assessment, these projective tests introduce some standardization into the assessment process and remove some of the individual variation from psychologist to psychologist. Elaborate scoring systems have been developed to allow comparison across clients in terms of the level of ego structure and emotional conflict. These tests take several hours to administer, score, and interpret and are therefore used sparingly today except in hospital or forensic settings where less costly clinical observation and interviewing have not produced a sense of understanding the client's problems.

Questions of predictive validity abound in the empirical literature on these assessment instruments (Lilienfeld, Wood, & Garb, 2000). Skilled interpreters seem to at times be able to make quite striking predictions from the symbolic interpretations of narratives evoked by these stimulus cards (e.g., Karon & VandenBos, 1981). Many clinicians have found that clients may reveal new aspects of their lives when responding to ambiguous projective assessment instruments, as opposed to the more straightforward questions of the clinical interview or objective tests. In 2006, the Alliance of Psychoanalytic Organizations published the *Psychodynamic Diagnostic Manual* (PDM Task Force, 2006), which for those working from a psychodynamic perspective has been useful. However, it is not accepted in place of *DSM–5* diagnoses and the related *ICD–10* categories by insurance providers as a basis of billing.

Humanistic–Existential Theory

A third approach to abnormal psychology comes from the humanistic–existential tradition. In the 1960s the humanistic psychology movement under the leadership of Abraham Maslow (1908–1970), Carl Rogers (1902–1987), Rollo May (1909–1994), Charlotte Buhler (1893–1974), and Virginia Satir (1916–1988) invigorated psychology departments with a "third force" and spawned the growth of the mental health counseling profession. They initially tended to reject all diagnostic terms as labels that categorized people and detracted from individuality. They referred to such aspects of the practice of psychology as "dehumanizing." In psychiatry, they thought this led to an acceptance of dehumanizing treatments such as compulsory sterilizations, electroconvulsive therapy, and prefrontal lobotomy.

Humanistic counseling and psychotherapy was less time-intensive and less expensive than psychoanalysis. The humanists believed that psychological pain was part of the human condition and that their "clients" (they rejected the term *patients*) primarily needed support, encouragement, and hope, through which they would find their own way to a solution to their problems. They said that the person who was suffering needed a relationship, not an interpretation. Humanistic psychologists have written extensively about the phenomenological or felt experience in areas such as psychosis, depression, and anxiety. They also explored the experience of freedom and freedom of the will, pointing to the everyday manner in which we are capable of determining, at least partly, our own destiny in life, as much by what we refuse to do as by what we actively do. They pointed as well to the freedom in human creativity in which we speak, write, draw, compose, or imagine ideas, images, and sounds that no one before us has ever conceived of in exactly the same way (Rychlak, 1981). Such freedom is not limited to creative artists but also extends to everyone in how she or he chooses to live each day. William James (1896/1966), writing over 100 years ago, pointed to how, by choosing to believe we are capable of a difficult task, we increase the likelihood that we will actually complete it. Granted, our exercise of free will is not without limits, and external social forces and physiological conditions may limit our options, but this does not mean that our actions are determined entirely by forces outside our personal control.

Humanistic–Existential Developmental Theory

Rogers's (1961) developmental theory focused on the growth of self-awareness and self-worth through relationships with one's parents. He believed that there was a positive growth potential that would lead to a positive sense of self and healthy relationships, unless obstacles were placed in the child's path. Those obstacles were messages that invalidated the child's own felt sense of what was happening around them. Parents, caregivers, and teachers who are highly judgmental or critical or who withhold love in attempts to mold their children into who they (the parents) wish their children to be, rather than allowing their children to be themselves, create these obstacles to "healthy" growth.

Maslow's (1971) theory of self-actualization also follows a developmental course, with basic physical needs having to be satisfied early in life, social needs next, and then transpersonal needs of self-actualization later in life. *Self-actualization* is finding a meaning for living that is beyond personal self-interest and that contributes to a connection with the community and furthers the culture we have been supported by. It is an experience as well of creative liberation from the constraints of living in fear of disappointing others or receiving criticism for being the person we each feel we are meant to be.

Charlotte Bühler (Bühler & Massarik, 1968) viewed human development as a process of becoming free and creative, and she examined how children sought such experiences at different ages. Although the infant is limited to need satisfaction, he or she can find creative ways, if only through trial and error, to increase the chances of those needs being met. Buhler saw moments when children between ages 2 and 4 spontaneously recognized what they truly loved, enjoyed, and could take comfort in. This is one of the building blocks to a creative self that cannot fully develop while the child and early adolescent is dependent on adults for survival. One must self-limit to be accepted and to avoid isolation or punishment. Yet during this self-limitation, we begin to demarcate how this self will live in the world when liberated from conformity to authority. Between 8 and 12 years the child is focused on developing a sense of self built on mastery and competence, often in the context of school and other forms of training and education. With adolescence comes an increased freedom to begin defining who one is and what one believes and values. All of these are elements of a tendency to develop a creative self that is influenced, but not controlled by, one's biological nature and social environment. We must take into account various limitations and restrictions in these areas (nature and nurture), but we need not be controlled by them unless we choose to abandon our own self and its potential for creative living (Derobertis, 2006).

Humanistic–Existential Diagnosis

Humanistic–existential psychologists have been skeptical of formal assessment procedures (Rogers, 1961). Rogers was particularly aware of the power differential in the assessment setting and the extent to which the psychologist is set on knowing more about a person than she or he knows about her- or himself. He thought such assessments set a horrible tone for later psychotherapy sessions; however, he developed a scale for research purposes to assess the overall level of psychological functioning. His experiencing scale allows one to assess a client after a session of psychotherapy for his or her ability to express his or her own thoughts, feelings, and conflicts in a spontaneous manner without denying responsibility for those inner experiences and at the same time not judging him- or herself for having them. The experiencing scale provides a window into the process of humanistic assessment and psychotherapy. I have modified it to clarify the conceptual content of the scale; this appears in Table 3.1.

Rogers noted that most people in the first or second stage of experiencing would not voluntarily seek psychotherapy or counseling. He noted that for many people the final stage of experiencing is difficult to fully achieve. He has shown in various research studies that progress in therapy can be gauged by clients' ability to move from the early phase of Stage Three into Stages Five and Six (Rogers, 1961). In terms of assessing an individual for psychotherapeutic services and assessing the outcome of those services, this is a potentially useful scale.

Contemporary humanistic psychotherapy researchers (Elliott, Greenberg, & Lietaer, 2004; Stiles, Barkham, Twigg, Mellor-Clark, &

TABLE 3.1
Carl Rogers's Process of Experiencing Scale

Stage	Quality of feelings	Content	Self	Freedom to change
One	Denial of all	No problem	Rigid	None
Two	Exhibited, not recognized	Externalized	Objectified	Fatalistic
Three	Present but distant ideas	Past, shameful contradictory	Reflected by others	Ineffective effort
Four	Intense differentiated	Mostly in past	Awareness of contradictions	Responsibility (beginning)
Five	Free, present, full	Internal, spontaneous	Authentic "me"	Seeking responsibility
Six	Immediacy, clarity	Unrestricted	A process of being	Integration of self/problem
Seven	Trusts own experience	Here/now	Fluid (feeling)	Internal (self-directed)

Cooper, 2006) have adopted measures of therapeutic relationships and more traditional clinical symptoms, such as anxiety or depression, to establish humanistic therapies as evidence-based treatments to qualify for government health care or private insurance payments. In addition, Fischer (2000) used a phenomenological framework in conjunction with traditional testing procedures (for intelligence estimates, personality traits, and clinical symptoms) in a collaborative manner with clients. Her approach is to ask the client what she or he has learned about her- or himself from each step in the testing process, also asking for the client's input into the final draft of any report that must be submitted to others. The report focuses on the individual's life goals and how the assessment may further the process of reaching those goals, rather than focusing on the usual comparison of the individual to standardized normative data.

Division 32, the Society for Humanistic Psychology of the APA, circulated a petition opposing the last draft of the *DSM–5* before it was published. The petition questioned the validity of the research program used to justify the diagnostic system and was signed by 15,000 mental health professionals (including this author) and 40 international organizations, including several divisions of the APA, the rather conservative British Psychological Society, the Danish Psychological Society, other division boards within the APA, and many other counseling and psychotherapy associations (http://dsm5-reform. com/). Current efforts are underway by these groups to develop alternative systems of diagnosis that might displace the *DSM–5* for clinical practice (Elkins, 2012).

COGNITIVE–BEHAVIORAL APPROACHES

The cognitive–behavioral model is the predominant clinical model taught in psychology graduate programs, particularly those clinical psychology doctoral programs that follow the Boulder model of training scientist–practitioners. As noted in Chapter 1, this model of treatment is based on the assumption that symptoms can be unlearned using the principles of learning theory developed in behavioral and cognitive psychology. It focuses on changing behavior and thought processes as a means of altering painful emotions and relationships (J. Beck, 2011). Using the same principles, behavioral psychologists have also offered training in behavior modification to parents, teachers, human services, and business organizations.

The major contribution of the cognitive–behavioral approach has been to bring to abnormal psychology a constant awareness of how much of what we think, say, feel, and do is actually learned from our experiences of living. Through experimental investigation under tightly controlled conditions of the laboratory, cognitive–behavioral psychology has provided a constant reminder of the critical role that specific environmental stimuli play in the processes of development. Experience alters the rate and direction of development in all areas of psychological functioning. Our bodies (through genetics, injuries, and illnesses) can place limits on what we become and accomplish, but these limits are usually broad, and the environmental influences on behavior select from within these broad ranges who we actually become. Particularly in our first decade of life we are quite malleable. We are organisms designed for learning, and thus in an environment attuned to an individual's strengths and weaknesses there is the potential for successful adaptation to human existence. The environment consists of both physical and social stimuli, with the social stimuli becoming increasingly powerful as our social world develops and expands throughout childhood and adolescence (Bandura, 1969; Skinner, 1953; J. B. Watson, 1924). Cognitive–behavioral theorists have emphasized learning as a continuous process rather than as occurring in specific stages of development.

Early pioneers in cognitive therapy (Albert Ellis, 1913–2007; Aaron Beck, 1921–) and behavior therapy (Joseph Wolpe, 1915–1997) had traditional training in psychoanalysis prior to developing their own approaches and adopted many of Alfred Adler's (1870–1937) earlier ideas about the role of conscious decisions to think, feel, and act in symptomatic ways in middle childhood. Adler was one of Freud's earliest followers and was heavily influenced by Freudian theories, though he did not agree with their universality (Adler, 1959). In recent years, J. Beck (2011) has acknowledged that some of the cognitive thought processes that heavily influence emotions and behaviors are the "scripts" from childhood (e.g., "I'll never trust an adult again" or "I'll never succeed at anything"). These scripts are not deeply unconscious; they operate outside of awareness, in the realm Freud called the *preconscious*—accessible without enormous effort but not thoughts or feelings we are aware of under most circumstances.

Also recently introduced in the second wave of cognitive behavior therapy (CBT) is acceptance and commitment therapy (ACT), which incorporates several humanistic ideas about the importance of awareness and acceptance of one's own stream of consciousness and the need for the client to make decisions to improve their own situation, rather than placing responsibility in the hands of the behavior therapist who will modify the client's behavior by manipulating the environment (Hayes, Follette, & Linehan, 2004). Motivational interviewing (W. Miller, 1996) has reintroduced Rogers's idea of unconditional positive regard and empathy as the central feature of the therapeutic relationship with highly resistant substance abusing clients.

Cognitive Behavior Therapy Assessment

Because of the similar assumption of the importance of quantified scientific-like indicators of psychological problems or disorders, the CBT and trait-measurement approaches to assessment have also been adopted in the more biomedical approach to diagnosis by those looking for measures that are more quantifiable than *DSM* diagnoses. As a result of this collaboration and the general scientific-like formulation of CBT principles, one often sees CBT as the primary therapy recommended other than medication in most medical practices. Usually this is secondary to medications, but on occasion it is offered as an option instead of medication in milder cases. Behavioral assessment attempts to duplicate laboratory measures of the effects of the contingencies of reinforcement by defining measureable operants (voluntary behaviors in specific environments) in the client's behavioral repertoire and then taking samples of those behaviors in terms of the number of such responses in a given sample period. These frequency counts are then monitored (usually by the client or staff) before, during, and also sometimes after treatment to determine whether it has been effective. This can be quite intrusive in a client's daily life, but some agree to do it.

Some behavioral measures designed for the individual client are used in cognitive approaches, but because the goal is to determine what a person thinks and feels, brief surveys of a client's thoughts, feelings, and behaviors that are associated with depression or anxiety have been developed (A. T. Beck, 1991). The client rates items on a 3-point scale measuring how frequently the content of the item is experienced; the total points are a rough measure of the extent of the problem to be worked on in CBT. For example, an item might read, "I am a worthless person," "When things go wrong, it is usually my fault," or "I have trouble falling asleep." These items are each followed by three choices, one of which is to be circled: *frequently*, *occasionally*, or *rarely*. The Beck Depression Inventory (Beck, Ward, Mendelson, Mock, & Erbaugh, 1961) is administered before, during, and after CBT to assess the effects of treatment. It has been administered to a variety of groups who do not identify themselves as in need of therapy, and although such individuals show a variety of scores, their average score is markedly lower than that from those who have requested therapeutic help. It should be noted that many such inventories are proprietary and are costly to purchase.

A number of behavioral inventories have been also been developed that are focused on child behavior problems (Achenbach, 1992; Conners, Sitarenios, Parker, & Epstein, 1998); these do not rely on frequency counts of specific behaviors over time. Since children are not generally viewed as good candidates for self-report measures because of difficulties with reading level, concentration, or cooperation with medical or psychological staff, when it comes to such assessment of children the patient/client does not respond to the behavioral descriptions on the inventory; instead, the person upset by the child's behavior—usually the parent and/or teacher—performs this task. These child behavior inventories standardize the assessment process in two ways: (a) One can be sure that the clients have all been asked about the same range of problems and asked in the same standard manner, and (b) the inventories permit developing age-related norms for children indicating how typical or unusual the child's behavior is for the same-age population (as seen by the significant adults in her or his life). Unfortunately, unless the clinician doing the assessment considers the extent to which the adults in question are fair in their reports of the child's behavior, there is nothing in these assessments that factor in distortions in the scores produced by relationship problems between the child and the adults in question. This is paid little attention, as the psychologist or mental health professional usually realizes that the parent is the "real client"; the child would not be present for an assessment unless the parent or school dictated her or his presence. In fairness, it might also be said that so long as the child must interact with these adults, their perceptions of her or him are critical to his or her well-being, and knowing the extent to which these adults see the child as problematic is critical to deciding on the type and intensity of treatment offered.

Objective Psychological Testing

Psychological testing is identified with a scientific approach to clinical assessment and is typically used by scientifically oriented psychologists from multiple perspectives (particularly biomedical and CBT) seeking to preempt, supplement, or shorten diagnostic clinical interviews. In psychological testing the client is presented with a standardized series of tasks to perform, and responses are scored according to previously established criteria. This tends to produce high interrater reliability, and because the tasks have been selected on the basis of their correlation with various outcome criteria (e.g., performance in academic settings, success in particular occupations, response to a specific treatment), the tests have respectable concurrent and predictive validity.

Psychological testing began with intelligence testing in the early 1900s. Individually administered IQ tests are still a major component of psychological assessment when a person's general cognitive abilities or school achievement are in question. These are labor intensive, taking several hours to administer, score, and write up in a report, and are therefore expensive to administer. It is only in the area of learning, developmental disabilities, and organic brain syndromes that these tests are commonly used and are of central importance in determining treatment planning (Wechsler, 1981). Neuropsychological testing is an extension of IQ testing and looks at specific cognitive or motor tasks that may be indicative of specific neurological deficits or illness. Such tests are required to be consistent with measurement and statistical theory and in this sense are far more scientifically credible as an assessment procedure than the DSM system. Clients must demonstrate their cognitive capacity through a series of increasingly difficult tasks that measure memory, vocabulary, abstract thinking, mathematical ability, visual–motor problem solving, and so forth.

The trait approach that arose out of personality research (Allport, 1937; Costa & McRae, 1988) identified important behavioral patterns, both healthy (e.g., sociability, conscientiousness) and unhealthy (e.g., H. Eysenck & M. Eysenck's 1985 work on introversion, neuroticism, and psychoticism), and led to "objective" (i.e., quantifiable) paper-and-pencil personality and clinical survey questionnaires in which an individual is asked to describe his or her behavior, attitudes, beliefs, and/or symptoms in questions that can be answered *true* or *false* or in ratings on 5- or 7-point Likert scales. The Minnesota Multiphasic Personality Inventory–2 (Butcher, Dahlstrom, Graham, Tellegen, & Kaemmer, 1989) has over 500 such questions (Graham, 1993) and screen people for being inconsistent or trying too hard to seem healthy or unhealthy. There are shorter screening and outcome measures used in general clinical practice, such as the 139-item Psychological Screening Inventory–2 (Lanyon, 2007), which takes a patient 15 minutes to complete, and the Patient Stress Questionnaire, a 31-item measure that can be completed in 5 minutes or less (Substance Abuse and Mental Health Services Administration, 2014).

These objective tests rely on self-report by the patient/client, and thus are essentially self-descriptions given in a format that can be quantified by the number of questions answered true and false related to specific symptoms or the self-rating on a scale of 1 to 5. This is objective in that the questions are standardized for every patient, and numbers have been assigned to answers so that a total score can be calculated and compared with other groups of people who have similarly described themselves. Because these are self-administered and now computer scored, they do save time. As screening devices in large organizations employing or serving hundreds of thousands of people (e.g., the government or military services), these objective tests have a legitimate role. The problem, as with the *DSM–5*, occurs when these become the primary means of understanding who a person is for the purposes of determining treatment. In time-pressured health care services this is always a risk: The person is treated as a diagnosis and not as a person who might be partially described by the test scores.

Another approach is for the clinician to use such an objective descriptive system for assessing the client after doing a formal interview or interviews. Structured interview rating scales or observational reporting of a client's behavior using a preset group of possible descriptors have also been developed (Shedler, 2012). These lack the cost-effectiveness of the self-report systems, but they do eliminate some of the individual variability in how clinicians report client symptoms and behavior by providing a standard format for doing so.

Granted, for the policy analyst or administrator who is interested in changing the average level of patient care in an institution, region, or society as a whole, group data has a different importance because it may suggest a need for policy changes. Improving the average level of care for all the patients is one way to approach social policy in a democratic nation. In such cases, the external validity of an assessment measure is critical in determining its ability to benefit the greater good. Unfortunately, external validity is the most difficult feature of an assessment variable to determine. Our research methods, primarily designed for answering theoretical questions, are far more successful at establishing the internal validity of our measures and findings by careful attention to matters of research design and statistical analysis.

COMMUNITY AND FAMILY SYSTEMS MODEL

The community and family systems model of abnormal psychology advises us to place all symptomatic behaviors, psychological problems, and psychiatric diagnoses into the social or institutional context in which the symptoms emerge (M. Levine, Perkins, & Perkins, 2005). The social work profession, which began in the early 1900s, had long held the view adopted from sociology that individual problems of functioning in society were almost always an expression of the failure of the major institutions of society to properly support and enculturate the individual. In other words, the real problems were in the family, economy, schools, churches, and governmental policies.

The profession of social work was built on a concern with issues of poverty, crime, substance abuse, racial or ethnic discrimination, and abusive family relationships, and these social circumstances were seen as the cause of psychological symptoms in the individual. About the same time, innovators in psychiatry and social work developed the first systematic programs of treatment for the entire family, and these family therapists also resisted diagnosing any individual family member, referring to the person who was most disturbed as the "identified patient" and believing that the real or true patient was the "family system" that could be diagnosed as dysfunctional in various ways as systems, not individuals (Hoffman, 2001).

This view also garnered support in the mid-20th century from the emergence of community psychiatry and community psychology within those professions (M. Levine et al., 2005). According to this model, paralleling social work theory and the experiences of mental health professionals working with World War II soldiers experiencing "combat fatigue" (now referred to as posttraumatic stress disorder), symptoms can only be understood in the context of reactions to the immediate social environment in which they were triggered, and environmental change is equal or more important than individual change (Herman, 1995). Working with family groups, employers, schools, community agencies, the police, and correctional system was key to reducing the stressful impact of these devastating life circumstances on individuals.

Developmental Family Theory

Social change must accompany personal change. Many psychoanalysts and humanistic psychotherapists have attempted to integrate these sociocultural ideas into their theories as well, particularly by developing approaches to family therapy. One might not expect to find much useful information about individual development from family systems theory, given that it is focused on a network of relationships and not on any one separate individual within that system. However, this expectation could not be further from the truth. By elucidating how family dynamics contribute to the emergence of problems in living (particularly in difficult problems such as psychotic thinking and refusal to eat [anorexia]), family systems theory is an invaluable addition to developmental understanding. In addition, attention to the family's life cycle and how it is superimposed on the individual's life cycle is of critical importance. The difficulty of adolescent identity issues is exacerbated if the adolescent's parents are experiencing their own mid-life crisis, marital discord, empty nest syndrome, and so forth. Births, deaths, and life milestones, such as weddings and divorces, affect and are affected by the meaning such events have to the entire family, not to the individual alone (Haley, 1993). Individual problems in living that seem inexplicable or insurmountable when considered only from the perspective of the individual's life history and development become intelligible and manageable once the individual crisis is seen in the context of the family's life cycle (Bowen, 1991; Satir, 1983).

A family has the potential to both nurture and support us when we are needy and feeling dependent and provide structure, discipline, and skills to face life's tasks independently. At the same time, the family life cycle introduces considerable stress and emotional conflict into the life of an individual. Marital conflict, the birth of a new sibling, sibling rivalry, an unemployed family breadwinner, moving to a strange house or school, a seriously ill family member, or a parent with an addiction or other serious problems of her or his own can result in a withdrawal of attention, support, and structure from a child's life. What the family giveth, the family can taketh away. We cannot understand the individual family members' paths of individual development without understanding the family's life cycle as well.

Family Systems Assessment

When an individual is having difficulty, she or he is involved in difficult relationships. Human actions only take place in the context of human relationships—even the hermit is defined by his avoidance of other people. Thus, the purpose of an action can usually be detected by examining what it accomplishes in the important interpersonal relationships, social groups, families, or communities with which the individual is involved. Actions taken to promote or avoid attachment, separation, loss, competition, rivalry, and jealousy are all familiar sources of personal concerns ("abnormal behavior"). Family therapists have defined patterns of family interactions that impede clarity of communication (Bateson, Jackson, Haley, & Weakland, 1956; the "double-bind"), prevent the emergence of autonomy (Bowen, 1991; "undifferentiated ego mass"), or create conflict (Minuchin & Nichols, 1993; confused role assignments, as when the child is expected to parent the adult and the adult takes the role of dependent child). Family therapists have developed systematic assessments of family dynamics that replace assessment of any one individual in the family (Moos & Moos, 1994; Skinner, Steinhauer, & Santa-Barbara, 1983). These are based on self-report, sometimes aided by observations through one-way mirrors or videotape analysis (Gottman, 1999).

AN INTEGRATIVE MODEL FOR A PRAGMATIC PSYCHOLOGY

Erikson's (1963) definition of good mental health as the ability to love and to work has been widely adopted in the psychodynamic tradition. By this it is meant that we must learn how to manage and participate in close interpersonal relationships so that we can ultimately feel close to other human beings and that we must learn how to manage our external physical and economic environments so that we can survive or even thrive in the world. Despite many attempts to offer different theories of human motivation or definitions of mental health, it seems in retrospect that all are simply slight modifications of Erikson's formula. The best modification is to be found in McAdams (2006), who writes of the need for agency and communion. *Agency* is the ability to intentionally alter the world around one in such a manner as it expresses how one wishes or wants the world to be, and *communion* is the process of drawing close to people and caring about their well-being.

Inherent in these definitions of mental health or goals of living is the notion of inevitable conflict. Our pursuit of work (agency/power) may interfere with our ability to attend to or promote our close relationships. Balancing work and family for working parents is a common theme in our culture today, as well it should be. However, there are other versions of this conflict that are subtler. One can consciously or unconsciously carry over a successful way of rather aggressively interacting with other people in the workplace to one's family life, only to discover that it pushes people away and interferes with close interpersonal relationships. One can also do the reverse, carrying over a supportive interpersonal style from close relationships to work, only to discover that this leads to a perception one is not competitive enough to succeed.

Erikson began his studies as an art history student, joined the psychoanalytic movement as a young man, and developed a map of psychological development that modified Freud's individual approach to include sociocultural influences on the development of our ability to love and work (communion and agency). Erikson's model, like Freud's, put a great deal of emphasis on early childhood, but unlike Freud, he saw crucial developmental processes also occurring during and after the adolescent years. A modified version of Erikson's model appears in Table 3.2.

Erikson's model is intended to supplement, not replace, Freud's theory of psychosexual development. He did not deny the power of pleasurable or painful experiences in our bodies to motivate us toward or away from various experiences, people, activities, thoughts, or wishes. Erikson also accepted Freud's theory that the same person or experience may be both pleasurable and painful and that such circumstances create an inner psychological conflict that may be and may remain unconscious—outside of our awareness. He also accepted the idea of fixation, meaning that if a period of development does not go well, if it involves too much pain or conflict, we arrive at the next stage unprepared for its challenges. Thus there begins an accumulation of difficulties because our psychological capacity to cope with the new challenges is not likely to be up to the task. For example, the problems from the oral phase of age 1 year increase the chances that we will have difficulty cooperating

TABLE 3.2
Life-Span Developmental Processes

Age (approximate)	Developmental psychological structures
Childhood and adolescence	
0–1	Work = Mastery of body to obtain food; use hands, feet, and body to navigate
	Love = Development of trust (attachment) in caretakers, avoidance of excess of mistrust
1–2	Work = Exploring the world, controlling the body in socially acceptable ways
	Love = Moving toward autonomy, avoidance of excess shame
3–5	Work = Continue to explore the world, learn in larger world
	Love = Seeking special relationships in the family without excess guilt
6–12	Work = Sense of productivity, industriousness
	Love = Development of friendships outside the family without excessive feelings of inferiority
13–21	Work = Continued growth in preparing for self-sufficiency in the environment outside the family
	Love = Beginning romantic/sexual relationships, a sense of identity without excess of identity confusion
Early adulthood	
22–35	Work = Continued development of job skills, advanced education, etc.
	Love = Search for true intimacy without excess of isolation
Middle adulthood	
35–55	Work = Mentoring junior members of one's profession
	Love = Building a legacy through promoting the next generation, without an excess of stagnation
Late adulthood	
60+	Work and Love = Developing wisdom about one's life's journey, the successes and failures, without excess of despair

in our toilet training or other social training we receive. We cannot tolerate the pain and frustration of foregoing pleasure because we have had too little of it in our lives. This is why the earlier there are difficulties in child development, the more severe the later psychological problems. Each stage builds on the previous one, and as the child matures physically, the demands on her or him continue to increase in difficulty and complexity until the psychological pain and suffering of later stages reaches a point at which the child becomes completely unable to function in work or love.

The original Freudian model did not leave much room for hope for children with traumatic early childhoods. The Freudians thought that without intensive psychoanalytic treatment, such individuals would always be locked in the pain and suffering of their pasts. Erikson, and then all later psychosocial theorists, argued that later relationships occurring in the natural world of the individual might be sufficiently therapeutic so that formal psychological treatment might not be necessary. Erikson talked about how fortuitous events might bring a person into the child's life who could build missing trust, autonomy, initiative, industry, or intimacy. A neighbor, relative, or teacher who sees the child's pain and makes the effort to offer extra nurturance, encouragement, guidance, or opportunity to develop talents and skills might be one source of such a naturally occurring therapeutic experience. This parallels what Sullivan (1953/1968) called the *chum*—where school-age children find a peer who befriends them and who affirms one's value and importance in the social world. Such fortuitous events cannot be counted on to happen and are more the exception than the rule. The life histories of "resilient" children who survive terrible early life circumstances often include accounts of such fortuitous relationships (Luthar, Cicchetti, & Becker, 2000). Therapeutic daycare centers and preschool education programs, such as Head Start, were designed by educators and psychologists who were attempting to institutionalize such resources from outside the family for children and families who may be in need of these developmental supports.

COLLEGE AS A DEVELOPMENTAL CRISIS

For many readers, the developmental milestone that is most salient and easy to remember and describe is the process of leaving home and moving into a college environment. Although it may have been anticipated and even planned for over several years, the actual physical act of moving into one's first college dorm room can be an overwhelming experience filled with intense mixed emotions—joy and sadness, fear and excitement, liberation and homesickness, to name several possible reactions. (For those who do not attend college after high school, similar feelings may be associated with the first time one moves out of the family home into one's own place, joins the armed services, starts full-time employment, etc.) These transitions are difficult in that they often feel like a "natural," inevitable part of growing up and becoming a mature adult, yet their compulsory nature is entirely a function of social conventions, often tied to income and social class variables. In agrarian communities or societies, the expectation in farm households is to get married at about this same time of life, have children, and then, depending on the accommodations at the parents' house, move out and start one's own household.

Those who are not ready for these kinds of big steps at the end of high school often feel stigmatized and under pressure to demonstrate their independence. Those who take the steps toward independence often feel overwhelmed, terrified, nauseated, and confused and feel the need to hide these feelings, again for fear of being seen as "not very mature" or independent. These feelings of being overwhelmed may last well into the second semester of the first year of college. Sometimes such students are referred to the college or university student counseling service.

Unlike many mental health contexts that are dominated by a medical model of symptom diagnosis and treatment, college and university counseling centers have long taken a developmental and problems-in-living approach to the work of counseling and psychotherapy. Even in today's highly medicalized world in which problems and suffering are converted to symptoms of illnesses, college counseling centers continue to focus on the daily problems in living faced by their students (Bland, Melton, Welle, & Bigham, 2012). Benton, Robertson, Tseng, Newton, and Benton (2003) reported that over an academic year students at a large Midwestern state university counseling center focused in counseling on the following problems in living: relationship issues 56%, family issues 45%, situational issues 58%, educational/vocational issues 22%, developmental issues 41%, abuse 12%, medications 22%, academic skills issues 34%, health problems 13%, grief 9%, legal problems 3%, and sexual assault 3%. The rates of all problems increased significantly and even dramatically over the 13 years of the study (except for educational/vocational, abuse, and legal problems, which either remained constant or fluctuated slightly up or down at the midpoint of the study). Problems with medications tripled over the 13-year period.

Case Study: A First-Year College Student With "Academic Problems"

The following is a case study based on the work of an intern at a college counseling center in New England. I was the case supervisor. Some details of the case have been changed to preserve the confidentiality of the client, but not in a manner that changes the fundamental clinical reality of the case. Cases were assigned to counseling center interns on the basis of the intake coordinator's assessment of whether the problem appeared to be primarily in the academic realm or the interpersonal realm. New interns were assigned academic problem cases because they tended to be less demanding. The intern was in her second year of graduate school, 24 years of age, and married with one child. She was relatively inexperienced, so she was assigned academic problem cases. The student/client was a young woman who had just entered the college as a first-year student 4 weeks before the first counseling session. She was concerned that she was not able to concentrate on her work. Having always been an excellent student in high school, this was a new and frightening experience for her, and she was extremely motivated to find a solution to her difficulties.

Because the experienced intake worker at the college counseling service had determined that this was likely to be a case with primarily an academic problem, the intern explored with the student (who will be referred to using the pseudonym Sally) her study habits and skills. She had been an excellent student at a competitive private high school in New England and had developed in her 4 years there a capacity to do a great deal of academic work effectively and efficiently. However, now at college she had a complete block, staring at her study materials for hours without being able to stay focused for more than about 15 minutes. The intern made a number of inquiries hoping to isolate the interfering stimulus:

- Was her roommate or room distracting? No, she mostly studied in the library, but her roommate was great.
- Was the work too difficult for her level of preparation in high school? No, in fact, the college work so far seemed a bit easier than what she was used to in her senior year of high school.
- Perhaps the course instructors were too distant, not like the warm supportive teachers she had in high school. No, in fact, the instructors had been super—she had even shared with a few of them the trouble she was having, and they had offered that she could wait to take her midterms until after semester break in a few weeks.
- Perhaps she was not sleeping well and was too tired to focus on her studies. It was true that she was not sleeping well because she was so worried about the upcoming exams, but she slept well the first week of the semester before she realized that she could not concentrate on her work.

At the end of the first session, the intern thanked Sally for coming in and said that she was sure that if they kept exploring the difficulty they would get to the bottom of it, and her powers of concentration would return. In supervision we discussed how the first session had gone. The intern liked working with Sally, who she saw as intelligent, warm, and attractive as a person and sincerely motivated to make a change. We discussed what else might be interfering with her studies. Could it be course selection or course content? Perhaps she had first been anxious about her grades and then could not focus, rather than the other way around.

In the second session, the intern explored these other possibilities. Sally was happy with the courses she was able to register for in her first semester and actually enjoyed listening to the lectures, but then her mind would wander. Feeling she was against a brick wall, the intern branched out and inquired whether Sally might be feeling distracted because she missed her old school friends or home. No, she was happy to be making so many new friends and loved living in a college town. Nonplused by continually running into dead ends, the intern suggested that the search for the cause of the poor concentration was not necessary and that instead they should work directly on changing Sally's study behaviors by altering the "contingencies of reinforcement" controlling her concentration on work. The intern asked for a blow-by-blow description of how Sally studied in the library.

Sally reported that she would enter the library either after classes at about 2:30 p.m. or after dinner at 6:30 p.m. She would stay for a minimum of 3 hours, but often after 15 minutes of trying to study she would get up from her chair, get a snack, walk over to the magazine rack and read a weekly news magazine, or just sit and people-watch. Occasionally, she would return to her textbooks and make another feeble attempt to study, but to no avail. The intern then suggested a behavior-shaping plan in which Sally would gradually increase her study time in 5-minute increments, beginning with 15-minute study blocks and increasing eventually to 1-hour blocks of time. Each time she met her goal, she would reward himself with 5 minutes of snack, magazine, or people-watching time. After receiving the reward, she was to increase the reading time target by 5 minutes using the same reward as the incentive. The intern explained that in just a few hours of shaping her own behavior, Sally would be reading for 1 hour at each sitting. If she got stuck at a particular step in the process, she was to repeat the last successful step two times before increasing the goal by the next 5-minute increment.

Sally thanked the intern for her thoughtful analysis and said she was eager to implement the plan that evening. However, when Sally returned for the third session of counseling, she was quite distraught. She had failed at implementing the plan after the second step. She had improved to 25-minute study blocks but then could not get herself to study anymore, no matter how good the incentives. Worse yet, Sally was now beginning to fear that she would be unable to succeed at college because of this new difficulty. In fact, she was so upset about that possibility that she reported calling her uncle to discuss what to do. Her uncle had been calm and reassuring, and that seemed to briefly help Sally to calm down.

Surprised by the introduction of the uncle into the session, the intern asked how he had been chosen to be the recipient of this call for help. Sally explained in a matter-of-fact, almost nonchalant, manner that she had lived with her aunt and uncle for the summer before coming to college; she really liked and respected her uncle, and so he seemed like a good person to call. Sally presented this information in such a casual manner that it took the intern until almost the end of the hour to ask Sally why she had chosen to call her uncle rather than her parents. Sally then made it clear that she had lived with her uncle over the summer because 3 weeks before her high school graduation her father had passed away, leaving her uncle as her guardian. She commented that the hardest part of her father's death was having so much responsibility for planning and arranging the funeral and dealing with the lawyers about her father's estate.

The session ended on that surreal note, with the intern's head spinning. It was only in supervision that she realized that Sally had presented the account in such a matter-of-fact and detached manner that she (the intern) had never thought to inquire how Sally's father had died, whether there were other siblings, or why she had gone to live with her uncle rather than her mother. The intern was also feeling somewhat overwhelmed because it was now clear that this was not simply a case involving a straightforward academic problem, and she worried whether she could handle the sadness she feared uncovering in the next session.

As the fourth session began, Sally noted that all her professors had given her extensions to take midterm exams after the semester break, and she felt somewhat relieved. Nevertheless, Sally noted that she was worried because she still was not able to concentrate on her work, and she feared that these extensions were only delaying inevitable failure. The intern asked how she had felt about the third session, and Sally remarked that it was fine. The intern then asked how Sally's father had died and whether it was unexpected. Sally reported that her father had committed suicide by taking a drug overdose, and Sally had been the one to find him dead on the living room floor. She had known her father was depressed, but she thought he was going to snap out of it with time. When asked about the nature of her father's depression, Sally was quite vague and evasive. When pushed, she allowed that her father's suicide might have been in reaction to the loss of his wife (Sally's mother) the previous year. She had a long history of health problems, and he never got over her death. They had been married for 40 years, and Sally was their only child. It was nearly halfway through the session before the intern realized that Sally had done it again. She had for the second time managed to tell the story of a parent's death without indicating how the parent had died.

Bracing herself, the intern asked Sally how her mother had died. Sally haltingly answered that her mother had died as a result of a lifelong battle with alcoholism. This time, the details of a parent's cause of death opened the floodgates, and Sally sobbed inconsolably for the last 20 minutes of the session. The intern did the best she could to comfort her, but mostly she just sat by her side as Sally wept. At the end of the session, the intern commented to Sally that all that pent-up grief might impede concentration on schoolwork, and it was good for her to grieve. Sally was appreciative of the opportunity to unburden herself, yet she found it hard to believe that grieving would interfere with her schoolwork. After all, she had taken her final exams in both her junior and senior years of high school within a few weeks of both her mother's and then her father's death.

The next week was the semester break, and Sally returned to counseling the week after to report that the midterms had gone quite well and that while in Boston her uncle had advised her to not worry so much about grades as a first-year student. She seemed genuinely to have been grieving the loss of her parents and at the same time freed up to fully engage in college life. Sally was seen another six sessions and terminated a month into the second semester because she was far too busy with friends and activities to make time in her schedule for the counseling sessions. By the time she terminated she could avow that perhaps the loss of her parents within the span of 12 months might have contributed to her concentration problems.

Reflections on the Case of Sally

Sally was a first-year college student whose life had both been blessed with privilege and opportunity (affluent family, private schooling, concerned extended family) and cursed with tragedy. We must assume that despite the benefit of material wealth, both her parents must have been overwhelmed by other life circumstances that were not explored during Sally's relatively brief psychotherapy experience. Counseling centers often do brief problem-focused work, and though Sally may have a lifetime of suffering to work through over the loss of her parents to their self-destructive acts, her immediate need was to be able to master the challenge of starting college after these twin tragedies. People often do the psychotherapeutic work they need to in segments on the basis of the degree of subjective pain they are feeling at any one time and the time and financial resources available at that time.

Moving through the later adolescent period and clearly anticipating being launched into the adult world subsequent to attending college, Sally was intensely alone in her first few months of college. She lacked a trusted supportive adult who could help her to navigate this new phase of life when she had to be more autonomous and self-directed than at any prior stage of her development. The graduate student intern was able to form a relationship with Sally in which Sally could trust that there was someone on campus who was fully on her side and available to hear about all aspects of her experience, including the horrible sense of grief and loss that would come over her in waves at unexpected times during the day and night. Without that support she might well have withdrawn from school so that she would not fail her courses, but then she would have new problems in living with which to cope: where would she live, with whom, how she could maintain old friendships or develop new ones with so many of her old friends away at their new colleges and new friends she made at college moving ahead while she was left behind? Her sense of self-worth would have taken yet another blow, after she already been abandoned by both her parents to survive in a life they did not wish to participate in any longer. Success at college and the building of new relationships had the potential of strengthening her sense of self both in work and love, giving her a sense of a future with opportunities of her own making, rather than being a prisoner to the past in the tragedy her parents had created.

4

PSYCHOLOGICAL SUFFERING IN CHILDHOOD

The typical emotional and behavioral problems of childhood and adolescence are the result of the inability of the social and emotional environment to offer the support and structure required for psychological well-being. Children vary greatly in their need for such support and nurturance, and environments vary greatly in the ability to offer the required levels of support. This does not mean that the adults are to blame for the child's problems, but it does mean that all such problems can be prevented or greatly reduced if the social environment can rally to support the child. Young children have almost no power to change their environments for the better. There are always adults somewhere in the child's environment who have the power to change the circumstances under which the child is being raised, though for various reasons they may not be able or willing to exercise that power.

The psychological disorders of childhood are always a result of an interactive process between the child and his or her social environment. In the absence of sufficient support, children develop emotional and behavioral

http://dx.doi.org/10.1037/14693-004
Not So Abnormal Psychology: A Pragmatic View of Mental Illness, by R. B. Miller

problems. These may include a wide variety of symptomatic behavioral problems that disrupt the expected pattern of development in a child or adolescent in the following areas: feeding and eating; ability to fall into a diurnal sleep and waking pattern; speech and language development; attachment to caregivers; motor and coordination development; toilet training, bedwetting, or soiling; sibling and peer relationships; learning in school; disobedience and defiance of adult caregivers or teachers; basic sense of security and safety in the world; intense sadness or discouragement; self-worth or self-confidence; habitual repetitive behaviors for self-soothing.

The range of childhood expression of emotional and relational distress is dumbfounding. It leads to a great deal of confusion among theorists, researchers, and practitioners who fail to consider the symbolic and metaphorical aspects of symptoms and who therefore believe that each of these problem areas is a "different" problem. Children often lack the ability or vocabulary to directly express their emotional states, and we are often in the position of deciphering a coded language for which we only know some of the code. Instead of learning how to decipher and understand the coded communications, enormous energies are invested in studying the presumed biological, cognitive, or environmental factors that differentiate these problems, rather than examining the common elements. A 2009 National Research Council and Institute of Medicine report concluded that psychological and behavioral problems in youths co-occur and that these conditions stem largely from the same conditions: physical, sexual, and emotional abuse predicting severe problems, and chronic parental conflict, criticism, insults, and teasing (coercive interactions) predicting hostile and combative and oppositional behavior in childhood (Biglan, Flay, Embry, & Sandler, 2012; Felitti et al., 1998).

Children vary in how much support or direct assistance they require to achieve various developmental milestones (e.g., walking, talking, toilet training, tolerance of separation from attachment figures), and equally important, caregivers and parents vary considerably in how much support and guidance they are capable of offering a young child at a particular time and place. Mismatches between the needs of the child and the capacity of the adults are critical in producing disruptions in the desired path of development. It may be that the child is not able to use what is offered, even though what is offered is what most children could use effectively for development. When the child does not thrive in the "average expected environment," we tend to attribute the resulting problems as internal to the child. Similarly, if a child is making demands for attention and support that seem age-appropriate and the attachment figures do not offer sufficient support, we attribute the problem to a deficient family or attachment environment.

When the child needs more than the average expected environment typically provides, it is still possible for the caregivers to identify this and provide greater than average support and attention. Of course, parents may need the assistance of others in doing so (grandparents, friends, community services). If it is sufficient, the child returns to a more average developmental trajectory, and there is no diagnosis remaining to be explained (Block & Block, 1980). Even when parents cannot personally compensate for a child's needs that are greater than the environment can support, child play therapy is often effective in steering the child's development back on course (Bratton, Ray, Rhine, & Jones, 2005; Moustakas, 1997).

At other times these environments of social and emotional deprivation may exist in society at large (as in a war-ravaged area of the world); in a subculture, such as living as a member of a persecuted minority in an economically depressed region of a generally prosperous country; or as the result of being part of a nuclear or extended family in which the adults raising the child are severely stressed by the following sorts of family problems: loss of a job or low income, health problems, ethnic or racial isolation, physical or sexual abuse, substance addictions, intense intrafamilial conflict, and divorce. These may occur even though the surrounding neighborhood may not share those difficulties. Another way of saying this is that the social and emotional climate may be adverse for the child on the macro (regional/national), local, or micro (familial) level.

Often environmental and family stresses fall harder on one child in a family. The reasons for this can be many and diverse. It can be as simple as the child being born from a pregnancy that was physically taxing, leaving the mother's health compromised, or a child born right before or after the death of the mother's own mother. It can be as complicated as a child being born and triggering the parents' own unresolved pain from childhood traumas. A similarity in physical appearance, health problems, shyness, or learning problems can trigger a parent's overidentification with the child, and this, if it is not worked on by the parent, can trigger either overprotectiveness or abandonment. Such factors are much more subtle, hidden, and difficult to discover and identify than the more obvious issues of parents' loss of employment, disability, divorce, eviction, and so forth.

Unfortunately, in traditional approaches to child psychopathology or behavior disorders, these contextual or systemic factors are only mentioned in passing, and instead, the child's disturbed (or disturbing to others) behaviors are the focus of the diagnosis and treatment. It is assumed that the adults will not, or cannot, change their contribution to the child–adult problem, and thus the least powerful person in the situation, the child, is required to alter her or his behavior or be regarded as "treatment resistant" or incorrigible.

Given the enormous range of physical and psychological individual differences among children and the wide variety of differences in family structures, supports, and dynamics in which children are raised, how is one ever to know what can be done to promote healthy development for children who are showing signs of disruptions in healthy development? The answer is to listen to the child, and if the child is not speaking in a coherent manner, then observe carefully her or his actions and consider those actions a means of communicating feelings and needs. Of course, one must also listen to the parents and caregivers in an equally open and compassionate manner. They have important information to share about the child and themselves. In the vast majority of situations the parent is not to be blamed for the problems in development. Few parents deliberately harm their children (Karon & VandenBos, 1981), but some act impulsively out their own desperation and unhappiness. Nonetheless, if the child is to have a chance of improving, a parent must take responsibility for changing the circumstances that are contributing to the child's misery.

TYPES OF "DISORDERS"

Traditionally, empirical studies have classified childhood diagnoses into two main subgroups (Achenbach, 1992):

- *Internalizing problems* in which the child is the one who suffers, though their suffering results in adults attempting to reduce their symptoms and complaints. These are children who show separation anxiety when they are required to attend school or preschool or who are withdrawn or shy with adults or other children. This may be manifested in psychosomatic (somatoform) complaints such as nonspecific headaches, stomachaches, injuries due to accidents, and so forth. Female children receive these diagnoses much more than do males, in a ratio of at least 2:1. Over time, these anxiety difficulties can develop into childhood depression.
- *Externalizing problems* in which the child does not complain, but the adults do quite vociferously. Here, the child who is anxious "acts out" their anxiety rather than containing it and shows anger and frustration in direct and indirect ways. Diagnoses in this group include attention-deficit/hyperactivity disorder (ADHD), oppositional defiant disorder, conduct disorder, and as the child becomes a late adolescent, antisocial personality disorder. This is a set of diagnoses largely given to male children, at a ratio of 3:1. Many children with ADHD diagnoses are also labeled with at least one of the other three diagnoses.

The externalizing disorders are defined in terms of defying adult expectations or disobeying adult rules either at home or at school (or in the community at large). Of course, this kind of aggressiveness may also be directed against peers. The adults who are offended or inconvenienced by the child's behavior are seen as the source for the most "objective" reports of that behavior. The Achenbach Child Behavior Checklist (Achenbach, 1992) is a widely used method of assessment in this area, but there are no generally accepted independent tests assessing the behaviors listed in the *Diagnostic and Statistical Manual of Mental Disorders* (5th ed.; DSM–5; American Psychiatric Association, 2013) as criteria for these diagnoses. One little-appreciated aspect of this division of problems into internalizing and externalizing subgroups is that this is a grouping of reported behavior problems, not of the children themselves. Many children, especially after the primary grades, begin to show behavior problems in both groups. For example, a child may show signs within the same day of being withdrawn or anxious and then later aggressive or disobedient. Both children and adults who report that they feel "depressed" or hopeless and discouraged may also be angry and embittered.

Diagnoses using *DSM–5* are problematic in that they show a misplaced concreteness and pseudoscientific objectivity. One need only examine the quasiobjective criteria for the diagnosis of ADHD, one of the most rapidly increasing diagnosed psychological problems in childhood in the United States, to arrive at this conclusion. The criteria for diagnosing ADHD in children are divided into two subgroups (A and B) of nine behavioral criteria (American Psychiatric Association, 2013). Group A determines the diagnosis of attention deficit, and Group B determines the diagnosis of hyperactivity. One must meet six or more of the criteria in each group to receive the corresponding diagnosis. Group A includes behaviors such as inattention to detail, not listening when spoken to, not completing one's work, distractibility, and so forth. Group B includes behaviors such as inability to play quietly, excessive movement around the classroom, talking out of turn, being intrusive, and so forth. The behaviors must be present prior to the age of 12 years in two different environments (e.g., home and school) and result in clear evidence of social impairment in daily functioning. In addition, the behaviors cannot be due to another mental disorder—for example, childhood depression, anxiety, or pervasive developmental disorder. The child who meets the criteria in both Group A and Group B receives an ADHD diagnosis. A child may be diagnosed with just attention deficit or just hyperactivity, but that is relatively rare.

To the uninitiated, or to a worried parent at the pediatrician's office, these seem like straightforward descriptions of problem behaviors, and the three possible resulting diagnoses seem equally clear. However, if one considers the actual instructions for making such a diagnosis—namely, choosing any six symptoms in a set of nine and then repeating that process for each of the Group A and Group B subtypes—there are in principle 84 possible ways a child might be diagnosed with a disorder. However, for the full diagnosis of ADHD there are actually 84 × 84 = 7,056 distinct symptom patterns for the full diagnosis of ADHD.

Granted, several of the additional criteria (age of onset, perception of clinical significance) might restrict the number of children receiving the diagnosis, but not the number of combinations in those so diagnosed. Of course, these numbers would only apply if the criteria really were distinct behavioral indicators, but clearly they are not. In fact, even the wording of several is almost indistinguishable. Others are clearly different but highly correlated behaviors. Teachers and mental health professionals do not judge distinct symptoms but behaviors that are causally related: If I cannot pay attention, I probably will not remember what was said or where I left my pencil; if I am moving around, I am probably not listening to the teacher and cannot remember what she or he said or follow the instructions she or he is giving. There is an underlying question in all of this that is not being addressed in diagnosing Johnny: Is Johnny suited to classroom learning in the class that this teacher is teaching, in the way that this teacher teaches? Am I as a parent providing a home environment before and after school that supports Johnny in being able to focus and cooperate at school? These questions invite the adults involved to consider their own role in the problem, rather than focusing on Johnny as a child with a defect in self-control and concentration.

IS ATTENTION-DEFICIT/HYPERACTIVITY A BRAIN DISORDER?

The rate of ADHD diagnosed among children 4–17 years of age reached 11% in 2011. The Centers for Disease Control and Prevention (2014) reports that "rates of ADHD diagnosis increased an average of 3% per year from 1997–2006, and an average of approximately 5% per year from 2003–2011" (para. 2). Once diagnosed as "minimal brain damage" for children who had sustained a known physical assault to their central nervous system (by injury, birth trauma, or infection), it is now diagnosed on the basis of behavior, but treated with brain-altering substances that are essentially psychostimulants—the same stimulants (e.g., amphetamines and related substances) that when consumed recreationally by adolescents and adults are considered drugs of abuse. It is important therefore to examine what evidence there is for the medical model of ADHD.

Biological Etiology

Literature reviews on the biological etiology of ADHD in recent years have focused almost exclusively on the search for molecular genetic evidence.

It is frequently noted that children are often diagnosed with both ADHD and either oppositional defiant disorder or conduct disorder, all three being examples of externalizing behavior problems. The areas of the brain associated with the wide range of behaviors in these externalizing behaviors are extremely diverse: prefrontal cortical areas, basal ganglia, cerebellum, and temporal and parietal cortex. Although researchers using twin and adoption studies have asserted that heritability is quite high, between 70% and 80% (Faraone et al., 2005), the first wave of molecular genetics studies (referred to as candidate gene studies) searched for gene variations related to producing and transporting serotonin and dopamine in the brain (because these are neurotransmitters most affected by the stimulant medication thought to be effective). Wallis, Russell, and Muenke (2008) found 215 reports of candidate genes tested for their association to ADHD. Only 36% of the tested associations were positive, 47% were negative, and 17% were equivocal. There were serious statistical problems in all the studies due to small sample size. Even when there was a positive finding, the amount of variance in symptoms explained by the genetic marker association was small.

In a comprehensive literature review, Banaschewski, Becker, Scherag, Franke, and Coghill (2010) observed that all the positive findings in candidate gene studies accounted for no more than 5% of the presence of symptoms in the ADHD populations studied. As a result, researchers have adopted a new approach, genome wide association scans, which searches the entire genome of each person in the study, looks for gene variations in common between patients with ADHD and their first-degree relatives, and then searches the chromosomes where these variations are found for gene variations that maybe linked to ADHD. Two large genome-wide association studies have been done, one with children and one with adults. The results were meager and difficult to interpret. There were no significant findings in the study of adults, and when ADHD was diagnosed using traditional methods, there were no significant results for children either. When the results were reanalyzed using a quantitative measure of ADHD, there were two genes that were significantly related to ADHD. The authors concluded, "To date, the findings from genetic studies in ADHD have been somewhat inconsistent and disappointing" (p. 247).

The Case of Max

Max is a 10-year-old boy attending the fourth grade in a rural public school. He lives with his parents, a 16-year-old brother, and a 13-year-old sister. The parents are both employed and have their own home, though they seem to struggle financially. Each year, Max falls further behind in meeting academic expectations at school. He does not pay attention to oral instructions or the content being taught. He does not complete reading or writing assignments in class and refuses to do homework after school. He mostly just waits for recess where he can engage in rough and tumble play organized around various fantasy adventures he creates for himself. Occasionally, other boys will join him in these adventures, but when they do it often ends in a verbal or physical altercation when the other child refuses to follow Max's orders or instructions.

At home, Max enjoys the company of his sister, and they are able to play well together unless the older brother is present, at which point Max provokes his brother by taunting him verbally or ambushing him with a physical assault. The older brother often takes these attacks without retaliating, but when this becomes too much, he will lash out; Max will then run to his parents for comfort because his big brother tried to hurt him. He is unable to either restrain himself from provoking or see his own part in creating the fights in which he is injured. In addition, Max is difficult at mealtimes and bedtimes. He refuses to eat most of what the rest of the family is served at each meal, and he seems to only need about six hours sleep, not falling asleep until close to midnight each night and then waking up at the crack of dawn. Every meal is a struggle, as is every bedtime, and he seems to control the social and emotional climate of the household.

When required to do chores, clean his room, or do homework, Max complies until the adult leaves the room, at which time he becomes engrossed in other activities, usually a video game, watching television, or his own fantasy play. When called out on this pattern, Max frequently becomes enraged, telling his parents that he hates them and that he wishes he had better or different parents. After consulting with her own psychologist, Max's mother brought him in to be evaluated as a potential candidate for child play therapy. In the initial interview with the parents, Max was described by his father as "a wild animal" and by his mother as a "Neanderthal-like creature." Both parents have developed quite punitive relationships with Max, taking away privileges, sending him to his room for long stretches, and attempting to shame him into good behavior. His mother indicated that she could identify with Max because she had struggled to succeed in school, but often this became unproductive because she found it too painful to relive the torture of her school experience. Nevertheless, she does find it quite easy to be with Max one-on-one, and she loves to watch him as he plays out his adventures around the house. His father too seemed to have a soft spot in his heart for Max, but he cannot relate to Max's school problems and becomes enraged at Max's refusal to do chores or homework. In discussing Max with his parents, the child therapist observed a great deal of nonverbal communication between the parents that suggested that they were having trouble not blaming one another for the problems with Max.

The child play therapist agreed to see Max once per week for an hour and referred the parents for parent counseling with a colleague (the author) with whom she worked closely. Max loved the play therapy room that invited just the sort of fantasy play he so enjoyed, and he quickly formed a positive attachment with the therapist. The parent counseling was not as easy. Both parents indicated during the initial session that they did not want to discuss any aspect of their life other than how to handle Max more effectively. In the second session, the father revealed that both of the older children had also struggled in school, but they were now doing fine, thanks to the intervention of their pediatrician who had referred them to a behavioral psychologist who specialized in ADHD. After being assessed, both children were placed on standard doses of medication used in the treatment ADHD. The initial medications produced severe side effects, but after 2 months of trying different medications, one was found that seemed to work without causing severe side effects. Still, they acknowledged that both children looked forward to the summer months when they could discontinue the medication because they were not in school.

During the third session of parent counseling the parents announced that they did not see much point in continuing the parent consultations because Max seemed to be doing a bit better, and they hoped he would continue to improve. As I explored with them how things were going better and what they had done to improve the situation, they indicated that it probably was not anything they were doing; rather, it was more likely the play therapy or his ADHD medication. Because I had not realized Max was also medicated, I inquired further, and the father responded, "He has been on medication since the start of school this year, about six months." They had not seen any improvement in his school or home behavior since starting the medications, and that is why they had brought him in for play therapy.

Because they were about to terminate the meetings with me, I decided to take a calculated risk—to discuss the side effects ADHD medications can have that can produce some of the difficulties they were having with Max. I pointed out to them that as a psychologist, I could not prescribe or unprescribe anyone's medication. However, as a psychologist I found it necessary to be informed of the behavioral consequences (positive and negative) of psychotropic medications. I asked how long the eating and sleeping difficulties had been going on, and it turned out that this coincided with beginning the ADHD medication. I informed them that these medications often create mood fluctuations as the medication wears off, so the child constantly has to adjust to inner cognitive and emotional states unrelated to what is happening in his or her life. In addition, I discussed how learning differences not addressed by changes in teaching styles can create the same pattern of behavior as ADHD, as can childhood anxieties. Furthermore, the medications "work" for ADHD in part by creating a desire to compulsively perform repetitive cognitive tasks of the kind often used by uncreative teachers to teach math and vocabulary skills (Breggin & Cohen, 2007).

Their response was quite surprising. They acknowledged seeing almost every one of the negative effects of the medication, but first in their older two children. It was as if lightbulbs were going off in the room for them every 10 seconds for about five minutes. They thanked me for the information and said that they had a lot to think about. I did not work with them again for about two months. When they returned they had discontinued the ADHD medication for all three children and were seeing a general improvement in each child's spontaneity and enjoyment of life. Schoolwork was not deteriorating, and they were pleased. Max was still miserable at school, but the mother was beginning to think about moving him to a private school that had small classes, where he would not be subjected to the teasing and ridicule he received in the public school for being different. I heard from the child therapist 6 months later that Max's mother was seeing him as a "different child," almost unrecognizable from the child who had started therapy a year before. He was eating well and was experiencing a growth spurt, and she was terminating the therapy because he had so many new social activities after school.

CHILDHOOD BIPOLAR DISORDER

Bipolar disorder was not diagnosed in children or adolescents before the last 20 years. Between 1994 and 2003, the rate of diagnosing bipolar disorder in youths went from 25/100,000 population to 1003/100,000 population—or 4000% (Moreno et al., 2007). For this to happen, there had to be a change in the definition of bipolar disorder in children and youth, and indeed there was. Instead of looking for alternating periods of depression and mania (overly happy and exuberant behavior) in children and youth, the task became to identify periods of withdrawn or sad behavior preceded or followed by periods of angry or defiant behavior. In other words, children and youth who show their anxiety in both internalizing and externalizing ways were now diagnosed with bipolar disorder.[1]

What is ironic about this sudden epidemic of bipolar disorder is that internalizing and externalizing behavior problems were never seen as exclusive descriptions of children; in fact, such patterns were defined as distinct exactly because the behaviors were statistically independent (uncorrelated), meaning that they were just as likely to be associated with one another as

---

[1]In an attempt to address growing concerns about the overdiagnosis of bipolar disorder in children, DSM–5 has introduced disruptive mood disregulation disorder.

not associated. Thus, one would expect some individuals would be described in both ways (as both internalizing and externalizing in how their problems were evidenced), and other individuals would be described as only one or the other (either internalizing or externalizing).

MEDICATED CHILDREN

Science journalist Robert Whitaker's (2011) scathing critique of the medical model's impact on children in the *Anatomy of an Epidemic*, has garnered much public attention. Yet, within the mental health professions, the heavy reliance on medications in the treatment of children with psychological symptoms continues almost unabated. The number of children on stimulant medication for ADHD increased from 4.8% of the children 4–17 years of age in 2007 to 6.1% in 2011 (Visser et al., 2014). Physicians and drug companies continue to publish studies in professional journals showing the drugs "work" and are "well-tolerated." Long-term follow-ups on large groups of children diagnosed with ADHD and then medicated in elementary school show no average difference in academic performance at high school graduation compared with a control group with similar academic difficulties who were not medicated (Lambert, 1988). Children on the medication report frequent side effects: difficulty sleeping (often treated with a second psychotropic medication), stunted physical growth, hallucinations, and blunted affect (referred to as the *zombie effect* in pharmaceutical company drug packaging literature). Of course, these side effects are described as part of the main effects of such drugs in drug-abuse literature aimed at preventing adolescents from abusing stimulant drugs. Another problem with stimulants is their rampant illegal use for cognitive enhancement by high-achieving students wishing to cram for high-stakes exams or to complete important term papers. Often, students with the prescribed stimulants are pressured by friends to give or sell them the pills for such use (Breggin & Cohen, 2007). Yet, the rates of prescriptions keep rising yearly, driven by marketing and advertising and the short-term behavioral improvements sought by teachers and parents. The children are more manageable without the adults having to change their own behaviors in any way, other than purchasing and dispensing the pills.

CHILDHOOD TEMPERAMENT

A different physiologically based view of personality is built on the concept of temperament. Many pediatricians and obstetricians have observed that at birth infants do not all behave identically (Thompson, Winer, &

Goodvin, 2010). Newborns seem to have a proto-personality in terms of whether they are calm versus emotional, active versus relaxed, reactive versus accepting of new stimulation, and receptive versus resistant to adapting to adult expectations for routines (e.g., eating, sleeping, bowel movements). Thomas and Chess (1977) originally proposed three general categories of child temperaments. The *easy child* is calm, mildly active, accepting of new stimulation, and settles easily into a pattern of waking and sleeping, eating, and bowel movements. The *difficult child* is the opposite: He or she expresses intense negative emotional reactions, is highly active, is highly reactive to changes in stimulation in the environment, and cannot settle into a regular pattern of sleep and wakefulness, eating, and having bowel movements. The *slow-to-warm-up child* is born with the characteristics of the difficult child but gradually shifts toward the easy temperament as she or he becomes more familiar with his or her new environment.

Though these distinct temperaments can exist at birth, only about half of all newborns seem to fit clearly into one category or the other. It is tempting to think that these are inherited characteristics, but the evidence for this is not as overwhelming as it might seem. First, one must consider intrauterine factors that seem to also affect the sorts of infant behaviors that make up this proto-personality. The health of the mother during pregnancy; toxins that may enter the mother's bloodstream, including prescription and nonprescription drugs; and environmental stressors experienced by the mother while carrying the child are just some of the physiological and social factors that might alter the child's temperament at birth and are not genetic.

A second factor undermining the importance of temperament at birth is that child development in the first 6 years of life is so rapid and the changes in cognitive and social abilities so complex that temperament measured at age 6 is only marginally correlated with a child's temperament at age 3. Development of self-control by age 6 will alter the expression of emotionality in many children, thus reducing the consistency of that temperament characteristic. Looking for behavioral consistency during childhood and adolescence is a daunting task because these are times of life marked by dramatic changes in cognitive abilities and social experiences within and outside the family (Thompson et al., 2010). Adjustment to school, peers, and the community at large introduces a great many new influences on our actions and interpersonal style, as do changes in the family structure and functioning over time.

A third factor that it is clear from both clinical and research data is that there are strong parental and social influences on those behaviors associated with the concept of temperament. Adverse events in the life of the child can move some children from an easy to difficult temperament, and highly supportive and nurturing environments can move the difficult child to behave in more "easy" ways. The birth of new siblings, loss of grandparents, having to relocate because of a change in parents' employment, illnesses, separations, and divorces, all have an enormous impact on factors that might be indicative of temperament in later childhood or adolescence—for example, moods, adaptability to change, a healthy diet and pattern of sleep, and so forth. It has been suggested that difficult children are most susceptible to their environments, whether positive or negative (Belsky, Bakermans-Kranenburg, & van IJzendoorn, 2007).

There is some evidence that normal variations in temperament-related behaviors such as exploratory and impulsive behaviors are associated with normal variations in the genes that influence the brain's ability to respond to the neurotransmitter dopamine ($D4$ receptors), and expression of fear, anger, and sadness may be associated with serotonin transporter regions (*5HTTLPR*). These genes may regulate the reactivity of the sympathetic and parasympathetic nervous systems, as well as brain functioning (Thompson et al., 2010).

THE PSYCHODYNAMIC VIEW OF CHILDHOOD PERSONALITY

Begun in 1968 at the University of California, Berkeley, by Jack and Jeanne Block, the "Block Study" followed 100 children over a period of 30 years (Block & Block, 1980). The children were evaluated eight times during this period. The Blocks identified two themes of personality they thought were central to personality development, especially to a sense of self-worth and self-respect: ego control and ego resiliency. *Ego control* concerns the ability to delay gratification (impulses) and to think ahead to the future. Children are classified as controlled, undercontrolled, or overcontrolled. Undercontrollers are prone to acting on impulse without planning. This means that those who are governed more by emotion than careful thought are undercontrolled. As psychoanalytic research in psychology, the Blocks assumed both innate (genetic) and environmental determinants of personality. *Ego resiliency* is the ability to adapt to new environments and to realize when it is necessary to be more or less controlled in one's actions. Ego control is closely related to control of emotionality, a key aspect of the easy or difficult child. However, ego resiliency is related to adapting to one's circumstances and environment and is related to interpersonal and practical intelligence—the ability to be flexible in one's behavioral response to people and challenges in the environment. A child may be high or low on either of these dimensions, because each is a relatively independent dimension of personality development.

Ego control and ego resiliency can be measured in children by the third year of life and remain stable indicators of a child's ability to cope with stress and challenges. However, when there are extreme environmental stressors over protracted periods (e.g., loss of a parent, divorce, parental unemployment, and substance abuse in parents), there can be important shifts in either dimension of childhood personality. Conversely, a child who is low in ego control and/or ego resiliency may be positively affected by parents who are capable of being patiently attuned to the child's developmental needs, accepting the child in spite of the lack of control and adaptability to the needs of the social environment and then gradually encouraging movement toward greater control and accommodation to the environment as the child becomes ready to meet new demands. Granted, there are only 10% to 15% of the potential parent population capable of such patient attunement (Block & Block, 1980); thus, the typical child who comes into the world with such difficulties will appear to be driven by internal forces into such behavioral styles, but it is not quite the predeterminism that it appears to be, because the child is likely quite malleable under the right environmental conditions. Nevertheless, we do seem to have a sense that part of understanding ourselves is knowing what we like and do not like and what we prefer to do or not do, but sometimes it does not seem that we have complete freedom to choose these attributes.

PARENTING STYLES

In addition to psychoanalytic and experimental studies of attachment and attunement processes (Ainsworth, 1969; Bowlby, 1969; Mahler, Pine, & Bergman, 1975), we also have impressive data from Baumrind's (1991) studies at the University of California, Berkeley, on parenting styles and their impact on children and adolescents. She identified and studied the parent–child relationship for three basic styles of parenting: authoritarian, authoritative, and permissive.

The *authoritarian* parent exerts powerful control over the child's behavior using punishment and fear as the primary means of affecting that control. The child yields and conforms his or her behavior to this parental style if the parent is also providing for the child's safety and security and is consistently present in the child's life. However, when this kind of punitive control is provided by a parent who is inconsistently present or nonprotective, the children become aggressive toward the world in much the same way the parent has been aggressive toward them. Courts are familiar with these children as they reach adolescence and begin to act out their feelings of abandonment and rage at the parent's largely punitive approach.

At the other end of the spectrum are the *permissive* parents who believe that control is unnecessary and that children are naturally good and self-directed. They provide assistance if asked, but largely leave their children to figure out how to behave and what to learn. These children also have difficulties as they reach adolescence, but they are more likely to become withdrawn and uninvolved in the world than aggressive. They have trouble finishing high school, finding work, and becoming self-sufficient.

Authoritative parents are involved in their children's lives and provide direction. However, they attempt to explain the reasons for their directives and engage children in dialogue and discussion about rules, consequences, and likely outcomes of various choices the children might make. This parenting style is seen by some as consistent with a democratic society, just as the authoritarian style might be more suited to a culture used to autocratic rule. But this is oversimplistic; it has been found that in high-stress, multiproblem families living in urban poverty authoritarian parenting is necessary to simply keep children alive, and the children respond to it differently than in contexts in which the control and punitiveness may seem to them unnecessary. Children raised in a more democratic manner in such environments do not have the expected good outcomes found in studies of middle class White children.

Recent work has attempted to integrate the roles of parenting style with child temperament, family dynamics, and culture differences in parent–child roles and relationships. Somewhat surprisingly, the authoritative parenting style has positive effects wherever it has been studied. In some cultures, corporal punishment is integrated with an otherwise authoritative (not authoritarian) style without apparent harmful effects (Morris, Cui, & Steinberg, 2013).

CHILD ABUSE

By focusing on a child's behavior and then on hypothesized defects within the child's nervous system, neurophysiology, or neuroendocrinology (hormones interacting with the nervous system), psychology can easily lose sight of the horrific events in a child's life that explain the need for extreme defense mechanisms (and therefore extreme symptoms). Some of these horrors are in the larger world (e.g., neighborhoods dominated by illegal drugs and violence, civil wars, or natural disasters), but other horrors occur within the confines of the home. At one time, the home was off limits to outside interference from the Western legal system ("A man's home is his castle"). Consequently, parents were free to interact with their own children within their own home however they saw fit. Through the late 19th century, children were often seen as miniature adults, and little that transpired in the household was kept from them. In working class families, children as young as 7 or 8 years of age would be expected to join in the task of supporting the family through their labor on a farm or in a factory. Corporal punishment was commonly used, and the intensity of whippings was at the discretion of the parents. Perhaps in this context we should not be so shocked at the statistics on child abuse in the United States, but it is difficult not to be.

It was not until the 1960s that all states in the United States required the reporting of child abuse and neglect to a governmental agency responsible for investigating such allegations. Those laws were inspired by the collaborative efforts of the professions of social work and medicine (pediatrics). By the mid 1970s, 60,000 cases were reported annually. By 1980, the number of reports topped one million. In 1990, there were two million cases reported, and in 2000, almost three million (Myers, 2008). It should be noted that there are about 75 million children in the United States in a given year. These reports are required to be investigated by child protective services workers, and in about 70% of the reported cases maltreatment is not substantiated. In about 20% of the cases maltreatment is confirmed and action taken. The remaining 10% are in a gray area where, even though no current maltreatment can be confirmed, the family voluntarily accepts supportive services aimed at improving the care provided to the children in the household. One way of looking at the numbers is to consider the rate per 1,000 children. The rate of investigations for child maltreatment is about 40 per 1,000 children in the population. The rate of confirmed child maltreatment is about 9 per 1,000 (U.S. Department of Health and Human Services, 2013).

Child maltreatment is broken down into four categories: neglect, physical abuse, psychological abuse, and sexual abuse. *Neglect* refers to unsafe living conditions such as failure to supervise a child by leaving them alone in the house or a car for extended periods of time or failing to keep the child adequately fed, clothed, clean, or cared for when seriously ill. *Physical abuse* involves deliberately doing physical harm to the child's body by, for example, striking the child in such a manner as to risk serious injury or confining a child with physical restraints or in a small physical space (e.g., a closet or box) for extended periods of time. *Psychological abuse* involves ignoring the emotional needs of a child to the point where a child is chronically terrified, humiliated, and either socially withdrawn or highly reactive. *Sexual abuse* involves fondling, raping, or engaging in sexually stimulating activities with a child.

In 2012, there were about 1,600 child deaths from abuse or neglect. In addition, there were almost 700,000 confirmed cases of child maltreatment in the United States (just under 1% of the 74 million children in the country). Of these cases, about 80% involved neglect, 20% involved physical abuse, 9% involved psychological abuse, and 9% sexual abuse. The rates of child maltreatment are higher for children in the first year of life, 21 per 1,000; at age 1 through 5 the rate is about 11 per 1,000, and then it declines to about seven per 1,000 in adolescence. The rates for sexual abuse do not follow this pattern. In 2012, 1,600 confirmed cases involved children in the first 2 years of life; by ages 3 to 5 the number increases to about 8,000 cases per year then steadily rises to a peak of 16,000 cases per year at ages 12 to 14 and slightly declines through ages 15 to 17, when the number is about 13,000 cases.

It is estimated that in 80% of the child maltreatment cases the complaint named one or both parents as the perpetrator of the abuse; in 20% to 30% of the cases the abuser was believed to have an alcohol or drug abuse problem. In addition, almost 30% of the child victims were reported to also have been exposed to domestic violence in their households. Oddly, the report does not include the socioeconomic status of the perpetrators or children, though it does acknowledge that the rate in minority communities is slightly higher than among Caucasian children.

We do have an understanding from confirmed cases of childhood abuse that the impact on the child is profound and long-lasting. Intense difficulty with the control of anger, terror, and situations that trigger memories of the abuse are common. The child may be extremely aggressive or alternatively extremely fearful and timid to the point of withdrawal from social contact. The sexually abused child may be terrified of physical contact or may exhibit hypersexualized behavior. Abuse histories are common in adults who ultimately are hospitalized with severe psychological difficulties (psychoses, major depression, borderline personality, severe substance abuse) and in those who end up in prison. Although most victims do not themselves become abusers of children, a significant minority of 40% do (Sroufe, Egeland, Carlson, & Collins, 2005).

THE CASE OF RACHEL

Rachel was a 5-year-old girl who had recently begun first grade at a rural public school in New England. Her mother, an insurance company actuary, had taken a leave of absence from her career to raise a family. Rachel's father was also an actuary for a large insurance company. When Rachel was first seen for an evaluation she had two younger siblings, a brother age 3 and a newborn sister. Rachel's presenting problem, as indicated by her mother at the initial interview, was that she hated going to school. Her mother was determined that Rachel be successful in school (as both of her parents had been), and over Rachel's protests and despite her clinging and desperate cries for her mother not to leave her, she would drop Rachel off at school each morning. Once in the school, Rachel tended to stop crying, but she refused to interact with the other children and frequently ignored the teacher's instructions and attempts at conversation. On several occasions, exasperated with Rachel's failure to cooperate, the teacher asked the principal to remove her from the classroom, which he did quite forcibly. Rachel then began to hide under the teacher's desk, wedging herself in so that it was very difficult to dislodge her.

The Assessment

Rachel was in good physical health, as were the other members of her family. She was highly verbal and seemed ready for school, already counting and doing simple problems in addition and subtraction. Her memory for information was quite exceptional, and if anything, her parents were worried that she might become bored in kindergarten. Rachel's home and family life was physically safe and secure. She lived in a bucolic semirural neighborhood of middle and upper-middle class families that had many facilities for outdoor exercise. Rachel's father was successful in his work and provided well for the family, though he and Rachel's mother looked forward to a time when all the children would be in school and she could return to her successful actuarial career and double the family's income. Similar to many hard-working, upwardly mobile young American parents, Rachel's father and mother seemed to have it all, but they had paid a price for their success at being almost the perfect all-American family. They seemed chronically stressed and anxious and did not seem to be enjoying the life they had achieved. To make matters worse, they seemed almost unaware that this was so.

On inquiry, Rachel's mother identified three stressful areas of family life. Rachel had been a model infant and toddler. She had gone through a normal period of separation anxiety at about one year of age, but then had become more independent. When her mother became pregnant with her brother, Rachel, age 2½, was excited to become a big sister and seemed unaffected by the birth. However, about six months before school began, her brother, approaching age 2, began to really emerge as a person in the family. Bobby was active, was into everything, was agile and strong, and was now speaking in complex sentences. Rachel regarded him as a pest and a nuisance and would occasionally lash out at him. She had also recently become clingier herself, reacting whenever her mother was out of her sight.

At first, her parents thought she was just "going through a phase" and expected that Rachel would be able to tolerate Bobby better when he got beyond his version of the "terrible twos." However, they had not factored in the birth of their third child, which had also coincided with Bobby's emergence as a person in his own right. Still, Rachel was thrilled to have a baby sister, and she devoted her attentions to the baby especially when Bobby was around, much to her brother's displeasure. Although this sibling conflict was of some concern, both Rachel's parents thought she was doing pretty well at home.

The second area of family stress was related to the fact that Rachel's parents now had three children under 6 in their home and they were living in a rural area of New England, hundreds of miles away from their own family support networks. They felt isolated and at times overwhelmed just by the daily responsibilities of parenting three young children virtually on their own. The mother was doing most of the parenting and looking after household responsibilities, and the father worked long hours at his job.

The third source of stress was worry that the family history may be repeating itself. Rachel's father had a sister who had died about ten years earlier of a drug overdose. In fact, Rachel had been named after her, and now her parents were horrified that somehow her emotional outbursts at school were a harbinger of things to come. What if this continued and she became a volatile, angry, withdrawn teenager? Are these problems not genetic? What could they do to keep Rachel from meeting a similar fate?

Play Therapy

First, the therapist reassured the parents that Rachel was not doomed to a life of paralyzing anxiety and depression. Research on the genetics of such problems is still in its infancy, and there is more reason to believe her mental state will be a result of her life experiences than a fixed inherited characteristic. Second, the therapist did what she did in every case, she met with the school teacher to assess the teacher's and school's perspective and to determine their ability to provide Rachel with a supportive environment that would maximize the chances of her being able to adapt to school successfully. Generally, this means having a teacher who is willing and able to adapt the classroom and her relationship to the needs of the child until the child is strong enough to begin making the adaptations she needs to be successful at school.

Unfortunately, the school in this case took the position that Rachel was a "spoiled child" and that nothing about the school environment was contributing to the problem; in their view it was all "the family's fault." They did not think Rachel shy and timid, but demanding and aggressive. The therapist, who had worked with many teachers and schools over the years, left the meeting with a sense that this was not the place for Rachel to work out her shyness and separation fears.

Also of concern were reports from Rachel that the principal was physically restraining her when she tried to run away from the school. The restraint was described as being forceful and terrifying. Although if true, this was not an illegal use of restraint by the principal, but it was odd that at the meeting the teacher specifically denied that any physical restraint had been used at all with Rachel.

During this period, Rachel began her play therapy sessions with the therapist. Play therapy was conducted in a humanistic manner (Moustakas, 1997). The child is seen in a large playroom and can decide which toys and activities to play with (e.g., sand table, art supplies, doll house, board games). The therapist enters into the child's play as invited by the child and they build a relationship through the play in which many emotions can be expressed and worked through (e.g., fear, rage, jealousy, love, trust, sadness, pride in one's work).

From the play therapy sessions it was clear that Rachel was afraid of being emotionally hurt in relationships with other people. Yet, her reports of the terror she felt at school seemed to go beyond her general anxiety level. She felt trapped in a hostile environment where no one understood her or even seemed to be trying to understand her. She was reprimanded for her fears, over which she had little control. These reprimands made her even more frightened; it was a vicious circle, leaving her demoralized.

With Rachel's permission, the therapist spoke with her parents about the therapist's assessment that this school environment was not a good place for Rachel and was exacerbating her separation anxiety. The parents responded immediately by enrolling her in a private school in the area in which they lived. Almost immediately her school behavior improved noticeably. The new school accepted her shyness and reluctance to play with other children and used her keen intellectual abilities as a way to connect with her. They did not discipline her when she resisted the control of adults but talked with her and found ways to ease her transition into group learning activities. Several years after all this transpired, the local newspaper reported that the principal at the first school had resigned amidst allegations of excessive use of physical punishment with defiant children.

Rachel remained in weekly play therapy to help her overcome her shyness and separation anxiety. Her parents saw this as a preventive measure, in light of their earlier fears about the family history of severe emotional problems. The play therapy was not necessary to keep Rachel in school, but it allowed her to more rapidly adapt to the school environment and lessened her sense of being overwhelmed in the first 2 years of school.

In play therapy it became clear that Rachel found it extremely difficult to trust adults, and at the same time she struggled to express emotions of any kind, particularly if these related to the feeling of being betrayed by those she had begun to trust. Her family provided her everything in the way of physical care and security, but both her parents themselves struggled with the expression of emotions. Discussions of sad or angry feelings were avoided at all costs in a family where "positive thinking" was taken to the extreme. Rachel also had difficulty with the related process of differentiating her own feelings from those of the people around her. When her parents were seemingly discouraged or worried, Rachel would feel the weight of the world on her shoulders. She was capable of sensing this even when her parents were not verbalizing their con-cerns. At such times she appeared quite depressed for seemingly "no reason."

As she began to trust the therapist, she began to explore in her play the feelings that people have. For quite a while she was convinced that her feel-ings were entirely unique and no one else had similar experiences. She would teach the therapist the feelings she had that the therapist might not have expressed. Over time it became clear that she was comparing herself with family members who never discussed upsetting feelings, and so she assumed her feelings were unlike those of anyone else on the planet (in essence that she was an "alien"). Gradually, over a 2-year period, her emotional devel-opment caught up with her advanced cognitive development, and her play became more creative and spontaneous. There were periodic setbacks, espe-cially when conflict with siblings led her to feel isolated in the family. As the eldest child she was expected to tolerate aggression from the younger ones, and if she became angry and pushed or fought back, she was scolded or punished. At these times she would become more withdrawn from adults and other children at school. As difficult as this was for her parents and teachers to witness, it provided a clear focus in the play therapy for working out feel-ings of anger and betrayal felt in the parent–child and sibling relationships. Rachel learned to express her sense of outrage directly without withdrawing, striking out, or feeling guilty for having the feelings and then clinging to her mother out of fear of retaliation for her anger.

Over the 2 years of play therapy and occasional parent consultation, Rachel's separation anxiety, disillusionment with adults and other children, and withdrawal gave way to her emergence as a young girl fully engaged in learning at school, playing with peers, and accepting of her younger siblings and their greater dependency needs. Her parents no longer worried about her as a future angry and depressed adolescent and were able to apply what they learned in the parent consultations to raising all three of their children.

PERVASIVE DEVELOPMENTAL DISORDERS

As difficult as were the problems of the children discussed earlier, they pale in comparison with those of the group of children with some of the per-vasive developmental disorders (PDD). These include primarily the autism spectrum disorder and PDD not otherwise specified. During my own training period, and for many years after, the chief diagnostic task related to autism was to distinguish it from childhood schizophrenia—both featured a refusal to join the reality of the parents and other children in the family and the inability to use language. The differential diagnosis was made on the basis of whether the child had initially during the first few years of life seemed to develop reasonably normally, especially in terms of language usage. If that were the case but then at age 2 or 3 the child regressed and stopped using language and withdrew from the family's shared reality, the diagnosis was childhood schizophrenia. In either case the rate of these disorders was extremely low: less than 3 in 10,000 for autism (Blaxill, 2004). Current data put the rate at about one in 100 children. No doubt the astronomical increase is due in part to the creation of a spectrum of the disorders rather than the continued use of the categories of autism or childhood schizophrenia. Current rates are given for the number of children on the spectrum of mild, moderate, or severe. Previously, the category was only used for what today would be considered the severe end of the spectrum. It is hard to find data today just for the rate of severe cases. Nonetheless, there does seem to be an increase in the number of children showing autistic spectrum disorder beyond the mild end.

Another confusing aspect of the diagnosis of autism or severe autistic spectrum disorder is the fact that most of the children with this diagnosis are also viewed as intellectually disabled (IQ less than 70). There are those at the higher range of IQ as well as some with unique abilities (the "savants"), often involving the calculation of numbers and patterns of numbers. Further confusing the picture are those children born with clear-cut severe intellectual and physical disabilities that make them unable to communicate, along with the often concomitant behavioral disturbances that can appear quite bizarre or psychotic. All of this is further complicated by the difficulty of doing psychological testing with such children and determining an accurate estimate of intelligence.

Whenever behavior is extreme and an individual is unable to make any meaningful contact with another human being, it is only natural to question whether he or she might be in some sense "other," not fully human, not really one of us. When that happens, we are even more likely to seek a physiological explanation, because our psychological access to the person seems completely blocked, and we think they resemble in their behavior people who have known brain injuries or infections. Thus, the search for a biological answer to autism has been vigorous. Unfortunately, the result of the search for the autism "gene" has been unproductive so far. Reviewing this literature, Losh, Sullivan, Trembath, and Piven (2008) wrote,

> The last decade has witnessed the development of an armamentarium of genetic techniques and tools for studying the genetic basis of disease. . . . Although these tools have led to major breakthroughs in medical genetics, we have not yet witnessed successful disease gene discovery in psychiatric diseases. Autism has proven particularly frustrating to genetic dissection. Despite compelling evidence from twin and family studies indicating a strong genetic involvement, the unequivocal detection of autism susceptibility genes remains an elusive goal. (p. 829)

Rossignol and Frye (2012) reached a similar conclusion:

> Although several genetic syndromes, such as fragile X and Rett syndromes, have been associated with autism spectrum disorder [ASD], empirical studies have estimated that genetic syndromes only account for 6–15% of ASD cases. Therefore, the majority of ASD cases are not due to simple single gene or chromosomal disorder. (pp. 389–390)

Rossignol and Frye (2012) went on to suggest an entirely new physiological strategy for understanding the cause of ASD—namely, systemic rather than central nervous system specific deficits. They suggested that ASD may be related to inflammatory disease, immune system dysfunction, and environmental toxins, among other systemic problems that damage the entire body including the nervous system. Because these hypotheses were all based on correlational findings after the children were diagnosed with ASD, no causal conclusions are drawn or warranted.

A third thread in the search for a physiological basis for autism can be found in brain imaging studies. Dickstein et al. (2013) performed a meta-analysis combining 42 previously published studies searching for brain regions that function differently in autistic children, autistic adults, and control groups of children and adults when engaged in both social and nonsocial tasks. Differences in brain activation were found between the autistic children and their controls, the adults with ASD and their controls, and between children and adults with ASD. The areas of brain activation that differentiated autistic and control group children were *not* the same brain areas that differentiated autistic adults from their control group. The authors described their findings as "highly speculative," which seems fitting. Nevertheless, they curiously recommended changes to the treatment of autistic children based on these highly speculative findings. This can only be understood in light of how desperately the mental health professions are in need of new treatments in this area.

The mainstream literature on autism is clear that there is no cure for autism and that behavioral and psychoeducational strategies produce at best modest gains in language and social development. When these children reach adolescence, if they are still essentially psychotic in their behavior, they are medicated with antipsychotic medication (discussed in Chapter 8). Suffice it to say, although such medication may subdue them, it also decreases their availability for learning to overcome their disabilities.

In cases of moderate–severe autism, parents have always faced grim options. Even the most scientific and professional approaches such as behavior modification offered little hope of recovery from the debilitating symptoms. In the 1970s, Barry and Samahria Kaufman faced this reality with their young son, Raun (Kaufman, 1995). They had been advised by physicians and behavioral experts in the 1970s to institutionalize their child when he was 3 years of age because he showed many signs of severe autism. Instead, they kept him at home and attempted to reach him by modeling his behavior rather than trying to get him to share in what they were doing. The parents spent many hours a day in a specially designed playroom, joining in their child's autistic activities (spinning, rocking, flapping, etc.). Over a period of several years and thousands of hours of one-on-one nurturing and lovingly joining in his world, their son Raun began to come out of his isolation and use language. Ultimately, he was able to attend a regular school, and then college at Harvard University. He now is the managing director of the treatment center they developed to train other parents in the approach they found worked for their son. In a number of remarkable cases they have reported dramatic improvements to the point that other children as well have developed speech and social behaviors that leave them indistinguishable from peers who have never been so diagnosed.[2]

The Kaufmans went on to develop a humanistic growth and personal development center for people of all ages who wish to have a more fulfilling life. The cost for parent training on how to work with one's own autistic child is only a fraction of the cost of the disability payments or special education programs that most children with severe autism will receive over their lifetime. In addition, parents set up volunteer-led support groups with other parents implementing this Son-Rise Program. For years the scientific community has dismissed the program as quackery, but recently three published studies on families implementing the procedure have appeared. Houghton, Schuchard, Lewis, and Thompson (2013) conducted an experimental study comparing the effects of the central feature of the Son-Rise Program (empathic modeling of the child's behavior) with a conventional special education approach to teaching language and social development. This was done for several hours per day in an educational setting rather than the home. There was a statistically significant greater improvement in the group of children receiving the empathic modeling. Williams and Wishart (2003) and Williams (2006) have developed and administered a longitudinal survey to parents in the United Kingdom who had received training through the Son-Rise Program and who had implemented the program in their homes. As with any longitudinal survey, there was considerable attrition in responders. At the 12-month point less than half of the parents responded to the survey. Of these, about 50 percent indicated that the program was "very beneficial" to their child ("very beneficial" being the highest rating available on the survey). In contrast, about 40% indicated that they thought the program was mostly having

---

[2]Note that this author has no financial relationship with the center.

negative effects on the rest of the family who seemed not to have sufficient time for one another.

In addition, the Kaufmans' Autism Treatment Center has expanded steadily and has interested parent groups in the United States, Canada, and the United Kingdom. Numerous other parents have reported positive results, including complete cures that parallel the experiences of the Kaufmans. Because cures are unheard of in the scientific community, most people are skeptical. However, we see in the case of schizophrenia in Chapter 8 that in fact there is an identical pattern with the most severe of adult disorders, except in that case the cures have been confirmed in multiple scientifically conducted studies involving both psychologists and psychiatrists working independently in the United States and Europe.

The work of these schizophrenia researchers too was dismissed as quackery until recently, so perhaps we should not be so quick to dismiss the Kaufmans' work. There is an extensive website (http://www.autismtreatment center.org/contents/other_sections/) the reader can consult to make up her or his own mind. What strikes me as most intriguing is that the treatment method devised by the Kaufmans, while being innovative, actually uses the basic ingredients of Rogers's (1960) humanistic person-centered therapy developed for use with adults and Moustakas's (1997) adaptation of that approach for working with children: empathy, acceptance, and genuineness. We know that for many people these are the ingredients that allow for personal growth and change. The Kaufmans found a way to communicate those interpersonal attitudes and conditions to a 2-year-old screaming, flailing, and terrified nonverbal little boy. I am perhaps less skeptical than the average reader because humanistic psychology had a theory that predicted this approach would work long before it was attempted.

Pragmatically, there is no hope of a systematic cure offered in the medical or psychological literature for severe autism. Therefore, those trying the Autism Treatment Center approach will not be doing so instead of using a known proven cure. The treatment is strenuous for parents and families, yet in the studies cited above (Williams, 2006; Williams & Wishart, 2003) 40% of parents have reported that they benefited from participating in it. Those reporting dissatisfaction focused on the strain on the rest of the family, but not on worsening of symptoms in the child. If one fourth of that group were to experience the remission of symptoms and to maintain that improvement, the cure rate would be 10% of the severe autism spectrum disorder group. This would be a major step forward for the field and for thousands of families.

5

ANXIETY AND RELATED FORMS OF SUFFERING

Understanding anxiety and depression is the key to understanding the psychological pain and suffering encountered in the mental health system. Objectively, the behaviors associated with anxiety and depression appear on the surface to be quite different, and the *Diagnostic and Statistical Manual of Mental Disorders* (5th ed.; *DSM–5*; American Psychiatric Association, 2013) attempts to clearly differentiate the two psychological states. It is only when one considers the subjective experience of the person and the development, meaning, and course or progression of the symptoms that the distinction begins to break down.

The term *anxiety* was used by Freud to refer to states of fear that seemed irrational either because the individual did not know what she or he was afraid of or because the intensity of fear seemed out of proportion given the actual level of threat. For Freud, many irrational behaviors (e.g., obsessive hand washing, unprovoked states of panic) resulted from the attempt to keep out of awareness feelings and emotions that were abhorrent to the self. He

http://dx.doi.org/10.1037/14693-005
Not So Abnormal Psychology: A Pragmatic View of Mental Illness, by R. B. Miller
Copyright © 2015 by the American Psychological Association. All rights reserved.

believed that such intense emotional states were traumatizing in just the same way that combat traumas produced shell shock in World War I soldiers. After the trauma, the soldier is left with a heightened sense of danger. He is jumpy and overreactive to loud noises or sudden changes in the environment and often experiences nightmares, even when safely home. The person with neurosis has similar troublesome psychological states but without a history of external trauma.

This idea that our anxiety and experience of stress may be derived from our internal emotional conflicts rather than external conflicts is a critical one. Freudian psychoanalysis directs our attention to our own internal world of conflicting thoughts, memories, feelings, desires, wishes, and judgments, and an awareness of nonspecific or irrational fear may be linked to these conflicts. This unease is often the beginning of ill-conceived behavioral defenses wherein through substance use, avoidance of situations that arouse the anxiety, mistaking the unease for disease, and so forth, one tries to eliminate the feeling without addressing the underlying problem. The feeling that one is physically ill is not uncommon in those experiencing anxiety because in fact in a heightened state of anxiety we have many of the psychophysiological reactions associated with the fight or flight syndrome—namely, arousal of the autonomic nervous system. In panic attacks, for example, this heightened state of arousal produces a burst of activity in the sympathetic branch of the autonomic nervous system in which heart rate is elevated, as is blood pressure, with accompanying dizziness and the fear that one may be having a heart attack.

Often a period of depression is preceded by a prolonged period of anxiety. The depression is exhaustion from the hyperaroused state of dread and worry. Depression includes feelings of hopelessness, helplessness, and emptiness. This can lead to periods of panic. There is a fear that nothing will get better, and one will have to live in this state indefinitely. Suicidal ideas may arise, often as an unwanted intrusion, but sometimes as welcome relief.

Anxiety is often triggered by anticipated losses or separations, whereas depression is triggered by actual losses. These losses may be related to relationships, work opportunities, physical possessions such as one's home, or physical disabilities as a result of illness, injury, or the aging process. Anxiety and depression may also be triggered by the fear or perception that one is not meeting the expectations of others one depends on for love and support. There may be in addition the fear of criticism or actual punishment that is not within one's power to avoid (Blatt, 2004). A loss of self-respect leads often to attempts to punish oneself as well.

Despite the clear links between anxiety and depression, they have traditionally been dealt with separately in the literature, and therefore this chapter focuses largely on anxiety and related disorders, whereas depression and related disorders are the topics of Chapter 6.

THE MEDICAL MODEL: PHYSIOLOGICAL SYMPTOM, ERGO PHYSIOLOGICAL CAUSE

In anxiety states we may notice an increased heart rate; increased perspiration; muscle pain, spasms, or stiffness; accentuated startle response; difficulty falling asleep increased or decreased appetite; headaches; heightened or lowered sexual interest; increased frequency of urination or bowel movements; and so forth. Surveys of patient visits to the practice of primary care physicians for adults and children suggest that somewhere between one third and two thirds of all visits are primarily for symptoms associated with personal stress at work, in the family, or in relationships with significant others (Gatchel & Oordt, 2003). The medical profession, not just the subspecialty of psychiatry, is the profession of choice for such patients, and these sorts of problems are seen as the province of medicine to treat and "solve."

Faced with the growing challenge from the newly emerging mental health professions in the post–World War II era, both psychiatrists and medical professionals in general have looked to neuroscience and psychopharmacology research to justify their positions as providers of choice for services to such patients. This research took three directions: (a) attempts to establish through genetic research that people with psychosocial problems in living are biologically different from the successful members of society, (b) attempts to show that the brains of people with such problems are structurally or physiologically different from the brains of successful people, and (c) new pharmaceutical discoveries allowing physicians to prescribe medications that would correct for the brain defects found in (b). When one focuses on the physical symptoms of anxiety and depression, such a biological view of problems in living seems entirely plausible.

This push to medicalize problems in living also fits with the social, economic, and political agenda of powerful corporations, government agencies, and political leaders who wish to avoid the enormous cost that would come with addressing the underlying pattern of social and economic inequality that gives rise to so much psychological suffering in our world. By turning the psychological and social consequences of inequality, discrimination, economic insecurity, and powerlessness into a problem of the biological deficiencies of the persons who have suffered such harm, we individualize and psychologize the most glaring social and institutional problems of contemporary society (Jansz & van Drunen, 2004). By placing the power and prestige of science, major research universities, and U.S. government watchdog agencies, such as the Food and Drug Administration and the National Institute of Mental Health, behind the psychologizing of such structural problems in society, and by permitting as well the direct marketing of psychiatric medications to consumers, we have become a society in which individuals increasingly believe that the medical model is the only way that an intelligent person should think about anxiety and depression.

Genetic Factors

Genes are the segments of chromosomes in the nucleus of human cells that determine the physiological functioning of the body. Until the first phase of the three-billion-dollar Human Genome Project was completed in 2000 (Hall, 2010), genetic research on human beings was limited to indirect methods that consisted of various kinds of family studies. The basic model in family studies is to look at relatives who share a given level of genetic similarity (25% for grandparents and their grandchildren, 50% for parents and their children, 50% for siblings or dizygotic [fraternal] twins, 100% for monozygotic twins) to see whether these groups share psychiatric diagnoses roughly in proportion to how much they share genes. We would expect that if anxiety or depression were strictly a genetic disorder, monozygotic twins would be concordant for (share) such a diagnosis 100% of the time, dizygotic twins would be concordant 50% of the time, and grandparents and their grandchildren would be concordant only 25% of the time. Studies vary greatly in the rate of concordance reported, with monozygotic twins never reported to be 100% concordant for anxiety and depression, but it is true that the rates of concordance do decline in proportion to the decline in genetic similarity of pairs of family members. McGuffin, Katz, Watkins, and Rutherford (1996) found a concordance rate of 46% in monozygotic twins and 20% in dizygotic twins. Edvardsen et al. (2009) found similar results.

Another related strategy is to look for concordance rates in monozygotic twins who have been reared apart, in presumably very different environments. Because their only commonality is their identical genetic makeup, a high concordance rate would be strong evidence for the dominance of genetic factors in the emergence of depression. In the one major study that has looked at this question, the actual observed concordance rates for depressive personality traits in monozygotic twins reared apart was a mere 4% (Gatz, Pederson, Plomin, & Nesselroade, 1992). This is no different from the expected concordance rate for depressive traits in pairs of randomly selected members of the population, which is about 4%.

Confounding Genetic and Environmental Variability

Ignored so far is the critical weakness of familial studies—namely, that as people in a family share less genetic material, they often also share less of the family environment. In other words, level of genetic similarity is confounded by level of environmental similarity. The comparison of monozygotic and dizygotic twins is a good example. Monozygotic twins are always of the same gender, and dizygotic twins may or may not be of the same gender because they grew from different eggs and were fertilized by separate sperm. If the gender roles are different in a family, as they often are, monozygotic twins not only share more genes in common than dizygotic twins but they also share a much more common environment within the household. Consequently, any difference in similarity of diagnoses for anxiety or depression may also reflect this difference in degree of shared environment. What it means to be a member of particular household in terms of responsibilities, privileges, and opportunities for learning and socializing may not at all be the same for the various members of the family. Oldest, middle, and youngest children may have different experiences growing up in the same family because of changes in the parents over the years and the presence of siblings in the environment. Researchers tend to assume that when differences are found in the psychological functioning of children in the "same" household they must be due to genetic variability.

The Heritability Statistic

Another little-discussed problem with all genetic research related to abnormal psychology is the use of the *heritability statistic*. This is generally interpreted to mean the degree to which a behavioral trait or symptom is caused by inherited genes rather than learned through the impact of the environment. This implies that the measurements of heritability are the result of experiments from which causal relationships between the genes and the behavior or symptom can be determined. However, the studies are all correlational and not causal, so no causal force can be inferred from a heritability statistic. When a study says that a symptom is 50% heritable, it does not mean that 50% of the time this symptom in an individual is inherited, nor does it mean that 50% of the symptoms one is experiencing are caused by genes or that when one was born there was a 50% chance that one would become symptomatic in this particular manner, and therefore one has no control over the symptoms being experienced.

The hereditability statistic means something quite different and far more abstract: If you take a large group of people who have different known amounts of genetic commonality and measure their level of a particular symptom or behavior, the heritability of that symptom or behavior is the amount of the variation in that symptom across the members of the group that is statistically correlated with the amount of variability in the genes in the group (Moore, 2003). What does this mean? First, the heritability statistic is about the effects of genetic variability on behavioral variability in a large group of people taken as a whole and not about the actual influence of genetics on the behavior of any individual member of the group. In other words, the heritability statistic is predictive of what is likely true for the group as a whole, not for any one individual in the group. Second, heritability can only be measured when there is a broad range of variability in the behavior or symptom in question and a broad range of genetic variability as well.

To illustrate the point easily, let us imagine a world of the future with human clones, 100 of which are identical genetically. We then measure their anxiety levels on a scale of 0 to 20, with 20 being panic levels of anxiety. Suppose the original human from whom they were cloned was highly anxious, so their scores, though not identical (e.g., because of measurement error or random effects), are similar, within a few points of one another: 17, 18, 19, and 20. The resulting heritability estimate would be zero because none of the variation in the anxiety scores corresponds to variation in genetics, because there is no variation in the measure of genetics—the genes are identical for all 100 clones. Clearly, using the heritability statistic to imply that a behavioral trait is "inherited" in a given individual is problematic, to say the least.

Hoping to overcome the limitations of familial genetic studies, behavioral geneticists looked forward with anticipation to the results of the Human Genome Project. At last, they believed, they would be able to use molecular genetics to examine the actual genetic codes of individual patients. They would be able to directly test for the presence or absence of specific gene variations (known as *alleles*) in persons with known diagnoses or in families with high concentrations of individuals with similar psychiatric diagnoses or behavioral traits. This kind of research relies heavily on statistical techniques that measure the rates of alleles (genes with common known variants in the population) in a group of patients with a specific diagnosis and compare that with the rate of that allele in the genes of a matched control group without the diagnosis. In all areas of medicine this approach has been largely disappointing. When differences in the rates of alleles in different groups of patients are found, these differences often fail to replicate, and either a different allele or no allele appears to separate the groups. Even replicated findings are disappointing, accounting for less than 4% of the variation in behavioral traits or physical disease (Hall, 2010). Some leaders in the field of molecular genetics are calling for a radical shift in strategy away from looking for common gene variants and toward the search for groups of extremely rare genetic variations that independently may contribute to the development of the same symptoms. In addition, epigenetic research is calling into question the definition of the concept of "genes" because it has been shown that biochemical substances in the nuclei of our cells previously thought to be of little consequence can control the material identified as genes (Hall, 2010; Moore, 2003).

A recent review of the literature (Schienle, Hettema, Caceda, & Nemeroff, 2011) estimated the heritability for generalized anxiety disorder (GAD)—the broadest, most diagnosed form of anxiety disorder in *DSM–5*—as ranging from

24% to 39%. This is considerably lower than found by previous researchers (Eley & Gregory, 2004) who cited heritability estimates from various researchers for anxiety disorders as "up to 50%." In fact, Tambs et al. (2009) estimated the heritability of all anxiety disorders even higher, at 54%.

Looking more specifically at the childhood anxiety literature, which tends to focus on the personality trait of neuroticism or behavioral inhibition rather than clinical levels of anxiety, the results are even more varied. Dilalla, Kagan, and Reznick (1994) estimated behavioral inhibition (fearfulness and shyness) in 2-year-old children at a heritability of 40% to 70%. Legrand, McGue, and Iacono (1999) found a heritability estimate of 45% in children and adolescents.

In terms of molecular genetics, Schienle et al. (2011, p. 121) found the state of research "too immature" to support any specific genetic loci as implicated in GAD, though they noted a great deal of interest in the serotonin transporter gene 5-HTP, which others have claimed to be linked to anxiety disorders. In response to these disappointing results, Gregory, Lau, and Eley (2008) cited two studies in which the short 5-HTP allele was linked to GAD, but only when adverse life events were accounted for—in other words a true Gene × Environment interaction (the interaction of nature and nurture). They posited that this might mean certain genes created a vulnerability or sensitivity to certain difficult environments. In this case, the heritability of GAD increased from 19% to 44% in adolescent girls. This enthusiasm must be tempered by a meta-analysis performed by Duncan and Keller (2011) that found that claims of Gene × Environment interaction involving the 5-HTP allele seemed to have been unduly influenced by small sample sizes and publication bias in favor of positive over negative findings.

What is often missing from these articles, and understandably so because the researchers are committed to biological research, is the preponderance of evidence suggesting that the environment accounts for 50% to 75% of the variance in anxiety scores for groups of adults studied for anxiety disorders. Yet, that is what the data show, if one regards this sort of group data as definitive in the field.

Brain Functioning

Postmortem studies of psychiatric patients have never revealed any consistent differences in brain anatomy between patients and normal control groups. Consequently, neuroscientists welcomed the newer imaging procedures, the positron-emission tomography and functional MRI methods, as ways to see the brain in action and to measure its physiology (i.e., how it functions) rather than just its structure or anatomy. Textbooks at all levels are generally peppered with images of healthy brains contrasted with the brains of psychiatric patients who are psychotic or severely depressed. The images have great impact, using bright colors to show different areas of the brain activated in the presence of similar stimuli or when in different mental states. The casual reader or the reader predisposed to the medical model sees these images as pure snapshots of reality, undeniable proof that the defective brain is the source of problems in living and extreme psychological suffering.

Recently, however, even some neuroscientists are showing reluctance to confer factual status on such claims. A distinguished international team of medical statisticians (Button et al., 2013) concluded that the established findings of neuroscience are largely based on faulty research methods, inadequate statistical procedures that are unlikely to reject false claims, and publishing practices that favor dramatic positive findings that are essentially statistical outliers so long as the findings expand on the dominant theories in the field.

Medications

Historically, prior to the 1980s when the selective serotonin reuptake inhibitors (SSRIs) began being marketed, the pharmacological treatment for anxiety was benzodiazepine medications. These drugs produce a rapid sensation of relaxation without complete sedation and were the number-one drugs prescribed in all of medicine in the 1960s and 1970s. Valium, Librium, and Xanax were extremely popular and also highly addicting. They potentiated alcohol and so could lead to dangerous accidental (or intentional) overdoses even when the patient was given less than a lethal supply. Due to wide publicity concerning their addicting qualities, by the time Prozac hit the market, the sales of benzodiazepines was in decline, though they remain fairly popular even today.

SSRIs were supposed to be "clean" drugs that targeted only one neurotransmitter in the brain. (The brain may have over 100 such biochemical messenger substances—we do not really know—but SSRIs supposedly affect only serotonin reuptake at the synapse.) Oddly enough, Prozac had an immediately noticeable effect on physiological symptoms of anxiety in many patients (though it also increased anxiety in others). The antianxiety effects are experienced immediately, though it may take weeks before the antidepressant effect is experienced.

As the complexities and vagaries of neuroscience multiply, the practitioner must make down-to-earth pragmatic choices as to what model to use in working with each individual patient/client. These choices may have life-altering consequences for the individuals in question and for the clinicians making those choices. In addition to knowing what one might or might not conclude from reading the research in the field, the clinician builds a body of her or his own work experience on which to draw.

THE FORMS OF ANXIETY

The most common form of anxiety is *free-floating* or *generalized anxiety disorder*. We feel agitated, tense, and worried "about everything and nothing in particular." There is a fear that something awful is about to happen, but one has no idea what that might be. When this kind of anxiety peaks with intense physiological sensations, the individual feels intense chest pain and lightheadedness and often fears that he or she is suffering a coronary event. (Rarely is this actually the case, but if you have never suffered from such an anxiety or panic attack, it is a good idea to have a physician check for an actual physical health problem before assuming it is psychological in nature.)

Most phobias are inconvenient but not incapacitating, with the exception of agoraphobia, which is the fear of leaving one's home. This is often symbolic of a fear of interacting with various individuals who one might encounter once outside the home. *Social anxiety* is a relatively new addition to *DSM–5* and represents an attempt to diagnose and treat shyness as a medical disorder requiring medication. Most surveys of the general population show that about 15% to 30% of the population characterize themselves as "shy," so one can see what the effect would be of medicalizing this personality trait.

Obsessive–compulsive disorder consists of repetitive unwanted and irrational thoughts often accompanied by repetitive unwanted irrational behaviors meant to ward off the thoughts. A person who has obsessive thoughts about harming another member of the family might repeatedly check the kitchen knives to make sure they have not taken one (and used it without remembering they had done so.) Most of us occasionally double-check to see whether we have done something right or wrong, but in clinical cases these rituals become incapacitating, consuming hours of the day. Between 1% and 2% of the population receive this diagnosis over their lifetime (Stein, Ford, Anderson, & Walker, 1997). Though Freud built his original theory on an understanding of the irrational guilt in obsessive–compulsive neurosis, talk therapies have not generally proven effective with this form of anxiety. Behavioral therapies involving exposure and response prevention have been as effective as medications (Barlow, 2004).

Psychodynamic, humanistic, and cognitive behavior therapies all report good results with the other anxiety disorders. The more intensive the treatment, the longer lasting the results (Shedler, 2012). Of course, one has to find a good match for a psychotherapist, and that can take some time and delay the onset of effective treatment. All the primary medications used in the biomedical approach produce addictive-like effects: increased tolerance and withdrawal symptoms on discontinuance. When SSRI antidepressants are used they also produce loss of sexual responsiveness in a significant minority of patients and undesirable weight gain for many. Most people assume that psychotherapy will be more costly than a medication approach, but in fact this may often not be true, especially if one is on a medication that is not generic and if one considers long-term health consequences.

SOMATIC MANIFESTATIONS OF PSYCHOLOGICAL SUFFERING

Somatic manifestations of psychological suffering have been called by many names: hysteria and neurasthenia in the late 19th century; psychosomatic, psychophysiological, and somatoform in the 20th century; and now somatic disorders in *DSM–5*. These are distinguished from malingering and other forms of deliberately simulating an illness or injury to obtain some benefit (e.g., sick leave or pay) and hypochondriacal complaints where a person believes they have a dreaded illness without any symptoms of the disorder being present and will not accept reassurance that they are not going to die.

In *somatic disorders* there is a change in physiological functioning of an organ system due to stress and/or psychological conflict, whereas in *conversion disorders* there is a loss of sensory or motor function without evidence of physiological changes. In the first group are individuals whose bodies seem to be a chronic (6 months or longer) source of concern though they have no known medical condition to explain their symptoms: episodes of pain in one or more areas of the body (e.g., gastrointestinal discomfort, pain in functioning of the reproductive organs, muscle and joint pain, and at least one vague neurological complaint). Less than 0.5% of the population meets all the criteria, though surveys of the general population have suggested that more than 50% of the population reports having at least some of these complaints at (Hiller, Rief, & Brähler, 2006).

Conversion Disorders

Some patients who are diagnosed using *DSM–5* criteria as having somatoform disorders have symptoms that Freud labeled at the dawn of the psychotherapy era as *conversion hysteria*. These patients have the appearance of a neurological disorder in the absence of any known physical cause. The may be temporarily blind, mute, or partially paralyzed; they may display seizure-like movements, numbing of skin senses, fainting spells, general weakness or loss of coordination, and so forth. What is atypical for true neurological diseases but common here is that the symptoms appear and disappear without any explanation, and the patients often seem to be indifferent to their plight (*la belle indifference*). The problem occurs in about 2% of the population, and the symptoms spontaneously remit after about two weeks. However, the symptoms frequently return. One follow-up study (Couprie, Wijdicks, Rooijmans, & van Gijn, 1995) found that perhaps as much as 50% of those who receive this diagnosis are found years later to have a medical condition that might explain the earlier conversion symptoms. Consequently, in somatic disorders, evaluation by a physician is also recommended.

Note, however, that unlike anxiety and depression cases for which no other physical explanation can be found and thus the psychological symptoms of anxiety and depression are taken at face value as suggesting a problem that is psychological in nature, in conversion hysteria there are no obvious psychological symptoms or problems. The psychological is converted into the physical, and there seems no trace of a psychological or social trauma to explain it—that is, unless one examines what Breuer and Freud referred to as *unconscious psychological trauma* (Freud, 1920/1966). There is a parallel with anxiety and depression when one considers the physical symptoms of anxiety and depression that are the result of similar psychological processes—upsetting relationships and overwhelming emotions that are shrouded in secrecy and shame.

Psychological approaches to these complaints that the body is either in pain or not functioning properly look for the meaning in the symptoms. In addition to expressing emotions through physical symptoms, the symptoms themselves may be preferable to the emotional pain that is represented. For many individuals, the terror of panic attacks or the despondency of depression is so unbearable that to have a localized pain or a specific physical difficulty is preferable. The physical pain is in effect a defense against or a diversion from the emotional pain. One has to wonder whether these interpretations of somatoform symptoms are valid ways to explain the different physical symptoms that individuals use to express their psychological pain. Why does one person express this pain in the digestive system, another in the respiratory symptoms of stress-triggered asthma, a third in chronic low-back pain, and a fourth not at all but then directly expresses concerns and frustrations with others and life circumstances?

That is the big unanswered question in this otherwise carefully developed and clinically useful theory. It seems the likely answer will involve some or all of the following considerations: (a) individuals seem to often have one organ system that is weaker than the others, and this is where stress gets expressed or communicated; (b) happenstance may contribute, as when a particular physical illness is witnessed or personally experienced as having a secondary gain—the individual realizes that he or she is treated better by others when ill than when healthy; and (c) another family member models using a specific illness to control the demands that others make on her or him.

Psychosomatic Suffering

Psychosomatic disorders are physical symptoms linked to psychological factors. These are stress-related illnesses, such as high blood pressure, asthma, and digestive difficulties, in which the body is not functioning properly and it is clear that either acute or chronic environmental stress or trauma has contributed to the initiation or exacerbation of symptoms. The difference between these problems and the others discussed so far is that in these cases there is in fact physical evidence of an underlying physical dysfunction or illness. Nonetheless, these individuals may become completely symptom-free with effective psychological treatment that alters the stressful environment. Thus, there is a third set of physical symptoms that are lessened or even eliminated by psychological rather than medical treatment, though medical treatment may be used as well to prevent an immediate health crisis (e.g., medication to lower blood pressure or reduce inflammation in the lungs or intestines).

Similarly, there is increasing evidence that behavioral or personality traits play at least some role in increasing the severity of serious medical illnesses such as heart disease and cancer. The common link seems to be the effects of stress on the immune system, which provides resistance to diseases. This sort of pervasive influence of psychological factors on fatal diseases was long denied by the medical community, and physicians who supported this view were ridiculed and ostracized within their profession (Siegel, 1998). However, this is increasingly becoming a mainstream view. Type A personality characteristics (hard-driving, perfectionistic, aggressive, competitive) are associated with heart disease, and Type C personality traits (passive, unassertive, unhappy, but suffering in silence) are associated with cancer proneness (Katz & Epstein, 2005). Interestingly, as with other personality trait psychological problems (see Chapter 7), individuals with these traits often are not consciously aware of the extent to which they behave in these ways or the effects these traits have on the success of their relationships or careers. In other words, we see again the influence on the body of aspects of our psychological life that Freud called the *unconscious*. In this case, however, what is unconscious to the patient is obvious to others who know the individual and even to their physicians.

Over the past 20 years we have seen tremendous growth in the area of health psychology, which addresses what the person does for and to their own body, especially in relation to chronic illnesses (Collins, Hewson, Munger, & Wade, 2010). This approach has received a major boost by being incorporated into key aspects of the Affordable Health Care Act ("Obamacare"; Patient Protection and Affordable Care Act, 2010). The new law requires a behavioral health expert to be a part of the primary care treatment team working with patients with chronic illnesses such as asthma, obesity, and diabetes. Over the past decade there has been increasing recognition of the role of psychological factors in the development of many illnesses previously believed to be solely the province of medicine. Most of this awareness has come from a study of the role of stress on the various organ systems of the body, including the heart and circulatory system and the incidence of coronary heart disease, the immune system that protects against infections and cancer cells, the respiratory system and the incidence of asthma, and the endocrine system and the incidence of Type II diabetes (Costa & VandenBos, 1996). There is clear evidence that psychological treatments that are aimed at reducing the impact of external stressors by changing one's environment and/or the psychological response to those stressors (e.g., expressing more emotion or increasing relaxation) does increase life expectancy in patients with these serious diseases (e.g., Friedman et al., 1996; Spiegel & Classen, 2000). Supportive–expressive humanistic group psychotherapy and cognitive–behavioral interventions both appear to be quite helpful in these health delivery system contexts.

Hypochondriasis (Illness Anxiety)

Hypochondriasis is the worry that one is terribly ill, without any obvious physical symptoms. The individual is convinced that she or he is dying and that some feature of the way her or his body is or works that had not been previously noticed (e.g., a bump under the skin, a random pain, a mole) is a sign of this dread disease and that doctors must take drastic measures to save his or her life. This is obviously a clear-cut anxiety disorder (once patients with difficult-to-diagnose physical ailments are eliminated, no easy task in itself). It is similar to an obsessive–compulsive disorder in which the obsession is "I am sick and dying" and the compulsion is to seek medical care. The problem with a medical approach in this case is that each set of expensive tests that the patient is convinced is necessary (and the doctor may be reluctant to refuse for various reasons of self-interest) only provides a short period of reassurance before the anxiety returns. Over time, this subgroup of patients in the health care system uses a tremendous amount of financial resources with no benefit obtained. Psychotherapy that deals with existential death anxiety, identification with relatives who have died unexpectedly or tragically, interpersonal problems that have pushed the individual to turn inward and become preoccupied with their own health, and guilt over deeds for which the individual thinks she or he deserve a death penalty are all potentially useful areas of exploration that have been found in individual cases to provide relief from the underlying anxiety. However, physicians rarely refer individuals to psychotherapists to address this problem.

Treatment: Hypnosis

Generally, the somatoform and stress disorders are difficult to treat because people are committed to a medical solution and do not see the point in psychological intervention. Their psychological pain is sufficiently outside of consciousness that a treatment that takes significant psychological effort does not seem like a good use of their time. The one exception to this is in the use of contemporary forms of clinical hypnosis for the reduction of pain in patients with many different physical and psychological problems.

Milton Erickson (Erickson, Rossi, & Rossi, 1976) became a psychiatric legend in the 20th century for his use of direct and indirect forms of hypnosis in a wide variety of medical and psychiatric conditions, especially in the treatment of pain. His approach to hypnosis permitted some individuals to undergo major surgeries (including caesarian sections and dental extractions) without the use of anesthetics. Even before Erickson, Freud had used hypnosis effectively with hysteria, but became discouraged because it did not result in a permanent cure (Freud, 1920/1966). However, only about 15% of the population is easily hypnotizable and 25% is quite resistant to hypnosis (Hilgard, 1965). The middle group can be taught with varying degrees of effort to enter into the trance-like state required for the technique to work.

Moene et al. (2003) used hypnosis in a randomized clinical trial to treat conversion disorders with motor symptoms and found that the hypnosis group did better than the untreated control group. Recent meta-analyses of the use of hypnosis in clinical populations show it to be efficacious in reducing pain in adult cancer and burn patients, with a moderate to large effect size ($d = .74$). Pain is perhaps the best example of the illusory difference between the mental and physical phenomena we encounter in the clinical practice of psychology.

TRAUMA AND POSTTRAUMATIC STRESS DISORDER

Freud used the experience of physicians with cases of "shell shock" as a model for understanding conversion hysteria. A severe psychological trauma, such as being trapped for hours in a life-threatening situation or watching one's best friend be blown to bits by a shell, would produce a psychotic detachment from reality, amnesia for the traumatic event, severe social withdrawal, nightmares, sleeplessness, loss of appetite, and so forth. It was found that such patients could recover if given supportive care, and in World War II psychoanalysis was widely applied with reportedly good results to help troops showing signs of what was then called *combat fatigue* to return to active duty in just a few days. Posttraumatic stress disorder (PTSD) was not formally a diagnosis until after the Vietnam War, when it was found that some soldiers who had not had severe trauma reactions would nevertheless develop symptoms years after returning home. Additional symptoms included waking flashbacks of being in combat, paranoia, and extreme reactivity to loud noises or visual stimuli that resembled the sights and sounds of combat.

Over the past few years, the U.S. military has reported unexpectedly high rates of PTSD (17%) in members who served in Iraq or Afghanistan (Black,

Gallaway, Bell, & Ritchie, 2011). Similarly, the Veterans Administration reported a shocking increase in suicides among veterans, and the U.S. Army has reported a disturbing increase in the rate of suicides among both active duty service members and veterans (M. Miller et al., 2012). Successful treatments have not been found (Institute of Medicine, 2007).

A CASE OF POSTTRAUMATIC STRESS DISORDER IN AN AFRICAN WOMAN

Edwards (2009) developed a model of cognitive behavior therapy (CBT) specifically for treating PTSD. The treatment model is based on a stage approach in which, depending on the client, the therapist decides what stage of intervention or treatment the client is currently ready to undergo. Edwards numbered his treatment stages from 1 to 3. In the first stage, the therapist and client must guarantee the client's safety and well-being (making sure the client is not violent or suicidal). The second stage emphasizes developing a strong relationship between the therapist and client and allowing the client to understand and comprehend the nature of his or her trauma. The third stage is designed "to initiate active interventions designed to activate the trauma memory and restructure problematic meanings, as well as to help clients build a life beyond the trauma" (p. 263).

The case of Grace by Boulind and Edwards (2008) followed this approach, a manualized form of CBT that also addressed responsiveness to the quality of the therapeutic relationship in a humanistic manner. Grace was a 22-year-old Black South African woman who suffered from moderate clinical depression and post-abortion syndrome. (Her name and other identifying information have been altered to protect confidentiality.) She was a university student and had a father who had died from AIDS and a mother who was HIV-positive. Grace had been feeling depressed for a while, and had been through a tumultuous few months. She had been experiencing frequent headaches, which made studying and making decisions extremely difficult. Within the 3 weeks before treatment the headaches had only intensified. Grace was also losing weight and seemed to be self-critical. A few months before, Grace had suggested to a friend that they both be tested for HIV. Although Grace tested negative, her friend tested positive. A few months later, Grace's friend died, and Grace felt guilty, believing that the discovery of HIV in her friend caused her friend to lose hope for life.

Grace entered therapy a few days after she had a panic attack that brought her into the therapy room. In the first session she and the therapist came up with the goals of her therapy to be: "(1) Not to be so hard on myself (less self-critical), (2) not to depend on others' approval, (3) to eat more healthily,

(4) to develop a more positive outlook, and (5) to worry less about my academic work" (Boulind & Edwards, 2008, p. 540).

In the third session, Grace revealed that the depressive symptoms had started in January, before the friend's death. When asked whether there was anything stressful that had happened around that time, Grace said that she had had an abortion earlier in December. Grace had hesitated to say anything earlier, because she feared possible judgment from the therapist. Her fiancé, the one with whom she got pregnant, was several hundred kilometers away when she found out she was pregnant. When she called him to discuss options on the telephone, he "did not actively offer his own views and, when she suggested she have an abortion, expressed no disagreement" (Boulind & Edwards, 2008, p. 541). She also did not tell her family for fear of being judged or called "a slut."

In this session, Grace seemed unaware that there could be a connection between the abortion and her depression. She revealed that only her fiancé knew that she had an abortion and had been keeping quiet about it. At the end of the session, Grace realized that all her goals were about overcoming this idea of herself as a bad person and that these beliefs started around the time of her abortion. The therapist concluded that she met the criteria for major depressive disorder and PTSD, primarily PAS (post-abortion syndrome). Grace felt upset when discussing her abortion and tried not to think about it. She felt less interested in or attached to other people and had sleep difficulties and other anxiety symptoms. Grace said she felt conflicted about ending the pregnancy, and because she coped by trying not to think about it, she was unable to reflect on the event. This repression of emotion and thoughts about the abortion led to her PTSD, and through that, her depression, which was exacerbated by her friend's death. Therefore, the aim of the treatment would be to "help her tell her full story of the abortion and the events leading up to it, to explore the personal feelings associated with loss shame and guilt . . . and to help her reframe those meanings in a positive direction" (Boulind & Edwards, 2008, p. 542).

In the next five sessions, Grace's experience of anxiety and depression lessened, which allowed her and her therapist to explore the aspects related to her PTSD that concerned her; however, she had not yet integrated the memory of the abortion. In the fourth session, Grace commented, "It's locked away at the back of my mind, and I don't know if I can take it out. . . . I just don't know if I can talk about it" (Boulind & Edwards, 2008, p. 542). The therapist, being mindful of Grace's unreadiness, changed the clinical focus from reintegrating the memory into her narrative to addressing other concerns, such as her eventual wedding, her academic life, and her ability to develop trust. In the seventh session, after finally reclaiming her life, Grace indicated that she was ready to discuss the abortion and told the full story. In the eighth session, she admitted that she felt rushed into making the decision and, for the first time in therapy, became visibly agitated, expressing anger at her fiancé for not discussing his opinions on the abortion with her: "He left me to make the decision alone . . . the biggest decision of my life and there was no one!" (Boulind & Edwards, 2008, p. 543).

In the 10th session, the therapist and Grace came to a joint decision to try and reexperience the trauma so she could have her emotions validated and reintegrate the experience. She began to recount the day she had the abortion, touching repeatedly on the sense of aloneness and distress she felt. Grace cried out, "Nobody knew . . . and nobody cared!" (Boulind & Edwards, 2008, p. 544). After the abortion, she did not talk about it with anyone, nor did her fiancé ever discuss it with her. The therapist recommended that she take time to mourn her lost baby and to discuss with her fiancé how she felt during that time, allowing her experience to finally be healthily incorporated into the rest of her narrative. In follow-up visits, it was obvious that Grace was progressing well and that her distress was rapidly diminishing. Within 3 months, her relationship with her fiancé was improving (they had a wedding date set), as were her other interpersonal relationships.

SEXUAL RELATIONSHIPS AND SUFFERING

Many modern-day students and readers decry Freud (1905) as obsessed with sexuality, as a man who saw in innocent objects and aspects of nature sexual symbols that were far-fetched, if not preposterous. This is quite ironic given that we live in a time when we are inundated with sexuality in the media to an unprecedented degree. Images that would have been considered pornographic 40 years ago are today commonplace on cable television stations that are rated suitable for young teenage viewers. Radio stations blast songs filled with overtly sexual lyrics, and on the Internet there is almost unlimited access to pornographic images. It is not only in the entertainment departments of the media that we find intense interest in sexuality but also in news departments. How many world famous politicians and athletes have seen their careers nearly destroyed by the "outing" of their sexual practices: President Bill Clinton; the former governor of New York State, Elliott Spitzer, who many thought was on the short list of potential future Democratic presidential candidates; Tiger Woods, the greatest golfer of his generation; war hero and CIA director General David Petraeus; and the list goes on. Lives great and small confused by, conflicted over, and sometimes destroyed by sexual behaviors that are both encouraged and forbidden within the same culture and society.

When couples are surveyed about the issues they fight about in their relationship, the top two items consistently on the list are money and sex.

Marital infidelity (affecting about 30% of all married couples) is one of the primary precipitants of divorce, though it may be a symptom as well as a cause of marital conflict. Love triangles are frequently cited as the source of conflicts in family homicides, suggesting how explosive the effects are of adding sexual betrayal to interpersonal rejection or conflict. In 2010, a young professor of psychology at the University of Idaho specializing in neuroscience killed one of his graduate students, with whom he had been having an affair. Just before she was murdered, she had broken off the relationship and notified the authorities that he was harassing her. He then killed himself. We seem to be a society that has little understanding of how to promote healthy sexual relationships and that can agree on only one thing: Freud made too big a deal about the role of sexuality in the human psyche.

DSM–5 takes a minimalist approach to defining sexual disorders. It separates sexual disorders into two groups: *sexual dysfunctions*, where an adult wishes to have a sexual relationship with another adult but is unable to do so in a pleasurable manner (e.g., male impotence, female inability to orgasm); and *paraphilia*, where an adult prefers sexual arousal with inappropriate objects or persons (e.g., fetishistic behavior, sadomasochistic behavior, voyeurism, pedophilia) over sexual behavior with another appropriate adult. Surprisingly, if the same behaviors are found between consenting adult partners, no diagnosis can be made, except of course for pedophilia, which is illegal.

DSM–5 notes that acceptable sexual behaviors are quite varied across cultures and that what might be considered deviant in one culture might be accepted in another. In fact, until the mid-1970s, the *DSM–II* (American Psychiatric Association, 1968) included homosexuality as a sexual disorder. Its removal came as a result of a vote of the membership attending the annual meeting of the American Psychiatric Association—a meeting that was the object of considerable political lobbying and protest by gay and civil rights groups. The culture was shifting its values, and so did the *DSM–II*. What is missing in all of this is the extent to which sexuality is a critical feature of relationships and the role of relationships in our lives. There is no sexual disorder diagnosis for sexual aggression or rape, for instance, although almost 20% of women in the United States reported having been the target of a sexual assault (World Health Organization, 2005).

Sexual abuse of children is far more rampant in our society than we would like to admit, with estimates ranging from 10% to 15% of the U.S. population (females in childhood are twice as likely as males to be sexually abused) having been the target of inappropriate sexual advances by adults. In multiproblem families with substance abuse present, the sexual and physical abuse is frequently life-threatening and may be inflicted on infants and preschool children. The rates of child abuse vary greatly across cultures because of different sexual norms and gender roles. The rate in South Africa is 61%

for men and 43% for women, whereas in Asia the combined rate is about 24% and in Europe about 9%. Of course, these numbers are subject to many qualifications, including the difficulty of doing cross-cultural survey research (World Health Organization, 2005).

Sexual dysfunctions, paraphilias, sexual aggression, and sexual infidelity all develop and exist within the context of close relationships or in the avoidance of such relationships. These behaviors represent (a) an inability to understand how to give and receive bodily pleasure with another similarly aged human being in a cooperative manner or (b) an intense fear or guilt about doing same. Many of the paraphilias are attempts to have sexual pleasure in the absence of on-going close personal relationships and are engaged in by individuals who have great social anxiety and awkwardness, an intense expectation of rejection or hurt in close relationships, and often intense anger over past rejections. These behaviors often are engaged in an obsessive–compulsive manner, again suggesting an underlying intense anxiety from which the individual is distracted by the symptomatic behavior. When the individual is less anxious, he or she does not engage in or think positively about the sexual behavior in question. However, when anxiety returns, he or she feels drawn to the sexual outlet he or she previously found shameful.

When sexual dysfunctions occur in the context of a relationship, the dysfunction serves to communicate a displeasure or frustration with the partner in nonsexual areas of the relationship. A spouse or lover who is feeling constantly berated and criticized is rarely a satisfying or responsive sexual partner. Sexual dysfunctions that carry over across relationships usually represent a more general sense of inadequacy as a person; sometimes individuals feel inadequate specifically in the sexual realm due to inexperience or guilt over the acceptability of being a sexually responsive individual. Sexual infidelity is often an aggressive act by a partner who is afraid to be aggressive in the relationship. It is often committed to get back at a partner for real or imagined transgressions within the primary relationship. One way we know this is an angry act is that it makes the person who has been cheated on angry when they discover the infidelity.

SELF-MEDICATING WITH ALCOHOL AND DRUGS

One can hardly get through middle school in the United States today without being exposed repeatedly to health education classes informing one of the kinds of addictive substances that are available in our society and the horrible aspects of addiction. This information is presented as though drugs and alcohol are so powerful that a perfectly healthy and happy individual could accidentally or involuntarily ingest or inhale such substances and be captured by the drug, immediately developing a craving that is irresistible (or if it is a prescription drug, a miracle cure). The presentation is reminiscent of morality plays from the Middle Ages in which a person gives in to temptation once, and the devil takes up residence in her or his soul. Missing from this simplified view of life is that incredible complexity of the interaction between substances that enter the body and the psychological state of the individual, both before ingesting the substance and after. We know from the long history of humanity and from contemporary research in social psychology that the social and attitudinal contexts in which one ingests a substance have a tremendous impact on how the substance is experienced. The placebo effect is a powerful human response based on expectations. A substance that we expect to make us sleepy, awake, sexually aroused, hungry, and so forth, is more likely to do so than the same substance ingested with a different expectation. This is true whether the substance is a drug or a food. Such expectations can be explicit (e.g., this drug will make you fall asleep) or subtle, as when a drug such as alcohol or a hallucinogen is incorporated into social or religious rituals, such as going to the pub after work for a few beers or smoking peyote to become one with the gods. The drug's effect is mediated by social expectations of how one is to behave in each context, though we may not be aware of it and may attribute the change in how we feel to the drug and not the social interaction or context (Jones, Corbin, & Fromme, 2001).

In this regard, my sense is that for the vast majority of substance abuse in the United States among high school and college students, and among their parents as well, the primary context is self-medication for low to moderate levels of anxiety or depression. Getting high or even wasted 2 or 3 nights per week is a form of escapism and what is being escaped is feeling anxious or depressed. The anxiety and depression is the result of the everyday stresses of life and the person's cumulative unresolved unconscious conflicts. In the absence of self-understanding and the psychological freedom that comes with it, most of us are in over our heads in terms of what we can tolerate emotionally.

This does not address the full-blown alcoholic or drug-addicted state to which only 13% of alcohol users and 30% of illicit drug users (Substance Abuse and Mental Health Services Administration [SAMHSA], 2013) progress, but often in these cases a person is attempting to self-medicate for a severe level of anxiety or depression. Of course, specific drugs (particularly stimulants and opiates) may have specific features that increase the speed of the decline in the addiction cycle or allow one to cover up the process for longer. It is also true that medical supervision of detoxification is needed in the early treatment phase because of the risk of life-threatening withdrawal effects such as seizures. Nevertheless, even in the midst of physical withdrawal or addictive cravings, the person's entire personality and social network can have a tremendous impact on how these "physical" effects are experienced and whether they are felt as unbearable and intolerable or simply as unpleasant. The psyche is never unimportant when considering how the person manages his or her own body. It is the person making decisions, giving up or holding out, or arranging for care or rejecting care that ultimately has the control, not some brain center's concentration of a neurotransmitter such as dopamine (thought to be involved in pleasure responses as well as psychosis).

Substances act in much the same way as psychological defenses such as denial or dissociation. *Denial* is the defense by which we tell ourselves that nothing unpleasant or objectionable has been felt, whereas in *dissociation* or *splitting* we allow one part of ourselves to feel a traumatic experience while keeping the trauma from being felt by another part of ourselves. When we split, we compartmentalize a negative set of feelings as only something to be felt in context A or B. The contradiction is not experienced by the person doing this, and when in one context, the other seems a million miles away and not relevant to who or what he or she is as a person. In dissociating, we may not be aware at all of the other experience and may deny that it ever happened. When these kind of defenses are overtaxed, they are no longer able to keep out of awareness the intense feelings of fear or terror triggered by current life events (and reminiscent of the feelings associated with childhood trauma), and substances are used to bolster the defenses.

The accuracy of this description is supported by the frequent observation that people with substance abuse problems use a great deal of denial or splitting to conceal from themselves the extent of the abuse, and how often in the intoxicated state addicts or alcoholics will engage in behavior that when sober they regard as foreign to their character. Who else's character could such behavior represent other than the person in question?

Substance Use Disorders

DSM–5 lists as disorders the ingesting of a wide variety of nonfood substances: tobacco, caffeine, alcohol, stimulants, opiates, and hallucinogens. It is a confusing list; the first three are legal substances from multibillion dollar industries, and the fourth category of substance is regularly prescribed to young children by their physicians to control their hyperactive behavior. The fifth category is regularly prescribed by physicians to control physical pain after surgery or injury, and the sixth has been used in experimental treatments or nontraditional healing rituals for various psychological disorders, including addiction to opiates and alcohol. Government-funded research on causes and treatment of addictions and policy aimed at changing the rates of use in the population usually focuses on illegal substances because it is much more difficult for producers and distributors of illegal substances to lobby the government for changes in funding or policy.

British researchers Nutt, King, and Phillips (2010) surveyed experts on substance abuse from the health and social sciences and asked them to rate a list of 20 substances according to not only physical and psychological damage to the individual abusers but also to their relationships and the community in which they live. They were asked to consider both direct and indirect costs in all of these areas to give a comprehensive picture of the effects on society of the substances in question. The experts' ratings were converted to a total score from 0 to 100, where 100 represented the most damage possible. The partial results were as follows: alcohol = 72, heroin = 55, crack cocaine = 54, methamphetamine = 33, cocaine = 27, tobacco = 26, amphetamine = 23, cannabis = 20, benzodiazepines = 15, methadone = 14; ecstasy = 9, LSD = 7, mushrooms = 6. The study was done in the hope of redirecting government research and prevention policy to the drugs at the top of the list, though given the power of the alcohol and tobacco industries, one can only wonder whether it will have any effect at all.

Substance Use in the Teen and College Years

The Substance Abuse and Mental Health Services Administration (SAMHSA; 2013) database revealed the epidemiology of substance use disorders in the United States:

- The rate for persons 18 to 25 years old is almost 20%, compared with 4.5% for children 12 to 17 years and about 6% for those 26 years and older. Males outnumber females by a ratio of 4 to 1.
- Among 18- to 22-year-olds who either were not attending or only attending college part-time, there was less alcohol binge drinking (36%) and less heavy use (12%) than among those attending college full-time (42% binge drinkers, 15.5% heavy users).

Clearly, there is something about the late teenage and early adult years—and something about college life in particular—that increases the risk of a serious alcohol problem. This is also reflected in estimates that about 1,700 college students die each year from alcohol-related causes. In a college population of about 12 million 4-year college students, this does not seem like many. However, that number is equivalent to the entire population of many small liberal arts colleges. Thus, this problem is equivalent to obliterating the student body of a different small liberal arts college every year.

These data suggest also that after graduation alcohol drinking patterns do change. The rate of substance use disorders in the general population drops from 20% to about 7%. Thus, it is clear that many heavy drinkers cut back when they graduate. Still, about one in three of the heavy drinkers will continue the pattern post-college. Although there are some controlled heavy drinkers who seem to avoid social and economic catastrophe, it is more common for the problem to worsen with the accumulating stress of career, marriage, and family life, the multiplying responsibilities yielding increased opportunities to overload the defense mechanisms that attempt to deny or dissociate negative emotional experiences.

The SAMHSA (2013) data on treatment is not encouraging. In 2010, about 23 million Americans were defined as in need of substance use disorder treatment. Only 10% or 2.6 million individuals actually received treatment at a specialty facility. Of the remaining 20 million, about one million indicated that they thought they needed treatment during the year, but 66% of those who said they thought they needed treatment actually sought it out. There are at least three reasons for these dismal treatment numbers. First, until the passage of the Affordable Care Act in 2011, many health insurance plans did not cover substance abuse treatment costs sufficiently to make the option realistic. Second, the denial and dissociation defenses of this population make them uninterested in pursuing treatment. Third, treatments for substance abuse are of limited effectiveness. Many people will "dry out" and detoxify during a 30-day inpatient stay at a rehabilitation center but relapse within the first 12 months after they return to the community.

Though a controversial approach, perhaps in part because it is not based on professional services or scientific methods, Alcoholics Anonymous (AA) is often the intervention that is the most effective. Practicing clinicians, even those who take a scientific approach, often encourage attendance at daily or weekly AA meetings for their patients. AA is a completely volunteer organization founded in 1935 by two men who had the desire to recover from alcoholism, Bill W., a New York businessman, and Dr. Bob, a physician from Ohio. To this day, people at AA meetings use only their first names, and meetings are open to anyone interested in learning about AA and how to become abstinent. Meetings are held wherever a group wishes to organize itself, and there are no fees or dues. Nor is AA affiliated with any social, religious, political, or professional group. A person who joins will be offered a "sponsor" who will be available any time day or night to talk the new member through the periods of intense cravings for alcohol that are associated with the withdrawal period. Depending on the size of the locale, one can find anywhere from one meeting a week to one meeting an hour to attend. In other words, there is an enormous amount of social support for quitting alcohol.

For a person whose social life has previously been associated with drinking at a bar or with friends, this is of enormous significance because otherwise one has to choose to give up not only alcohol but also one's social life. The twelve-step program created by the founders of AA is explained and developed through the *Big Book*, the AA bible (Anonymous, 2001). It outlines 12 steps to overcoming alcoholism that involve (a) admitting that one's life has been ravaged by alcohol and one is no longer able to control one's drinking; (b) trusting God to lend His will to one's attempts at sobriety; and (c) taking a moral inventory of one's actions as an alcoholic and asking forgiveness, making amends to those one has harmed and eventually reaching out to others to help them join AA.

In the context of the discussion about the defense mechanisms of denial and dissociation, one can see how focused these steps are on confronting first the damage done in one's life by alcohol and then the damage done to one's relationships with others. Of course, the even more obvious message is the nonsectarian but clearly theistic emphasis on recognizing a higher power outside oneself, a rejection of an entirely secular view of life in mechanistic and deterministic terms, what most would identify as a spiritual aspect to life.

I must say, when I was first exposed to an AA meeting as a graduate student preparing to work with a new DUI program being set up in Vermont, I was put off by this almost evangelical approach to alcoholism. Now, with the hindsight of 40 years of working with people in psychotherapy, I no longer object to this aspect of AA. I find that the suffering that people must survive and overcome calls forth from us a need for courage and the opportunity for intense human connections that can only be described at times as miraculous or spiritual.

Nonetheless, the quasireligious component of AA is alienating for some, and many individuals who drink to quell their social anxiety find the social group aversive. But despite its nonprofessional and nonscientific nature and its quasireligious feel, AA is a critically important community resource for the problem of alcohol use disorder. Many people have reported that the twelve steps have saved their lives, and there are several million people participating in the over 100,000 regular meeting groups held throughout the world (Alcoholics Anonymous, 2014). Family members of those with drinking problems have formed parallel organizations in over 100 countries—namely, Al-Anon for spouses and Alateen for offspring. In essence, AA has become a form of family therapy, in which all members can work on reducing the conflict within the household and learn to live with one another without the need for substances to quell their anxieties.

6

DEPRESSION, SUICIDE, AND ANOREXIA

In the current culture, depression is associated with the emotion of sadness or grieving, with the added condition that the emotions seem out of proportion to the actual harm or loss. The grieving process is suppressed and never really blossoms into grief, or it blossoms but then does not subside in a culturally acceptable length of time. Many of the objective criteria of depression are functional or behavioral equivalents to depressed mood and affect: low energy, weight gain or loss, sleep loss or gain, difficulty concentrating or remembering mundane matters, social withdrawal from previously enjoyed relationships and activities, loss of sexual drive, and being easily moved to tears for seemingly no reason. Physically, the person feels exhausted, heavy, and achy, with possible gastrointestinal problems from changes in eating patterns. Appearance is often noticeably affected, with sad facial expressions, hunched shoulders, slowed walking, little attention to physical appearance or dress, and so forth. There are sufficient physical symptoms to suggest the plausibility of seeking medical attention.

http://dx.doi.org/10.1037/14693-006
Not So Abnormal Psychology: A Pragmatic View of Mental Illness, by R. B. Miller
Copyright © 2015 by the American Psychological Association. All rights reserved.

But it has not always been thus. Prior to the 1970s, depression was seen as a rare (less than one in 1,000 adults) and serious psychological condition sometimes requiring hospitalization because the individual affected was unable to function in her or his social roles. It was diagnosed as melancholia and associated with the mid-life or late-life years. The recovery rate was generally above 50%, and persons who recovered rarely had another episode. Treatment with the first generation tricyclic antidepressants had mixed results, with some studies showing little better than a placebo response to the medication (Schuyler, 1974). Comparing this with the National Institute of Mental Health (NIMH) epidemiological study at the beginning of the new millennia (see Chapter 2, this volume), which found that almost 10% of the population showed evidence of meeting the *Diagnostic and Statistical Manual of Mental Disorders* (4th ed.; *DSM–IV*; American Psychiatric Association, 1994) criteria for a mood disorder, there was an increase from the 1970s by a factor of about 10,000.

Prior to *DSM–III* in 1974 and the introduction of the selective serotonin reuptake inhibitor (SSRI) class of pharmaceutical drugs as antidepressants, mental health clinicians were required to do a detailed inquiry to differentiate reactive from endogenous depression. This involved exploring both the psychosocial experiences of the individual's recent history of the year prior to the first emergence of the symptoms of depression and early life circumstances that might have created a vulnerability to depression (e.g., loss of a loved one, parental divorce, social isolation or rejection, school or job failures). If the symptoms could be reasonably thought to be a reaction to such life circumstances, the diagnosis was *reactive depression*, and medication was not to be prescribed. It was prescribed if two other conditions were present. First, no such precipitating life circumstances could be identified despite a thorough psychological assessment interview (generally about an hour in length). Second, and equally important, the predominant complaints were in the realm of persistent physical symptoms of depression related to fatigue, appetite disturbances, sleep disturbance featuring early morning wakening and an inability to return to sleep, and loss of sexual drive. The individual's sense of hopelessness and helplessness seemed focused on the effects of the physical changes on his or her ability to perform daily duties, rather than on the disruptions to his or her ability to perform daily duties after a change in the environmental circumstances. When both these circumstances were present, an *endogenous depression* was the diagnosis, and the first-generation antidepressants were prescribed. Many patients refused to take these medications because of the unpleasant side effects of continual dry mouth and constipation. Others endured or treated the unpleasant side effects to receive the mood-altering benefits of the medication. Medication was used in only a small percentage of the patients who were evaluated for depression in this manner. It was generally found that if patients who had reactive depressions were medicated, the medications were of little or no use.

All of this changed with *DSM–III*'s creation of the diagnosis of *major depression*, which focused on the signs and symptoms of depression, with duration of at least 2 weeks, without regard for the possible precipitating psychosocial circumstances or the life history. This radical shift was justified on the grounds that the new SSRI antidepressants were helpful to anyone with such symptoms regardless of the "cause" and claims that there was now evidence from heritability studies that depression was a genetically transmitted disorder. The other key factor at play was that the drug trials with the SSRIs showed that for most patients there were none of the objectionable immediate side effects that led to discontinuation of use. These studies were based on the 6 weeks of treatment required by the U.S. Food and Drug Administration (FDA) to approve a drug and the additional requirement that there be at least two separate studies showing a difference between those treated with the new medication and those treated with a placebo or a previously approved tricyclic antidepressant.

Critics of *DSM–III* and *DSM–IV* noted that the symptoms of major depression were common in persons who had recently endured the loss of a close loved one and that these often were present for at least 1 to 2 years in the case of the unexpected loss of a child, parent, spouse, or significant other. *DSM–IV* had specified that in such circumstances the symptoms had to be present for 2 months rather than 2 weeks, as in other cases of major depression. In another bold move, *DSM–5* (American Psychiatric Association, 2013) has eliminated this distinction, thus sanctioning the medicating of grieving after a 2-week period.

BIOLOGICAL EXPLANATIONS

As with the anxiety disorders, in this chapter I examine three aspects of the biological explanation: genetics; brain structure and functioning, and response to medication.

Genetics

The findings of Duncan and Keller (2011) on the inadequacy of the research design in Gene × Environment studies are even more relevant in considering the genetic theory of depression. Caspi et al.'s (2003) article on the short *5-HTP* serotonin transporter allele asserted that this allele is more prevalent in those with clinical depression than in control groups. It is cited over 1,400 times in the PsycINFO database despite the fact that numerous reviewers have cautioned against such a conclusion. Exhaustive meta-analysis reviews by Risch et al. (2009) and Munafò, Durrant, Lewis, and Flint (2009) agreed with Duncan and Keller (2011) that the link between depression and 5-HTP is not a statistically significant finding. It should be remembered that Caspi et al. had warned that because the 5-HTP allele is present in 50% of the population, it is not likely to be discriminative for any diagnostic purpose.

These reviewers (Duncan & Keller, 2011) ironically noted that the other major finding in Caspi et al.'s (2003) study, the link between stressful life events and clinical depression, has been repeatedly replicated, including by the Centers for Disease Control and Prevention's major study of adverse childhood events (Felitti et al., 1998) that showed that life stress in childhood was statistically linked to a host of other psychological symptoms and physical illnesses.

Brain Structure and Functioning

Button et al. (2013) found weak statistical procedures in the extant literature on structural and volumetric MRI neuroimaging studies as well as for genetic claims to have located the alleles responsible for various forms of psychiatric disorders. As for positron-emission tomography (PET) scans of regions of the brain with high concentrations of serotonin type 2A receptors, Smith and Jakobsen (2013) concluded,

> Sadly, studies carried out by PET with available radiogands have neither proved nor refuted conclusively any hypothesis concerning causal connections between molecular neurobiology and the severity of depression. . . . The richness of human motions, thoughts and actions, plus the complexity of molecular events in the human brain, caution against expecting PET brain imagining to provide rapid progress toward improving the treatment of depressive disorders. (p. 13)

There has been much work devoted to studying the activity in the hypothalamic–pituitary–adrenal (HPA) axis that links the prefrontal cortex to the glandular and hormonal system of the body. The HPA may play a role in depression and a wide variety of psychological disorders, though it is not clear whether stress causes this system to be altered or whether variations in the functioning of the HPA result in a lowered stress tolerance.

Medications

Breggin and Cohen (2007) noted a curious pattern in research on the effectiveness of psychiatric drugs. The patent on new pharmaceutical drugs is generally 20 years. During that time, pharmaceutical companies can sell their products for whatever the market will bear, often at prices a hundred times or more than it would cost to produce the drugs at an acceptable profit (the price a drug is sold at once it is available as a generic). Therefore, a company has a tremendous profit incentive to defend the original claims of drug effectiveness from critics for 20 years. The curious pattern is that most classes of drugs that have been used to treat psychiatric conditions have a life expectancy of about 20 years. It is only after the patents are about to expire that long-term negative side effects become widely known, or the lack of either short-term or long-term effectiveness is documented in the research literature. This happened with the use of barbiturates and stimulants in the 1940s and 1950s, minor tranquillizers in the 1960s and 1970s, the first generation of antidepressants and antipsychotics in the 1960s and 1970s, and now with the SSRI medications and second-generation atypical antipsychotic medications (Breggin & Cohen, 2007).

The SSRIs' fall from glory began with work that showed that they did not work any better than older antidepressants such as imipramine or desipramine. In fact, Kirsch and his colleagues (Kirsch et al., 2008; Kirsch & Sapirstein, 1998) showed in their reanalysis of data submitted to the FDA by drug companies seeking approval of SSRI-type antidepressants that their effects are equivalent to a placebo, except in a small subset of hospitalized depressed patients, and even in this group the result appeared to be from a suppressed placebo response rather than because of the effectiveness of the medication itself. As a result of these findings, the National Health Service (NHS) in the United Kingdom stopped prescribing antidepressants as the first line of treatment in depression. Citing studies showing that regular exercise was at least as beneficial to depressed patients as medications, the NHS began offering a 6-week free gym membership in place of the medications. The NIMH Depression Awareness, Recognition, and Treatment program also showed that there was a lack of clinical effectiveness in the use of SSRI medications in typical clinical settings, as well as numerous serious side effects affecting a large percentage of patients taking the medications (perhaps as much as 70%): weight gain, loss of sexual desire, general emotional blunting, agitation, insomnia, and in a small number of patients (2%–3%), violent out-of-character outbursts even resulting in suicide or homicide (Breggin & Cohen, 2007). There is also for many a difficult withdrawal effect even though patients are told that the medication is not addicting (Healy, 2009; Kotzalidis, Patrizi, Caltagirone, et al., 2007).

ANXIETY, DEPRESSION, AND ANGER

Feelings of powerlessness, a lack of assertiveness, and suppressed anger and rage are found in the clinical and research literature to be closely related to anxiety and depression. This initially seems counterintuitive and does not seem to fit with the picture of fear and sadness gone awry. It is only when we ask, "Afraid of what?" or "Sad about the loss of who or what?" that it begins to make sense. The answer usually is, "I am afraid (or sad) about being punished or rejected for speaking my mind." As mentioned in the previous chapter, the terms *anxiety* and *depression* have slightly different meanings and come from quite different theoretical schools of thought within psychology, but they essentially refer to the same psychological processes—namely, those that occur in interpersonal relationships in which one does not express one's own needs or feelings in deference to other people's needs, then feeling a good deal of resentment and bitterness, which also does not get expressed (Malan, 1995). This accounts for the sense we often have of people who are anxious or depressed that they can be surprisingly quite irritable and bitter about what has happened to them and how others have treated them (i.e., unfairly). When this irritability or bitterness surfaces, it is often negated by apologies or excused as the result of some extraneous factor (e.g., a poor night's sleep, headache, or other somatic complaint).

There is a clear developmental history in such individuals. Their families lacked a method for resolving interpersonal conflict, and either everything was swept under the rug or there were regular outbursts of anger that ruptured the safety and cohesion of the family. (Occasionally there is an alternating pattern of both avoidance and outbursts.) In this environment, children learn to keep safe by not expressing their own needs strongly, and when that becomes too burdensome, they pay a huge price in terms of fear and guilt for attempting to be heard. There is a sense that either the child will lose the love of a parent and be rejected, or that the parent will collapse or die from seeing that the child is unhappy. The only solution for the child who has to depend on the parents is to suppress the anger that is felt and to use defense mechanisms to keep the aggressive thoughts and emotions at bay.

As the individual matures, the defenses against angry feelings continue to operate, largely outside awareness, even though now the adult is no longer as dependent on the parents or the other people with whom this pattern of avoiding the experience of anger is replayed. Now the pattern has little advantage but great costs for the person. It undermines satisfying relationships at home and at school or work because the individual is always giving away to others the rights, opportunities, and satisfaction of needs that he or she requires.

A CASE OF A COLLEGE STUDENT ON PERSONAL LEAVE

Jerry was 22-year-old who had recently taken a leave of absence from a prestigious East Coast private university and moved to a small town in New England to live with his girlfriend. He had a job as a blue-collar worker in a local lumberyard that he found a refreshing change from the rarefied atmosphere of the university. His girlfriend had graduated from the same university the previous spring and was working for a nonprofit public interest company. Jerry called me at the urging of his mother and older sister after he had experienced several days of strange thoughts and feelings and an inability to sleep for more than a few hours per night. I asked him how urgent he felt the situation was, whether he could wait to be seen the next day, and whether he felt he could call family if he needed to talk to someone in the next 24 hours.

When I saw Jerry the next day, he struck me as a bright, well-spoken, attractive individual of average height and build. With long hair and a beard, he looked more like a woodsman than the senior he had been at an elite Eastern university. He described himself as having to get out of the house and walk for hours because he could not bear to sit or lie down. He was afraid he might be losing his mind because out of nowhere he would become terrified that he might be dying. He felt a sense of terror similar to what H. S. Sullivan described as the "uncanny," but he had no chest pain or other signs that might have been ambiguous and require referral to a physician to see whether there was a disease process involved. Jerry indicated that the feeling of needing to get out of the house had been going on for longer than the weird thoughts, about two weeks. When I asked what might have been going on in his life 2 weeks ago, he could not think of anything unusual or significant. Seemingly at a dead end, I backed up the time period and inquired about what it was like to move from his university to the small town.

On this topic he was more forthcoming, describing how in the fall term of his senior year he had just "burned out" on being a student. He had gone straight to university from high school, had worked hard to get good grades all along, and had just run out of gas. He was an English major; his senior honors thesis was on Hemingway, and the more he read Hemingway, the less he wished to be at school. At midyear, he asked for a leave of absence and moved in with his girlfriend. They had lived together for almost a year now, and he thought it was great. He liked the rhythm of going to work, having a few beers with friends from work at the end of the day, going home for dinner, watching a little TV, going to bed, and the next morning having the routine start all over again. The only problem was that he wanted to finish his thesis, was not working on it at all, and knew that he should. I asked him whether the thought of not completing his degree created any emotional reaction, and he said that it bothered him a little, but he thought the whole status-and-prestige rat race was a waste of time anyway.

Given that the school at which he was doing his thesis was the same school his girlfriend had graduated from the year before, I asked him how she was taking to his new lifestyle. Jerry indicated that she was fine with it, as was his mom. They were all intent on giving him space to sort this out on his own. I complimented them for their openmindedness, to which Jerry responded,

> Yeah, but my girlfriend has been complaining about other things. She says we are acting like an old married couple—me drinking beers with the guys after work and not wanting to go anywhere with her, which really surprised me because it seems to me we are both really tired at the end of the day, and she wouldn't want to go out even if I did.

I wondered how he had responded to her confrontation, and he said he had not handled it well at all. He had tried to defend himself from what he thought was an accusation that he was a boring person to be with by telling her she was being ridiculous and storming out of the house. He said he had walked around the neighborhood for hours before returning home after she was asleep. I asked him when this had happened. Jerry's response that "it had been about two weeks ago" seemed to surprise him as much as me. "I guess that is when I started feeling this way, but I hadn't put the two things together until just now," he added.

That began the process of unwinding the meaning of his weird thoughts and agitated feelings in his body. It turned out that he and his girlfriend had not discussed their argument at all after that night, and Jerry had thought everything was settling back down until 3 days ago. His girlfriend had invited a male friend of theirs to come over and have a beer with them after work. During the evening, Jerry had felt quite jealous of the attention she had paid to this friend, but he had been afraid to say anything for fear of losing his temper again. As the first session ended, I agreed to work with Jerry to get to the bottom of what was disturbing him so much, and I reassured him that the kind of agitation and weird thoughts he was having about dying were common forms of anxiety and were responsive to psychotherapy.

I saw Jerry weekly for about six months, and in the process explored his history of serious relationships with women, his family dynamics, and his feelings about himself as a male. He had a girlfriend the summer between high school and college who had ended the serious relationship, claiming that she was "bored" and needed to move on; that had precipitated a year of poor grades for him at university. Even more significant, his father had without any warning abandoned the family when Jerry was in ninth grade. His mother was so distraught that Jerry had to look after her and his younger brother for 18 months before she got back on her feet. Since then, there had been no contact between father and son and no financial support of the family. Prior to leaving, his father had been a loving but tough taskmaster, and Jerry frequently felt he did not live up to his father's expectations. He found his father's actions in abandoning the family completely inexplicable.

His weird thoughts turned out to be not only that he might die but also that he wished he were dead. It terrified him that he would think such a thing, and he was afraid his actions might be as uncontrollable as his thoughts. It turned out that, as his father's son, he feared that he might do something as inexplicable as his father had done. But that was only half the story. The other half was that he had never grieved at all for the loss of his father, because he was too busy holding his mother and brother together through the emotional carnage created by his father's departure. The feelings of devastation, rage, and fear that had been repressed to survive that time were just below the surface as he faced the threat of another abandonment in the new family life ("an old married couple") he had created for himself. His own feelings of hopelessness from the ninth grade emerged into awareness. These included at times the wish that his father would die and the fear that he, Jerry, might die as punishment for wishing his father dead.

As the relationship of his past family life to his present relationship became clearer and it became easier in therapy to face the painful memories of those years in high school, Jerry's anxiety, suicidal thoughts, and inability to finish his senior thesis all gradually lessened and then disappeared. He was able to face the end of the relationship with his girlfriend, move into an apartment with a friend, and begin to socialize with friends in ways that did not depend on going to the bars. By the point of termination he had no evidence of intense anxiety or suicidal thoughts and had not for several months.

This is not an unusual case by any means. Anxiety, depression, and suicidal ideas in college students are not uncommon, and the treatment success rate is extremely high (Shedler, 2012). Most forms of talk therapy in the hands of a caring, ethical, and well-trained therapist (or even a well-supervised beginning therapist) produce positive results. Sometimes therapist and client are not a good match, and it may take a few trials of therapy for the symptoms to be alleviated, but that is about as cautious as one needs to be about the claims for successful outcomes.

Unfortunately, given the mental health system of care currently provided to college students through primary care physicians or college counseling centers, it is more likely that such a student will either be immediately provided with an antidepressant or be seen for five sessions and then referred for medication, usually antidepressants. Unlike therapy, even in the hands of an ethical provider, these can produce serious side effects: addiction, withdrawal symptoms on discontinuance, and on average, less benefit than counseling and psychotherapy. Because these drugs work by dulling all emotions, the student may feel some relief of the symptoms after a few weeks of medication. However, the understanding of the problem will be short-circuited and the opportunity to learn what needs to be learned to prevent the kind of relationship problems that contribute to the problem developing in the first place forfeited. In the case of Jerry, the pattern of taking care of the women in his life rather than considering his own emotional needs, even to the point of not grieving the loss of his father, which did not emerge in the therapy until the tenth session, and the fact that he not only feared dying but also had intrusive suicidal thoughts did not emerge until the fifth session.

MORE SEVERE ANXIETY AND DEPRESSION

When current losses or traumas are severe, and/or with parallel multiple losses and traumas from early childhood, there is an increased likelihood that a person will be overwhelmed by anxiety or depression. In these circumstances, the individual will withdraw almost completely from their prior daily life routine, even to the point of refusing to get out of bed, engage in self-care routines, or communicate with other people in their social network. Sleep routines can be completely thrown off and eating and drinking greatly reduced. Weight loss of 15 pounds over 3 months in a person who originally weighed 160 pounds is not uncommon. Sometimes the withdrawal produces a loss of clear differentiation between dreaming and wakeful states or between what is referred to as fantasy and reality, in other words, hallucinatory experiences. There is no clear line between sleep-deprivation-induced perceptual distortions and hallucinations, even in people who are not depressed. In fact, in some surveys, 15% of the population has reported hallucinatory experiences of some kind. In this kind of social isolation one can begin to hear one's own repetitive and self-condemning thoughts as if they were being spoken by someone else (Johns & van Os, 2001).

If mild to moderate anxiety or depression is the common cold of mental health work, more severe forms of anxiety or depression are like a bad case of the flu. Most people recover from the flu without complications as long as they are well taken care of during the worst part of it. However, we tend to panic when someone is severely depressed and think they must be treated in radical ways or hospitalized. Assuming the individual is not acutely suicidal and that there are people who can keep a close watch on him or her, and assuming psychotherapy can be offered multiple times per week, severe anxiety or depression is responsive to psychotherapy. Such dark times have their own self-limiting features, as long as the environment does not exacerbate the situation by treating a person in this condition as a nonperson, depriving them of their freedom, and forcing intrusive biological interventions on them.

People, even people we love, are difficult to be around when they are experiencing overwhelming feelings of emptiness, dread, and meaninglessness. It is much easier to tell them in word or deed that these feelings are unwarranted and to buck up than to listen patiently to what they are feeling and allow ourselves to feel the desperate vulnerability that is part of the human condition and that we work so hard to avoid feeling. When our defenses are down and we are feeling the uncertainty, randomness, chaos, cruelty, and basic unfairness of human life, the distance between being the person holed up in one's room curled up in the fetal position and being the person who has stopped by to lend a helping hand is a small one indeed. Many times we are afraid to acknowledge our own vulnerability when trying to be helpful to someone who is feeling overwhelmed; we want to be strong for them. Paradoxically, this can result in the depressed individual's feeling even more inadequate as they compare how they feel with how we act, and they gather more evidence for how weak and incompetent they are. In moments of true crisis, when people are completely overwhelmed, they may need someone to take over for them and think clearly enough to get practical matters accomplished. Except in those circumstances, showing our strength to lend some of it to a depressed person often backfires and worsens the situation. Far better to listen and empathize with feelings that we recognize ourselves as having experienced and to share that we know what it feels like and that this person will make it better when they are ready to do so.

Just as in milder anxiety or depression, one of the most confusing aspects of severe anxiety or depression is the amount of hostility and rage that can be felt. This rage is proportionally greater, and often frightening, in the sadistic thoughts and feelings directed at those for whom one is grieving in the first place. To have thoughts of destroying, mutilating, or ripping the heart out of a person for whom one professes undying love is deeply confusing, guilt-producing, and shaming. This turns one into one's own worst enemy because one knows that to treat another person this way would be to lose their love forever. Malan (1995) called this the *depressive position*, referring to the way in which a seriously depressed person defends at all costs against becoming aware of the hostility she or he is feeling for fear that it will actually destroy the other person or at least any hope of reconciliation with that person. Intensive psychotherapy is well-suited for working through this conflict and finding ways to claim a seat at the table of life without feeling as though doing so is at the risk of life and limb, either one's own or someone else's.

MOOD SWINGS

The *DSM–5* bipolar disorder is a controversial diagnosis that has exploded in popularity in recent years. Previously termed *manic depression*, it involves wide mood swings from the depths of depression to manic highs in which the individual would behave completely out of character in highly impulsive ways. A person in a manic state would become impulse-driven and entitled, preoccupied by instant gratification for food, sex, and other forms of material gratification. They might run up huge sums on credit in an orgy of self-indulgence and then be unable to pay the bills, jump out of their car to direct traffic on a busy street when frustrated by the slow pace of movement, or impulsively have an affair after 30 years of marital fidelity. It was an extremely rare phenomenon, much less common than melancholia. It was generally treated with salts made from the naturally occurring metal lithium, a treatment that tends to dampen all moods and produce a semblance of stability in one's behavior. Lithium has two unfortunate drawbacks: (a) the dose at which it dampens mood sufficiently is close to the lethal dose, and thus a person must have their blood level monitored frequently; and (b) most people discontinue use of lithium against medical advice because they find the affectless state it creates aversive and they miss feeling the excitement and enjoyment of life they would have without it. Patients who discontinue use are at an elevated risk of relapse compared with untreated controls (Baldessarini, Tondo, & Viguera, 1999).

Psychodynamic theory views mania as an elaborate defense against feelings of severe depression and as an exaggeration of the defenses we all use to distract ourselves from our pain: keeping busy, going on vacation, being silly or foolish, shopping, seeking sexual gratification, or using substances to elevate mood. When depression is extreme, one can only relieve it by using such distractions and defenses in the extreme. If the defenses keep the depression from consciousness through denial, projection, or splitting, the manic phase will seem to come out of nowhere, surprising the individual her- or himself.

Since *DSM–III*, physicians have been permitted to diagnose bipolar disorder if a person has had a major depression preceded or followed by noticeable heightened mood, even if the mood does not reach manic levels. For this and other reasons that remain unclear but seem likely to be related to increasing prescription and street drug use by adolescents, the rates of bipolar disorder have been steadily rising, and this once extremely rare disorder is diagnosed in 5% of the population (Judd & Akiskal, 2003).

SUICIDE AND ANGER

Generally, what is true about the relationship between anger and anxiety and depression is true also for suicidal thoughts and actions. Suicide is about killing, and killing is usually about rage (except perhaps in the context of intractable pain and terminal illness). We tend to first think of suicide in terms of hopelessness in the face of loss and disappointment and a desire to end intense psychological pain and suffering, and there is some truth to that.

We all live in part to fulfill the roles we play in other people's lives; there is a great satisfaction in being needed and useful to others. A loss of one's primary relationship can be excruciatingly painful. When loss produces social isolation and the anger at the losses increases emotional isolation, there is no way to express the rage except against the self. This is when crisis intervention by others who care enough to reach out to support the individual through the most intense feelings in the immediate aftermath of a loss is so critical. By providing a bridge to interpersonal expression for the intense feelings that are emotionally isolated we provide a way forward out of the crisis.

Most important is affirming a meaningful purpose for the individual's life, even in the absence of the lost people or opportunities that precipitated the crisis. This must be done in conjunction with providing an outlet for the feelings of anger and rage at those who have left the individual behind, either through death or abandonment. The desire for revenge should be acknowledged as a wish that, although natural under the circumstances, cannot be acted on in a direct manner. I am fond of telling my clients that "the best revenge is a life well-lived." Although they rarely accept that idea at first, often months later they repeat it back to me as part of their plan for expressing their anger and triumphing over the loss.

Communications of suicidal intent, even when they appear to be attention-getting or manipulative, should never be dismissed without a careful assessment of the person and situation. It is a myth that people who say they will commit suicide never do; some of the people most determined to die conceal their intent in order to succeed. In those cases, behavior can indicate the intent even when there are not words to do so. Such people will withdraw from previously enjoyed social, occupational, and recreational activities and make arrangements to tie up loose ends by giving away property, pets, and so forth. They may quite suddenly appear less depressed because they now see a way out of their powerlessness and misery. The suicide plan gives them back a sense of control that had vanished from their life. These are the sort of people who probably cannot be stopped without bringing to bear the power of the police or hospital to hold them against their will.

Though I am in principle strongly against forced treatment in mental health work generally, on the grounds of both civil liberties (the right to liberty in the absence of conviction for a crime) and likely treatment failure, I am not opposed to the involuntary treatment of individuals who have made suicide attempts with a high degree of potential lethality and who have not had the opportunity to enter into psychotherapy. The truth is that anyone with the physical capacity to act and who is determined to die can find a way to do it, even in a maximum-security hospital. One regularly encounters clinical cases in which an individual was kept alive through such a crisis by involuntary psychological treatment and who is later both incredulous that he or she would have tried to commit suicide and greatly appreciative of the efforts to treat him or her against his or her will.

PROBLEMS WITH EATING: ANOREXIA AND BULIMIA

Most students in abnormal psychology are fascinated by anorexia and bulimia, disorders that are relatively rare, occurring in about 2% of the female population; males make up only 20% of the individuals with eating disorders within a clinical population (Smink, van Hoeken, & Hoek, 2012). Anorexia is, however, one of the few problems studied in psychology that has life-threatening consequences: One can in fact starve oneself to death. Estimates vary, but it seems that the death rate in the population is less than one in 1,000 in a given year. The diagnosis is made in females when the individual falls below 85% of expected body weight, stops menstruating, and has a distorted body image. Other physical changes are common: increased dental cavities, dry skin, brittle hair, diminished breasts, and anemia. Metabolic and electrolyte imbalances may be life threatening. Weight loss may be from restricted eating, from purging, or from other means of removing food from the body before it is adequately digested. There is an associated denial of severe weight loss and a fear of weight gain.

Short-term hospitalization and tube feeding can prolong life, and some people seem to manage anorexia the way some drug abusers manage their habits to stay just above the level of functioning that would bring ruin to their lives. Unlike drug abuse, most clients in this group alter their eating to a healthier pattern within 5 years of receiving treatment.

Both the psychoanalytic and family systems literatures contain published case reports of successful treatment in some cases (Bruch, 1978/2001; Papp, 1994). In these approaches, the adolescent is seen as fighting to establish a sense of autonomy and purpose in the face of overwhelming anxiety about becoming independent and leaving home. There is a sense of controlling others in the family and expressing hostility toward them by not eating. This can happen only when direct expression of frustration is ineffective in creating change in the family system dynamic. In other cases, a perfectionistic view of beauty and attractiveness leads to rigid dieting that becomes so central to the sense of self that it becomes the only way to try to contain anxiety about other areas of life (e.g., relationships, school performance, athletic prowess). Eventually, the dieting and exercise are pushed to the point that the symptoms of anorexia are present. Treatment involves finding a way around the perfectionistic defenses and beliefs that are often endorsed by other family members, even though they are not anorexic. The inability to assert one's own view of the family or the world despite feeling as though that world is destroying one's will to live seems implicit in the adolescent's refusal to eat. It is as if the adolescent is saying, "If I tell them they make me want to die they won't love me, so better that I die and they mourn for me than I tell them and they hate me."

A usually milder form of this problem is found in *bulimia*, a behavior pattern of regular binging with high-calorie foods followed by self-induced vomiting or use of laxatives to avoid weight gain. About 2% of the female population will at some point in their lifetime engage in this regular pattern of eating (Smink et al., 2012). These individuals rarely have the severe weight loss found in anorexia, but bulimia nonetheless creates social difficulties because the individual is ashamed of her or his actions and attempts to hide the pattern from others. It can nonetheless have serious health consequences, because the persistent vomiting of stomach contents includes stomach acids that may damage the enamel on teeth or the tissue lining the esophagus. Other more severe physical consequences may occasionally result from use of chemicals to induce vomiting or resulting electrolyte imbalances.

MALAN'S CASE OF PAUL

The following is a summary of a case study by the noted psychoanalytic psychiatrist, David Malan (1997). Paul was an 18-year-old student entering the first year of his undergraduate degree at the beginning of World War II. He was considered an exceptional science student up till that point in his academic career and was awarded a scholarship to university. One of the requirements Paul was to meet before beginning his studies at the university level was to pass an examination that would allow him to become a scientist. After failing the necessary examination twice, Paul consulted his tutor about what exactly he should do. This was an especially critical situation because it had been his academic promise in science that had contributed greatly to the amount of scholarship funds he was to receive. Paul was transitioning into this new life stage with an already desperate feeling of loneliness and isolation due to his new academic struggles.

Paul took the tutor's advice and approached the professor he would be working with, asking for extra assistance in the form of laboratory practice. The professor lost his temper when Paul made his request, shouting at him. It was later revealed to Paul, when contacted by his tutor, that the professor had a reputation for being a difficult man; therefore, the behavior was intended with no personal malice. After explaining this, the tutor promptly apologized for the professor's behavior. Unknown to the tutor, Paul had left his meeting with a devastated feeling. He was overcome by tears, feeling as though the "bottom had dropped out of his world" (Malan, 1997, p. 170). This feeling of total devastation was accompanied by a déjà vu sensation, as though he had experienced something such as this before. Sitting with this feeling over the next few days, Paul gradually came to the conclusion that he could no longer face the university and would kill himself. The final decision was made on a Tuesday, and the suicide was carefully planned for a Saturday afternoon.

Paul selected his particular date, time, and method for a number of reasons. There were no lectures held on Saturday; therefore, his absence from class would not be noticed. Paul accounted for the visit from the college housekeeper to make his bed the following morning by determining that he would do nothing in his suicide that would cause damage to his body should he fail, or raise any suspicion by onlookers. He therefore settled on suicide by means of chloral hydrate at a dosage of 28 grams, 10 grams being the fatal dose. He went to the chemist that day and, due to the nature of his major, had no trouble obtaining the substance without suspicion.

During the week leading up to the suicide Paul did not indicate any signs of distress, nor did he discuss his desperate feelings or plan of suicide with anyone. At least one opportunity presented itself to discuss this course of action, or the feelings related to it, with the tutor who had checked on him after his meeting with the professor. He continued to follow his regular schedule, completing weekly essay assignments and even showing up for his shift in the lab on Saturday morning. Early that same Saturday afternoon he returned to his dorm room and mixed the 28 grams of chloral hydrate into a glass of water and began to drink. The taste was so horrible that he stopped before finishing the liquid; however, he decided that he must "do the job properly" and finished the rest. Paul then said the Lord's Prayer aloud, just as he had been taught to by his mother before going to sleep.

Paul awoke many hours later with a desperate urge to get rid of the mixture of chloral hydrate and water that he had consumed earlier. He was physically compromised and rolled out of bed onto the floor, unable to reach his trash bin, vomiting all over the floor. He was unable to get back into bed; trying to call for help, he was unable to make anything but a hoarse croaking sound. He stayed in this position, attempting to call for help until he again drifted back into unconsciousness. The next morning he was found by the housekeeper and was taken to the hospital.

Background and Events

The immediate precipitating event to the attempted suicide was the interaction with the professor; however, on closer examination, this coincidence was unconsciously repeating trauma from Paul's past. If we were to look back at the course of Paul's life, we would find that the pattern of innocently approaching an important person and receiving an extremely negative response in an entirely unprovoked fashion was a typical experience for Paul from an early age. Although his early childhood was filled with security and happiness, at age 7 his father suddenly became ill and died within a matter of days.

His mother's oscillating reactions between emotional numbness and grief were not unnoticed by Paul. There were particular incidents right after his father's death in which he had been looking for his mother in her room and walked in on her crying. Not wanting her son to see her pain, his mother shouted at him and told him to get out. Her struggle in processing the death of her husband extended to the inability to be attuned with Paul and help him process his grief as well.

A second trauma, in which the core issue of uncertainty in his role in his relationship with his mother arose again, occurred when Paul left for boarding school soon after his father's death. Young children have not developed the cognitive capabilities to anticipate and prepare themselves for the experience of separation, especially from a needed caregiver, until they have actually had the experience. In Paul's case, he had recently had the experience but was unable to make sense of it in relation to himself. Going to boarding school and being separated from his parent who was not attuned to his needs for a smooth transition only further exaggerated the previous trauma of the loss of his father.

It is important to also mention the mother's motives. There was pressure put on Paul from a young age not only to minimize his emotional needs for the benefit of others but also to perform well academically. It was particularly important to his mother that he do well enough to receive academic scholarships, not just because he wanted them but also because his mother stressed that it would be both for his own benefit as well as hers. She believed that Paul's continued academic success would make her appear "legitimate" in the eyes of her deceased husband's family. This traumatic experience of continually living out a false self to ensure his value to important others in his life continued into his first romantic relationship, the conclusion of which further exacerbated his fragmented feeling of self, accompanied by the shame, hopelessness, and loneliness he felt as a young child in departing for boarding school and being separated from his mother.

The coincidental and precipitating event was the result of a development in which Paul's internalized self-structure and needs were constantly ignored or at crucial times negated at the hands of vital and needed others. The coping mechanism he had cultivated under the structure of his false self that had served to ensure his survival by warranting the attention of needed others was now breaking down in this new self-structure in which the emphasis on the importance of needed others was now focused on the importance of the abilities of the authentic self.

Treatment

Paul had originally received treatment from a psychiatrist following his suicide attempt. The psychiatrist was kind and helpful but lacking in psychodynamic training, so the full and complex implications of Paul's entire personal narrative did not emerge until his psychoanalysis many years later. Thus, Paul made little progress in the neurosis unit where he was originally placed directly following his suicide attempt. Despite the aforementioned underlying difficulties with his mother, they had a close relationship; she and her son had no problem making the mutual decision to bring him home from the unit, against the doctor's advice.

During his psychoanalysis, the exploration of his suicide attempt brought up five major contributing factors that were explored in their combined relation to that incident. One of the most important aspects of treatment was readjusting the conceptualization of suicide in Paul's life. Paul accomplished this in psychotherapy by exploring old affective states, reintegrating their meaning, and exploring the suicide attempt as an attempted annihilation of the internalized self. Paul's suicide attempt was viewed as a reaction to the convergence of repeated traumatic experiences throughout his life. This allowed for the maladaptive structure that perpetuated the selection of a coping mechanism such as suicide to be brought into conscious awareness and be effectively addressed and reintegrated in a way that was supportive, not lethal, to Paul's self-structure.

Although these varying factors converged to tip the balance in favor of a suicide attempt for Paul, they all shared the underlying theme of loss of relation with his mother. This would prove to be a crucial factor in the overwhelmingly positive outcome of his psychotherapy. Another factor that heavily guided treatment was Malan's belief that in Paul's case the cathartic effects of the suicide attempt provided enough relief to reduce the suicidal impulse to a point where it was no longer a current threat. The suicide attempt also allowed Paul to give himself permission to take the following term off because of a physical complication that had arisen from being in a coma. This break from school gave him a chance to reexamine the false self-structure he had begun to build. The pressure to be defined to the important others in his life by his academic performance was so embedded that its foundation and subsequent role in Paul's life could not be called into question outside these extreme circumstances.

In this time away from school reworking his current self-definition, Paul was able to rebuild his ability to cope in a manner that would prove much more authentic and helpful in the future. When he returned to school the following term, Paul was able to select an examination in a new subject, pass, and eventually go on to earn honors in his coursework. He kept in touch with his analyst and, importantly, was able to find an individual who appeared to be the real girl of his dreams, unlike the fantasy of what could have transpired between him and his first love. At follow-up more than 50 years after his suicide attempt, Paul said that the "ever-present longing to be released from the burden of life had completely disappeared" (Malan, 1997, p. 177). His self-concept shifted to one that was comfortable and authentic, and this allowed for much more positive and adaptive coping strategies in the face of continued convergent trauma.

7

PERSONALITY PATTERNS THAT ENGENDER SUFFERING

The concept of *personality* was introduced into psychology by Harvard psychologist Gordon Allport in the 1930s as a means of discussing the most central, enduring, and distinctive patterns of behavior, ways of interacting with others, and ways of being, thinking, and feeling that typified an individual human being—what defines a person as the person he or she is. Personality is the ultimate holistic concept in psychology because it attempts to show the degree of integration or fragmentation in the person as a physiological organism, a phenomenological being with private thoughts and feelings, an actor in the world of interpersonal relationships, and a performer of various social roles in various institutional contexts (e.g., work, family, place of worship, recreation, creator of goods and services for the local economy).

Carl Jung, one of Freud's early associates in the development of psychoanalysis, emphasized the difference between introverts and extraverts. *Introverts* like to spend a great deal of time alone thinking, reading, and working independently on projects, whereas *extraverts* want to be out in the world engaged

http://dx.doi.org/10.1037/14693-007
Not So Abnormal Psychology: A Pragmatic View of Mental Illness, by R. B. Miller

in activities. Extraverts are more comfortable around other people, but are so active and busy that they do not easily develop intimate relationships with others. Over the last 100 years, the trait of Introversion/Extraversion has shown up as one of the elements of personality in every major research program that has attempted to describe the critical behavioral dimensions on which human beings may be compared (Costa & McRae, 1988; Eysenck & Eysenck, 1985). Most people fall in the middle range on this trait, but 2% to 4 % of the population seems to be either highly introverted or highly extraverted. Other traits that have received a good deal of confirmation across many different research programs are those of Neuroticism (vs. emotional stability), Agreeableness (vs. hostility), Conscientiousness (vs. irresponsibility), and Openness to Experience and creativity (vs. rigidity and conformist or conventional thinking; Goldberg, 1993). These trait approaches have been mostly developed by experimental research psychologists using concepts that originated in clinical work (e.g., Jung's idea of Introversion and Extraversion).

Experimental psychology thrives on separating complex phenomena into the smallest elements that can then be studied systematically in isolation from confounding variables. The problem noted by Allport and other Gestalt psychologists of this period was that once one dissected the human personality into its narrow and specific behavioral components, it is extremely difficult to see how one is ever going to be able to "put Humpty Dumpty back together again." Trait theory is certainly instructive in teaching us to think about important personality traits that are dimensional rather than categorical. We do not have to think of ourselves as either introverted or extraverted, but as somewhere on a continuum between one extreme and the other, with no one being fully one or the other. If we carry this over to what are usually considered personality disorders, we have an advantage over those who wish to find clear distinctions between types of personality disorders. Although this approach has yet to provide a powerful theory able to guide clinical work with this difficult population, it has made a contribution to freeing us from the categorical thinking about diagnoses that has so crippled clinical treatment. It also ignores the critical individual differences that exist in areas of intelligence and achievement (or power), motivations that, although related to personality, have been seen as separate areas of research in psychology.

KAREN HORNEY AND NEUROTIC TRENDS

Karen Horney (1942/2013) was one of the first female psychoanalysts. She trained in Germany with one of Freud's earliest followers, Karl Abraham. Unlike Freud, she saw all symptoms and personality problems as the result of attempts to find safety and security in a world that childhood had taught was an extremely dangerous place. Threats to physical or emotional safety and security produce a sense of overwhelming, intolerable terror in the child. She described a dozen neurotic personality trends that are ways of adapting to the terrors of childhood and maximizing physical and/or emotional safety but that do so only by sacrificing a rich, full life of diverse experiences and challenges. These trends are observable to some degree in everyone, but when such trends become the dominant modes of being in the world, the individual's interpersonal relationships become stilted and ultimately unsatisfying. Not seeing any alternative, such individuals do not even consider seeking psychological assistance. Nor does the individual complain about his or her approach to life, believing it is the only way for him or her to survive.

Psychoanalytic theorists use the term *ego syntonic* for problems in living that an individual does not see as problems but as necessary means of survival and the term *ego dystonic* for problems in living a person recognizes as problems to be solved. Horney's approach is clear—these defenses against the terror of feeling unsafe and insecure in the world are ego syntonic, and we do not wish to change them, because we see them as essential to our own survival, and we all do this to some extent without realizing these patterns of thinking, feeling, and acting are defenses against childhood psychological injuries we no longer hold in our conscious awareness. With the exception of the biomedical view, all the other models of abnormal psychology discussed here have formulated explanations of how we unknowingly contribute to our own problems in living and of the central importance of understanding the process by which this takes place (e.g., restricted awareness, cognitive scripts from childhood, learned behavior, family roles or scripts).

Karen Horney (1885–1952) was a radical psychoanalyst in her day—feminist, humanistic, and interested in sociocultural influence and self-help. Though her ideas were rejected by many strict Freudian psychoanalysts, her theory of personality "neurotic trends" remains the most coherent and useful in the literature and is used here. Horney divided the neurotic trends into three groups: moving toward people (*compliant*), moving against people (*aggressive*), and moving away from people (*detached*). These groupings are the intellectual precursors to the current classification system of "personality disorders" in the *Diagnostic and Statistical Manual of Mental Disorders* (5th ed.; DSM–5; American Psychiatric Association, 2013), only more pragmatic. It is important to understand this approach to personality styles and difficulties because it begins to make comprehensible to us subgroups in the population who are otherwise incomprehensible. Common sense rarely helps us understand people who have become locked into these patterns.

Moving Toward Others

The first group, those who move toward other people, initially seem to have good interpersonal relationships. They want to be with people, and they are extremely solicitous of others and anxious to be liked and accepted. They are kind, loving, and considerate. However, they are terribly afraid of asserting themselves in any manner, for fear of complete rejection, and as a result are terrified of independence. They seek relationships of mutual dependence. In return for giving love, they expect their partners and friends to do for them all the things they find difficult to do—taking risks, being assertive, and exploring new opportunities. Needless to say, over time such relationships often break down because neither member of the relationship can grow or change once it is established. Dependency difficulties are often the result of problems in the attachment process in the second and third years of life. Individuals were nurtured and protected in these years, but for a variety of possible reasons unable to move on to independence. The current diagnoses of avoidant personality disorder and dependent personality disorder are similar to this group. As a feminist, Horney pointed out that this and many other "disorders" are simply exaggerations of the social role that women in Western societies were required to adopt to survive in a male-dominated society.

In the *DSM–5* dependent personality disorder the individual welcomes interpersonal relationships, but out of a fear of conflict or rejection they tend to submit to the will of others both at home and work. The dependent individual almost compulsively defers to the needs of others, and is often seen as exceptionally easy to get along with, and cooperative. In exchange, the dependent individual expects to be taken care of and avoid making decisions and feeling responsible.

In the *DSM–5* avoidant personality disorder the individual desires and seeks out relationships with others who will protect her or him from anticipated conflict, criticism, or failure in competitive social or work situations that demand assertiveness. In exchange for this kind of protection, the avoidant individual essentially submits and caters to her/his protector in their personal relationship, and deflects conflict that might arise with others onto the protector who acts as an agent for the avoidant individual out in the world. Over time, the protector can become tired of fighting these battles, and refuse to do so. If this happens the avoidant member of the couple will frequently go into a depressive state experiencing this shift as a loss and betrayal. ("After all I do for him, he couldn't even call the store and complain about the way they cheated me.")

Individuals with avoidant personality disorder are so fearful of being criticized or rejected that they restrict their interaction with other people by avoiding any environment where this might occur. The resulting isolation is felt as a real loss, because the avoidant person still desires to be accepted and enjoys human relationships that are free of risk of hurt or rejection. These individuals report a great deal of anxiety when faced with situations such as this that cannot be avoided (e.g., work, school, health care appointments) and may seek treatment for such symptoms.

Moving Against Others

In the second group, those moving against other people, one finds people who initially are engaging and exciting to get to know. They often enliven a room, entertain, and leave others feeling special and privileged to be in their presence. However, this is a mirage because members of this group care primarily about their own well-being, success, or protection. Four *DSM–5* diagnoses are similar to this group: histrionic, narcissistic, paranoid, and antisocial personality disorder. Individuals in this group have mastered the ability to generate in others a sense of special intimacy, allegiance, or closeness that seems more gratifying than with less-exciting people. Often substance use and other forms of "high living" are associated with these individuals' lifestyle. These personality styles leave behind a train wreck of relationships (both platonic and romantic) for which their significant others have given up homes, life savings, personal security, and families. These individuals are often attractive, talented, and/or highly intelligent, and therefore can be successful and respected in the public realm. Usually, the life history of such a person includes emotional or physical trauma in the first year or two of life or abandonment by loved ones in later childhood or both. They treat the world in the way they believe they were treated.

The *narcissistic personality* hopes to avoid rejection by (a) being sure that everyone believes he or she is the most wonderful person in the world and (b) not caring much about others' well-being unless injury to another results in a loss of the adulation he or she requires. Narcissists are charming and charismatic, often having exceptional artistic, athletic, or occupational talent or skill that serves as the original impetus to establishing the claim to superiority as a person. This seems to be a predominantly male trait, though as gender roles shift, there may be increasing equality in distribution of this personality disorder.

The *histrionic personality* is focused on appearing alluring and sexually seductive as a means of guaranteeing social and interpersonal acceptance. This is typically accompanied by a tendency to be intensely demonstrative of emotion and affection, though in a way that leads others to question the depth and sincerity of the emotions expressed, often leading to further attribution of manipulative and ingenuous behavior. Usually ascribed to females more than males, it is maintained by feminist critics of psychiatry to be merely a restatement of male stereotypes of femininity.

The *antisocial personality* disorder is similar to the narcissistic disorder in that there is little or no empathy for other people. The real difference is that whereas the narcissistic individual uses others for his own benefit, it is done with little intent to harm others, which would take too much thought about the other person and would detract from the goal of winning adulation from the world at large. Individuals with antisocial personality disorder, in contrast, have no desire for genuine relationships and in fact wish to benefit themselves, and sometimes even harm others, by taking from others what they believe to be "rightly theirs." They are indifferent to or even at times enjoy the harm experienced by others in the process. They tend to prefer having power and control over others to having relationships. The antisocial group is typically divided between the "con" or "flimflam" artist who uses false identities to defraud others without regard for the impact he or she has on others through such actions and the more dangerous psychopathic personality who wishes to physically harm others. Both groups tend to have a history of delinquency in childhood or adolescence and a high rate of school failure and substance abuse. This group shows up in the criminal justice system when the personality traits stop being effective as a means of controlling others.

Individuals with *paranoid personality* disorder show an intense distrust or disregard for most other human beings, but unlike the antisocial personality/con artist, the distrust is openly stated, and unlike the psychopathic personality, there is no attempt to seek revenge, but these individuals rather try to detect and catch those who wish to harm them before it is too late. Once harm is detected, they are unforgiving. It is almost as if the paranoid person is saying, "I want to like you people, but you folks are going to have stop screwing with me before I can do that." Because they continually scan the environment for potential harm, they periodically detect dishonest or manipulative behavior in others that might have gone undetected by a more trusting individual, and this confirms that their belief that no one can be trusted is accurate and that their strategy is working.

Individuals in both these groups (moving toward and against others) may eventually wear thin on partners and friends, leading to the one result that is most feared from childhood: rejection. When this happens, the individual becomes depressed and may seek help for the depression but not for the underlying personality traits, because those are not seen as the problem. He or she hopes to pull out of the depression and become more proficient at using his or her existing style of interacting with the world with a little more skill.

Moving Away From Others

In the third group we find those who are moving away from other people, either through physical isolation (e.g., a recluse or hermit) or psychological detachment. This detachment can be in the form of social withdrawal or interacting in ways that push others away by seeming odd, eccentric, or even bizarre. The *DSM–5* diagnoses that correspond to this group are the obsessive–compulsive, schizoid, and schizotypal disorders. When we try to form relationships with such individuals, they politely withdraw, not wanting conflict but also not wanting connection. It is easy to think that by using extra kindness such a person can be reached and will open up to a relationship. It is always worth making some attempts in this direction, but often such efforts come to nothing because schizoid, schizotypal, or obsessive–compulsive individuals find emotional connection terrifying and painful. They are protecting themselves from such painful early memories of rejection and abandonment that they cannot allow themselves to accept the kindnesses offered by others who are well-meaning.

The individual with *obsessive–compulsive personality* disorder seeks acceptance and approval on the basis of his or her demonstrated competence and responsibility and seeks to avoid the risk of being criticized or rejected by removing any possible grounds for such reactions in others. Individuals with obsessive–compulsive disorder attempt to be perfect in everything that they do. They are highly organized, hard-working, and averse to emotional displays by themselves or others. They want to keep everything businesslike so that human relationships are as predictable as a train schedule. Their partners and friends find them loyal, trustworthy, reliable, productive, and somewhat boring and judgmental.

In contrast to the individual with avoidant personality disorder, individuals with *schizoid personality* disorder from an early age seem to have given up on human relationships and wish to have minimal contact with other human beings except in the most perfunctory superficial manner (e.g., having to interact with a clerk at a store when buying needed goods). They do not report missing or longing for relationships the way avoidant individuals do, and they strike others as cold, distant, aloof, and at times even robotic.

Individuals with *schizotypal personality* disorder are those who are not psychotic or schizophrenic in that they are able to function in life, support themselves, and have some meaningful relationships. Yet, the thought processes and content demonstrated by such individuals parallel the description of schizophrenic cognitive dysfunction, though often in a milder form. They tend to deny the importance of physical reality, believe in parapsychological and occult forces, and endorse the truth behind many conspiracy theories of history or politics. There is, of course, serious scholarship exploring such conspiracy theories in history, political science, parapsychology, and so forth. Such scholarship carefully weighs the evidence on such topics with logical analysis, and aims to discern the truth about such matters. Thus, it is not the content of such ideas but an individual's use of the ideas as a defense against close interpersonal relationships that defines the schizotypal personality.

These behavioral and interpersonal patterns seem to justify a non-categorical approach to the concept of *thought disorder*, one of the key features of schizophrenia (discussed in Chapter 8), and seem to show the continuity between madness and sanity, psychosis and personality characteristics. In fact, unlike prior *DSMs*, *DSM–5* places the schizotypal personality disorder on a newly created "schizophrenia spectrum." Once we attempt to specify what we mean when we say that psychosis is a "loss of contact with reality," we are forced to admit the relativity and subjectivity in our understanding of what is actually real. All of the seemingly concrete instances of "loss of contact"—namely, delusions and hallucinations (discussed in Chapter 8)—are experienced occasionally by "normal" individuals and more than occasionally by the individuals that meet the criteria for the schizotypal disorder. Such people, if they manage to avoid the mental health services sector of the economy, will be referred to as "eccentric," "a little weird," or "odd."

BORDERLINE PERSONALITY ORGANIZATION

The one set of personality characteristics that Horney did not fully address, perhaps because it was collapsed into what was then called *hysterical neurosis*, is what is called in *DSM–5 borderline personality*. In psychoanalytic theory *borderline personality organization* referred to individuals whose psychological development was interrupted by a trauma in the third year of life and who were unable to develop a stable coherent sense of being an autonomous or separate person. Such individuals were thought to have symptoms that were a mixture of neurotic and psychotic features. They function in society more adaptively than individuals with psychoses and less well than those with neuroses. However, in *DSM–5* the term *borderline personality* is defined more in terms of self-destructive and erratic behaviors. These individuals self-harm, use substances, drop in and out of treatment, and exhibit a variety of symptoms that qualify for a variety of *DSM–5* diagnoses. In other words, they defy being categorized in biomedical or behavioral terms. In the interest of increasing the reliability of diagnosis (agreement among diagnosticians), *DSM–III* (American Psychiatric Association, 1980) introduced this personality disorder as a "wastebasket" term for all the people who were hard to diagnose. They were not a large percentage of the total patient population, but they demanded a disproportionate percentage of the time and energy of the mental health professionals from whom they sought services.

People with borderline characteristics vacillate greatly across all three of Horney's groups: They move toward people, and when frustrated in those relationships, they move against the same people; at other times they move away and become detached and unavailable. This is an incredibly confused and confusing way of being in the world. The transitions from one mode to the other can be triggered by an interpersonal event or life circumstance, and the shift can be abrupt and startling. The changes are not only sudden but also almost incomprehensible and can be followed by equally dramatic shifts back to an earlier personality state or to a third position. Substance abuse is common, as are threats of suicide and other forms of abandonment. These individuals often have had chaotic childhoods with little consistent sense of reliable emotional safety and security.

The borderline personality disorder is perhaps the most intriguing and represents an attempt to place into a diagnostic category the individuals who defy categorization because their symptoms change every few visits to the mental health practitioner's office. One week they complain of anxiety or depression; a few weeks later they are furious at the betrayal by a loved one but not particularly depressed or anxious. A few more weeks pass and they arrive for their appointment intoxicated or "high" on an illicit substance but with no discussion of the offending relationship of the previous visit. At a fourth visit, they seem more depressed, even suicidal, but they have no idea what has made them feel so awful. They reject any suggestion that anything said or done at previous sessions is relevant and threaten to fire their incompetent clinician. Nevertheless, they show up a few weeks later complaining that they feel empty and dead inside. Other branches of psychoanalytic theory that have done much to bring coherence to the concept of personality include the ego psychologists and object relations theorists whose work has been integrated in an instructive manner by Gertrude and Rubin Blanck (Blanck & Blanck, 1994). On the basis of the pioneering observational studies of mother–child dyads in the first 3 years of life, Mahler, Pine, and Bergman (1975) described the process of separation–individuation that takes place over that period, when we come to see ourselves as separate, independent persons rather than as extensions of our mother or primary caregiver. Mahler called this the *psychological birth* of the human infant, occurring subsequent to the physical birth. When this process is disrupted by a failure of the environment to be attuned to the child's ever-changing need for a balance between nurturance and opportunities for independence and stimulation, various intrapsychic processes are set in motion that disrupt personality development. There is a splitting of positive and negative feelings toward the same person and oneself, an inability to form a sufficiently autonomous self to withstand conflict with loved ones, and an inability to tolerate ambivalent feelings about ourselves and others. When successful, this period ends with a sense of self and a sense of others as largely separate beings in the world who, although imperfect, are basically good people who can be trusted.

PERSONALITY DISORDERS ACCORDING TO *DSM–5*

Anxiety, depression, attention-deficit/hyperactivity disorder, and substance abuse, especially in mild to moderate forms, do not define a person's entire way of being in the world, but personality disorders do. *Personality disorders* are regarded as equivalent to a basic style of life, personal character, or general way of interacting with the world and oneself that is not adaptive or effective. For example, an individual with narcissistic personality disorder is someone who feels that he or she is the only one in the world who deserves special treatment, attention, recognition, and approval. There is a general sense of extreme entitlement and a blindness to the needs of other people.

The personality disorders all involve a distortion in a mutually beneficial interpersonal relationship. There probably is not a consensus within our culture as to what counts as a mutually beneficial relationship, which should tell us how subjective such diagnoses will be. Interpersonal, psychodynamic, and humanistic theories assume that interpersonal relationships are healthy when partners can alternate being autonomous and interdependent (alternating between dependence and independence), enjoy being both physically separate and together, are in agreement on some basic life goals and values but can tolerate disagreement on others, and have a flexible yet stable relationship in which there is a commitment to mutual satisfaction and to problem solving where there are differences.

Intensive psychotherapy can be helpful in learning new ways to deal with the tasks and challenges of life without overreliance on defense mechanisms (Chessick, 1993). This kind of psychotherapy often requires meeting two to three times per week with a therapist for several years. Interestingly, few psychiatrists recommend medication for personality disorders, because there has never been any evidence that they work with these kinds of problems. Nevertheless, because psychiatrists using *DSM–5* diagnose both a personality disorder and a more specific symptom disorder (usually anxiety or depression) in the same person, such patients often end up on medication (usually antidepressants or antipsychotics, or a combination of the two).

Although I find the idea of describing another human being's personality as "disordered" to be offensive and demeaning, I do think that the concept of personality is a critically important one in psychology and that identifying patterns of personality characteristics (both positive and negative) is quite useful. The behaviors described in each of Horney's neurotic trends and the *DSM–5* personality disorders do often cluster together and often are tied to early patterns of relating to parents or siblings. Thus, if we remove the idea of disorder and just talk about personality patterns that have interesting consequences in people's lives—some negative and some positive—there is a lot to be learned that is valuable. For example, some of the traits in the obsessive–compulsive personality pattern (excessive orderliness, perfectionism, preoccupation with tasks rather than relationships) are actually required in professions such as accounting and chemistry and to some extent in any serious academic study.

This is true in many of the personality traits that can develop into "disorders"—they exist in part because they work in some contexts. The *disorder* refers to how the pattern does not work, but it tells only half the story. In fact, it is almost impossible to succeed in some demanding and high-status jobs unless one has a certain degree of perfectionism and self-absorption. True, these positions brings high levels of stress, limited time for pleasure or relationships, and perhaps some psychosomatic problems (e.g., irritable bowel, high blood pressure), but is it not possible that if the person has an annual salary of a million dollars, they may regard this as a good trade-off? Do we wish to diagnose such a person as evidencing a personality disorder? If we did, it probably would not matter, because such a person is unlikely to seek mental health services for such ego-syntonic traits.

Here is where *DSM–5* is clearly attempting to establish the norms of interpersonal relationships and behavior for the culture as a whole. Whether one agrees with the set of interpersonal norms or not, and despite the impending introduction of *ICD–10* (providers are expected to begin billing for insurance reimbursement according to ICD codes beginning in October, 2015), it is nevertheless important to acknowledge that the American Psychiatric Association is seeking to assert that kind of authority in our culture, and those who use the *DSM–5* personality disorder diagnoses in their professional practices are joining in that endeavor.

As with anxiety and depression, it is far better to consider personality characteristics as essential elements of human existence and to think of each of the categories of disorders as identifying critical interpersonal traits or characteristic ways of interacting with other human beings. In moderation, each of these traits can be a necessary mode of conducting oneself in the interpersonal world. Even the worst traits associated with the antisocial personality, a complete lack of empathy with others and disregard for anyone else's needs, may be a survival mechanism under dire circumstances (e.g., survival in a Nazi extermination camp such as Dachau or Auschwitz in World War II). When encountering excessively demanding people, it is sometimes a good thing to be avoidant of too many demands and expectations from others. When ill, one has to be able to allow oneself to depend on others for one's well-being, and when trying to survive in a highly competitive environment, one must be driven to garner attention for oneself. In a highly dangerous environment, suspiciousness and fear of strangers and the unknown are likely to increase the chances for one's survival. In a sterile and lifeless world controlled by goals of productivity and functionality, the intense volatile emotions and relationships of the histrionic and borderline personalities are a means of guaranteeing a passion for living in a drab world and protecting oneself from emotional abandonment.

All of these categories of personality diagnoses invite us to engage in stereotyping and treating people as though they were labels rather than human beings. The use of these diagnoses also invites us to deny responsibility for who we are and what we do: "I can't help criticizing you; it is my obsessive–compulsive personality disorder speaking." Alert to this, federal and state courts have moved to exclude the antisocial personality disorder as a qualifying mental illness for use in the insanity defense. This is because, as a mental illness present at the time a crime was committed, it was being successfully used to establish that defendants should not be held accountable for their actions before the law, since they could not control their antisocial impulses because of a disease. However, the understanding that these seemingly self-limiting and sometimes destructive patterns of interpersonal relationships are not just the irrational misfirings of a diseased brain but the self-protective mechanisms used by people who must live in an interpersonal world they find fraught with pain, fear, and humiliation is an important step forward in building a more humane world.

TREATMENT

Because of the ego-syntonic component of these neurotic trends and personality disorders, one of the critical ingredients in any process of change—namely, motivation for change—is missing. Such individuals experience profound anxiety or depression when their characteristic personality pattern stops working for them, and they ask for help to alleviate those symptoms. But what do they want help with? The narcissistic individual wants help returning to her path of glory, the antisocial individual wants help getting out of jail, and the dependent person wants help finding a new person to take care of him. To the extent that we sometimes need to make fundamental changes of direction in life, which may mean fundamentally different ways of viewing the self in relation to others, such requests for help are not likely to produce long-term change or benefit.

As noted previously, a biomedical approach is ineffective in dealing with the underlying personality process. A modified form of cognitive behavior therapy, dialectical behavior therapy (Linehan, 2013), has claimed some limited success in managing the self-harming behaviors associated with borderline personality disorder, and as with many behavioral approaches that have a psychoeducational focus, can be taught to public mental health service providers in a straightforward manner. One of the advantages of psychodynamic theory is its attempt to not only understand the development of personality patterns that contribute to interpersonal suffering but also to provide effective treatments that can produce at times an almost complete transformation in personality (Davanloo, 2001; Johnson, 2005; Malan & Della Selva, 2006). When this work is successful, there is no doubt that it is the psychotherapy that has produced the individual transformations, though it is difficult work and success is not easily achieved (Abbass, Sheldon, Gyra, & Kalpin, 2008). Next, I present two such cases, the first involving a narcissistic individual and the second an antisocial individual incarcerated in a maximum-security psychiatric hospital within a prison.

THE COLD-BLOODED BUSINESSMAN

This is a published case of intensive short-term dynamic therapy by Dr. Patricia Coughlin Della Selva with a 58-year-old married man and father of four daughters (Malan & Della Selva, 2006). I refer to him as CBB throughout. CBB came to therapy with complaints of depression and anxiety that were manifested in a hopeless outlook on life and psychophysiological complaints of erectile dysfunction and sleep disturbances that were affecting his work and home life. These symptoms had been present over the previous 12 years, ever since he moved his family to upstate New York so that he could take a new job. He had been in therapy with different psychotherapists and had been taking medications prescribed by a psychiatrist for the entire 12 years. He saw intensive short-term dynamic psychotherapy (ISTDP) as a desperate last attempt to find relief from his symptoms before he considered committing suicide. The ISTDP model requires the therapist to do a trial stage of psychodynamic therapy during the first session to determine how well the treatment is suited to the client. This involves directly though cautiously confronting the client's defenses to see whether he or she is able to tolerate examining his or her inner life without becoming destabilized.

Although he was initially eager to talk about his history, CBB was highly defended, refusing to discuss any emotions that were associated with these traumatic events. He continued to confuse being open with his feelings with sharing his thoughts and actions that emerged in conjunction with a traumatic event. He could identify the thoughts and behaviors that led his wife to describe him as "aloof" in their marriage and saw the connection between his depression and his weight gain over the past 12 years. There was not much more he could say about the inner experiences associated with these behaviors.

Dr. Coughlin Della Selva challenged CBB's avoidance of intense feelings and pushed him to recognize that his complaints of depression and anxiety manifest out of his emotional suppression. Even in the first session, she asked him how he felt about the way she asked him to express whatever feelings he was having about her as she directly inquired about his unexpressed inner thoughts and feelings. He was evasive, but she again gently but firmly suggested that he could not benefit from therapy unless he was more honest and forthright with her than he had been with previous therapists. By the end of the first session, CBB was able to demonstrate some ability to look at his own defensiveness and the need to move through it rather than to continue avoiding the painful emotions that remained hidden.

In the second session, the therapist took time with the client to obtain important aspects of his history. CBB thought fondly of his father, although his father had worked most of the time and struggled with self-confidence because of a physical disability. However, he disliked his mother, perceiving her to be mean and unintelligent. One of his most memorable experiences occurred at 7 years of age when his mother intentionally held his hand on a hot stove, burning him because he expressed disapproval about the meal she had cooked that evening. After that he refused to eat anything his mother made. This led to him becoming underweight, so he was sent to live at a health camp when he was 10. His parents rarely visited him there over the next 3 years of his life.

After the trial phase and the history taking, the third phase of the therapy required a return in earnest to the analysis of the defenses initiated in the trial phase. This phase of ISTDP lasted about 15 sessions. The therapist confronted the client's defenses that had allowed him to avoid his emotions. By facing the anxiety and not backing off to safety, he was pushed to recognize the way he had intellectualized all his life problems as a means of attempting to deal with them without feeling the intense pain that was repressed. He talked about his feelings, but he did not show them. When he was able to acknowledge his defenses and openly demonstrate his feelings, he was able to recognize that avoiding this in the past had caused his complaints of depression and anxiety (Malan & Della Selva, 2006, p. 130).

CBB gradually moved from intellectually recognizing that he was avoiding the nonverbal interconnection with the therapist, to slowly engaging with the therapist enough to experience the bodily sensations associated with his emotions of fear, anger, and sadness. Anger at the therapist was particularly difficult for him to acknowledge. When she noted his sarcasm directed at her, she asked for the feeling behind it. When he answered that he wanted to stand up to her and yell at her, she again confronted him as offering a behavior not a feeling. She directed his attention to the tension in his hands to show that his impulses were moving into his conscious action. Eventually, with the therapist's unwavering pressure on him to acknowledge his feelings, he acknowledged his uncomfortable feelings: "I'm afraid. I'm afraid I could hurt you" (Malan & Della Selva, 2006, p. 136). With the benefit of the therapist's interpretation, CBB recognized that by pushing his impulses of anger toward others away from awareness, he brought them on himself, causing behavioral, somatic, and emotional upset.

As CBB broke through the defense protecting him from one strong and painful affect, he and the therapist encountered yet another layer of defense protecting him from experiencing other painful memories and feelings. After being able to acknowledge his fear of his anger at the therapist, CBB grew uncomfortable with what came next. In wanting to harm her like she harmed him (i.e., in challenging his defenses rather than feeding his narcissism), he had fantasies of sexually abusing her and feeling a sense of relief as a result. The therapist encouraged him to explicitly describe the extent of his abuse of her, including how he would feel when it was all over. He realized that the end point for him in such an encounter would be terrible guilt and remorse. Recognizing the transference, the therapist chose to validate his guilt—she and he both knew that "might does not make right," that just because one is bigger and stronger does not give them the right to physically assault someone else. CBB replied, "It also relates to my mother and me." Here the therapist needed to merely affirm that what he had said at the first interview without emotion had contained a great deal of hurt, and she inquired whether he had ever felt anger at his mother for burning him as she did. He responded, "I want to smash her body and leave her in the sewer to die alone" (Malan & Della Selva, 2006, p. 142).

Now CBB could focus on the source of his narcissistic injury that had made him mistreat women he loved: the rage he felt toward his mother for burning his hand and later sending him off and abandoning him for years. Recognizing that feelings of love and attachment inevitably brought with them feelings of murderous rage, he could see why he had remained aloof with his wife these many years. He could only feel sexually attracted to anonymous strangers with whom he felt no love or attachment.

As CBB was able to liberate his anger and fear, he discovered loving feelings. Roughly 40 sessions into therapy, he explored with the therapist his intimate feelings toward her. In this fantasy he did not have purely sexual thoughts about anonymous women, as he had 4 months earlier. Rather, he wanted to be closer to the therapist in an intimate and loving manner. The therapist accepted these feelings as positive transference of the love he wished for from his mother and in more recent years from his wife. CBB was then able to redirect these desires for intimacy to his wife for the first time in his life.

Following the introduction of the new emotions he was experiencing, CBB spontaneously came to a deeper understanding of himself and came to see how his affairs and the way he mistreated the women in those affairs represented his unresolved longing for closeness with his mother and his furious rage at not receiving it.

In the following months, around the 50th session (at 1 year), CBB opened the session with an intention to reflect on the depression and anxiety he had gone through. He was nervous as he entered the session because he was sure that to talk about it meant that he was going to relive all the pain. Yet, by the end of the session he only felt relief, and he was surprised and encouraged that in the future he could trust that when he expressed his inner pain to a person whom he could trust, he would feel better, not worse. His stories, once emotionless tales of experience, turned into intimate and authentic experiences that he visualized and felt.

VIOLENT AND ANTISOCIAL PERSONS

The antisocial personality is regarded as essentially untreatable in the mainstream literature of psychiatry and clinical psychology. Much attention is devoted to the trait of *psychopathy*, which involves both a lack of empathic emotional arousal for those one has harmed and a lack of fear of getting caught or punished. A picture is painted of a coldhearted individual who is physiologically incapable of compassion, fear, guilt, or remorse (Hare & Neumann, 2008). Indeed, if one works in a prison setting, as I did for several years early in my career, one does occasionally encounter such individuals, and the description seems accurate. It was not until I encountered the work of the British psychiatrist Robert (Bob) Johnson (2005) that it became evident to me that the truth of this description is dependent on having failed to pierce the massive defensive armor that is easily mistaken for being all there is to the person so characterized. What Johnson did in his work inside Britain's maximum-security psychiatric unit was to show that if the mental health professional refuses to accept this almost impenetrable façade of no emotions, in some cases such individuals have revealed the real truth about their lives—namely, that they are massively defended against the experience of brutal, terrifying childhood experiences. Further, once those defenses are breached, fundamental personality transformation can take place that heals the trauma and removes the individual's need to be violent and antisocial. Granted, this is dangerous and extremely difficult work.

Johnson maintained that there are three conditions that must be met for such a transformation to be possible: (a) the therapeutic experience must be noncoercive and entirely voluntary, (b) the client must understand that they must be honest with themselves and the therapist and tell the truth about their own childhood and adult life experiences, and (c) the therapist and client must work to develop mutual trust.

Johnson developed this approach during a 5-year stint as a psychiatrist on a special unit at Parkhurst Prison, Isle of Wight, England. The unit was set up to house the most violent, unstable, and ill-disciplined men serving life sentences in the British prison system. These were prisoners even too dangerous to be kept at the infamous Broadmoor Prison. Over the 5 years, Johnson worked with more than 60 such highly dangerous offenders using his three-pronged approach: "truth, trust, and consent." Government records documented a startling reduction in violent attacks in this special unit. During the first 7.5 years of its operation, there were 42 such attacks, whereas in the last 2.5 years of Johnson's 5-year stint, there was exactly one violent attack. During this last period, use of tranquillizers by the inmates dropped 95%. Vague physical complaints and insomnia lessened, and there was an increase in enrollment in open university courses.

It is fair to say that not only was antisocial behavior drastically reduced but also that prosocial behavior increased. Once word of the success of the program spread, it received attention in the national media. The conservative government's home secretary, Michael Howard, asked the High Court to quash further publicity about the program on the grounds that such extreme murderous behavior as evidenced by the inmates of the special unit was biologically determined and incurable. The High Court ruled to allow news coverage to continue (Johnson, 2005). Not to be deterred, after highly publicized escapes from other units at Parkhurst, not long after the broadcast the government chose to close the special unit on which Bob Johnson worked and declared the report on the outcomes at the unit a state secret. Since then, with the help of the James Nayler Foundation, Bob Johnson has been lecturing and writing on his revolutionary approach to working with hardened criminals and murderers, as well as on other serious life-threatening problems such as addictions, anorexia, and psychoses.

Johnson's work with one particular inmate at Parkhurst was reported in an article in *The Guardian* (Davies, 1994). Davies described how Johnson had worked with a man referred to as "Des," who was in his 40s and tall and muscular. He had beaten a close male friend to death in a senseless argument over a seemingly trivial matter. In prison he had engaged in similar kinds of fights in which he would lose all control of his violent temper. He had been transferred from prison to prison and had been in and out of solitary confinement. He arrived on Bob Johnson's unit heavily medicated with sedatives and refusing to discuss his childhood.

Johnson persisted, and eventually Des began to talk about his childhood and permitted the discussions to be videotaped. Davies (1994) reported what he then witnessed on the videotapes. Des responded to Johnson in a flat, unemotional way about a childhood environment in which as a small boy he was subjected to endless violence captured in one single episode. His mother called to him from across the room, "'Come here, Des. I wanna batter you.' And so this small boy had trotted across to her, and she had battered him."

Over a period of weeks, Johnson began to make headway. He asked Des what he would do if his mother were to enter the room they were in at the prison, and he indicated he would have to flee out of fear for his life. Des revealed this as if he believed it to be a perfectly rational answer; of course, Johnson queried him about his mother's size and age. Without hesitating, Des reported she was 85 years of age and was a small but sprightly woman. Reluctantly, Des admitted that he could probably defend himself fairly well against her now and that he was responding out of the depths of the fears from his childhood. After 2 months of these talk therapy sessions, Des began to say that if his mother were to show up, he would simply say to her, "You can't hit me now, I am an adult."

Johnson then began to explore what had happened the night Des murdered his friend. They were out on the town and had no place to sleep. The friend suggested that they stay with Des's mother. Des said no to that suggestion, but the friend thought that was ridiculous and began to insist they go Des's mother's house. That is what triggered his rage—being badgered into returning to where he had been so badly beaten. He recalled that once he started hitting the man, he actually wanted to kill him. In discussions with Johnson over the following few months, Des became clearer in his own mind that his mother could never again attack him, and he reacted to this realization by becoming increasingly calm. Johnson began reducing his medication, and he still remained calm.

The following is Johnson's edited reflection on the case (personal communication, February 18, 2014):

> Des murdered because he was not thinking straight. My research indicates that the same applies to all homicides—criminal, terrorist, or political. . . . Setting out to alter a patient's view of their problem is entirely standard in ordinary medical practice—"I'm having a heart attack" is not something any doctor would accept unreservedly, without further substantial clinical evidence. This is especially so with crimes of violence—the accounts offered bear little relation to reality. After spending some 2,000 hours (unaccompanied) with the most dangerous prisoners in the British prison system, this was their most striking feature. When asked to explain why they murdered, all they could manage was "He had it coming," "He was asking for it," "A red mist came down, so I let him have it," or as with Des, "I just went too far" or "I snapped"— this might invigorate more orthodox views of "psychopathy," but does little to engage an investigative clinical mind.

Childhood traumas freeze the individual at an infantile emotional age, so solutions to life's insecurities are based on infantile strategies, which entail perceiving other adults as being of parental size and power, and therefore continuing to hold life-threatening capabilities. Another's life is thereby seen as relatively insubstantial. Emotional maturation means no longer being dependent on parent figments for survival—the true opposite of infancy. Interdependency, yes—infant-style dependency, no.

So why was Des not thinking straight? How could he possibly imagine that an 85-year-old weakling could injure, let alone kill him? And to misperceive this so thoroughly as to murder? The answer is painfully simple: The beleaguered infant cannot appeal to the Supreme Court—their "protector" is doing the opposite, the attacks being received have no physical remedy, so the child applies a mental one: "This isn't happening to me." This can be described as *denial*, *projection*, or *dissociation*; what it entails is remedy by fog—rather than think "Mum is about to batter me to death," the child elects to stop thinking at all. This is *cognitive fog*, a device or defense to stop being murdered, as the infant sees it. Thinking straight leads to inevitable demise, so do not think at all. Do not raise any objections—that would be fatal. The remedy then is as simple as it is not easy: persuade the sufferer that there is now value in thinking straight after all, to raising objections—in today's reality, Des's mother cannot harm him, because I, though powerful enough to be an abusive parent too, will stop her, will hold her off long enough for him to see the truth.

Does it work? What is the success rate? Again the answer is counter-cultural: Success depends not on the sufferer, but on the therapist—can one walk the crucial tightrope of being powerful yet benign, of being forceful yet entirely dependent on the consent of the sufferer? Can you build enough trust so that they can cease "fogging" their minds and can accept help from those more powerful, who so far have proved irredeemably untrustworthy. This cognitive fog underlies all manner of psychiatric pathology, from all varieties of personality disorder and indeed the full gamut of psychoses. It only fails when trust is lacking or consent is overridden, thereby ensuring that truth remains befogged. Whence comes my advocacy of truth, trust, and consent. But what fascinates me is that it shows the pattern below every psychiatric encounter: Like a crossword there are clues to an underlying infantile rationale, where the healthier outcome is more reality, more emotional maturity. What a privilege.

8

SCHIZOPHRENIA: PSYCHIATRY'S POSTER CHILD

In popular parlance the word *schizophrenia* is used to refer to a person behaving in a manner that is so out of character that it seems that they have become a different person. In fact, such "Dr. Jekyll and Mr. Hyde" transformations have a formal diagnostic label in psychiatry—namely, *dissociated identity disorder* (previously referred to as *multiple personality disorder*). *Psychosis*, however, refers to a psychological state in which the person's mind seems broken or deluded and includes symptoms such as hallucinations, delusions, incoherent speech, bizarre behaviors, disregard for personal safety, erratic dangerousness to self or others, becoming immobilized or completely withdrawn, or being uninterested in self-care and personal hygiene. When some of these symptoms are associated with severely depressed mood, it is labeled as *bipolar disorder* or *major depression with psychotic features*. More often, such behavior and characteristics are diagnosed as a *schizophrenic disorder*, though during the first 6 months of such symptoms, especially if they have come on quickly, the term used might be *reactive schizophreniform psychosis*.

http://dx.doi.org/10.1037/14693-008
Not So Abnormal Psychology: A Pragmatic View of Mental Illness, by R. B. Miller

Generally, the rate of complete recovery from psychotic episodes is poor in conventional psychiatry, and therefore most people who would properly be diagnosed as having a reactive psychosis are told that they have symptoms of what is likely to be a lifelong illness for which there is no cure and that will require a lifetime of taking high doses of antipsychotic medication. Recently, it has been questioned whether it might be the treatment itself that is turning these acute psychotic conditions into chronic lifelong disabilities (Fisher & Ahern, 2000; Mosher, Menn, & Matthews, 1975; R. Whitaker, 2011). Contemporary biological theories of schizophrenia (the dopamine theory) were developed to explain the supposed positive impact of antipsychotic drugs in psychotic symptoms. Given the dominance of this model on education and training in psychology and psychiatry over the past 50 years, it is helpful to look at some historical antecedents to our current predicament.

CULTURAL AND HISTORICAL CONTEXT

We can certainly see Ellenberger's (1974) themes of punishment, healing, and acceptance in the controversy over how to understand and treat schizophrenia in our culture today. The punishment approach is represented by the over 330,000 individuals with serious mental illness (i.e., psychosis, usually schizophrenia) incarcerated in local, state, and federal jails and penitentiaries, essentially being punished for behaviors resulting from their inability to cope with modern society (Litschge & Vaughn, 2009). This represents 15% to 20% of all persons incarcerated in the United States (estimated at 2.4 million persons). As for the contemporary "lay healers," spending on antipsychotic medications in the United States is over 18 billion dollars with over 57 million prescriptions for these medications per year (Lindsley, 2012).

The consumer advocacy movement is oriented toward accepting people who "hear voices" (http://www.hearing-voices.org), consider themselves "survivors of psychiatry" (http://www.chrusp.org/home), and often seeks to accept and celebrate aspects of psychotic experience (Fisher & Ahern, 2000). These consumer and patient rights groups often have support from humanistic practitioners of psychology and psychiatry (e.g., Fisher & Ahern, 2000; Szasz, 1960/1984).

One has to be cautious in deciding whether a particular organization or professional practice is primarily oriented toward one or the other of these orientations (i.e., to punish, heal, or accept/glorify). For example, the National Alliance for the Mentally Ill presents itself as an advocacy group for the parents of schizophrenic and psychotic children, yet they receive funding from pharmaceutical companies, and they strongly encourage the use of antipsychotic medications, which their children are likely to have refused to take voluntarily (Breggin, 1994). Of course, if parents believe that the only alternative is incarceration, it is easy to see how they might believe they are only doing what is best for their offspring. Yet, as a national organization they do not embrace the "acceptance" aspects of the recovery movement, which might be seen as even more supportive of their children.

Coercive or forced treatment of psychotic individuals in hospital or state hospital settings on locked wards blends elements of punishment and healing. Patients may describe the effects of medications as debilitating and dehumanizing (R. Whitaker, 2005) and yet be told by physicians or psychologists that they are required to take the medications and that they are incompetent to manage their own medical care and are thus subject to court-ordered treatment. Acceptance and healing approaches also may blend into one another. Humanistic psychotherapy of psychosis (Prouty, 2003), psychodynamic psychotherapy of schizophrenia (Karon & VandenBos, 1981), and the Soteria House project (Mosher et al., 1975) are models of treatment designed by mental health professionals interested in healing that use a great deal of acceptance and even glorification of symptoms to mobilize change in patients' lives. The key here is to not try to heal or change parts of the person's experience without the full voluntary consent from the patient (Johnson, 2005).

The modern medical school emerged as an educational institution in the mid-19th century, and German medical schools were considered to provide the best training in the Western world. It was in Germany that the first departments of psychiatry emerged around 1850. These departments were sometimes referred to as *departments of neuropsychiatry* because it was assumed that problems of behavior and mood were associated with illness in the nervous system. The discovery in the late 1800s that general paresis of the insane could be prevented by early treatment of syphilis with a drug that killed the spirochete gave encouragement to the neurological theory of psychosis. However, less than 1% of the patients suffering from psychosis had a history of syphilis, so the actual impact on the treatment of psychosis was limited. Still, it spurred an unwavering commitment to a biological explanation of schizophrenia and other psychoses that is still with us today in the field of psychiatry and, to some extent, in the entire mental health field.

In Nazi Germany, the first systematic killings of civilians who were considered "life not worthy of life" were children with intellectual and physical disabilities of the nervous system, followed next by adult mental patients (Lifton, 1988). It is also well documented (Bonnie, 2002) that during the communist control of Russia and the former USSR, state-sponsored psychiatrists regularly medicated political dissenters into vegetative states using antipsychotic drugs to treat the culturally bound form of "thought disorder" for which the only symptom was vociferously holding anticommunist views.

It was assumed by the state-run psychiatric profession that anyone of sound mind would prefer communist dictatorship to any other form of government.

In the United States, the American Psychiatric Association was established in 1908 by a group of seven psychiatrists, all superintendents of large state hospitals. Prior to Freud's work catching hold in psychiatry in the 1920s, there was not much demand for psychiatric services outside of institutional or hospital settings. Psychiatry had the job of managing those members of society who could not adapt to social expectations and social roles and who were not eligible for the criminal justice system. The behavior of such individuals was not criminal, it was disturbing or offensive, but either not strictly illegal or lacking in criminal intent. This social management was described as treatment in the patient's interest, not punishment. Nonetheless, it might be involuntary treatment, and some of the treatments were quite extreme and life-threatening (insulin coma therapy, electroconvulsive shock, and prefrontal lobotomies were used during the first half of the 20th century). Furthermore, during the eugenics movement in the United States (1920–1950), state hospital physicians involuntarily sterilized or castrated tens of thousands of "mentally ill" and "mildly retarded" patients so that they would not "breed" future generations of nonproductive citizens. There were 60,000 forced sterilizations in the 30 states that had passed eugenics laws. The sterilizations were done on the basis of an individual or family history of disability and poverty, though minority racial background also seemed to be a major factor (Reilly, 1987). This movement was created and funded by the financially and socially elite segments of U.S. society concerned about the growing demands of the poor and others unable to work for a greater share of the society's wealth (R. Whitaker, 2005).

There were dissenters in psychiatry, but their voices rarely attracted public attention. Exceptions to this included Thomas Szasz (1960/1984), a psychiatrist who published *The Myth of Mental Illness*, in which he argued against coercive medical treatment of people who had never broken the law, regardless of their medical status, and R. D. Laing (1959), a radical psychiatrist who made similar arguments in Great Britain and in fact became widely read by intellectuals outside of psychiatry and psychology. In the mid 1970s, the head of the National Institute of Mental Health (NIMH) schizophrenia research center, Loren Mosher (Mosher et al., 1975), shocked academic psychiatry by taking a similar position and demonstrating in his Soteria House treatment center that a nonmedical treatment that deemphasized the routine use of antipsychotic medications with a schizophrenic population was actually much more successful in the long run (2- and 4-year follow-ups) than conventional hospital treatment. His results were so threatening to the prevailing ideology within psychiatry that Mosher's funding from his own department at NIMH was cut by more than half because the peer reviewers could not believe he had not falsified his data to get such positive results.

HISTORY OF THE DIAGNOSIS OF SCHIZOPHRENIA

In many ways, schizophrenia is the poster child of biological psychiatry simply because most people, as well as most psychiatrists, cannot imagine a person with a healthy brain behaving in such a bizarre or unusual manner. Other people often find the psychotic population intolerable to live with, their unpredictable and unorthodox social behaviors occasioning fear and frustration. Spouses and parents of such individuals have in Western culture created a demand for residential and hospital care for such members of their families, and the medical community has responded to this social demand by creating an expensive service and a lucrative area of medical practice. Most people who have not lived with this level of psychological pain and disturbance find it not only intolerable to live with but also intolerable to be around for any length of time. It is terrifying to see another human being in such a state of terror, rage, despondency, or debilitation.

Since the 1850s, psychiatrists have been divided on whether the psychotic states of mind associated with schizophrenia (then called *dementia praecox*, Latin for early loss of mental functioning) are due to a disease or adverse life experiences. Eugen Bleuler, a Swiss psychiatrist, coined the term *schizophrenia* to replace *dementia praecox* because he had observed that the thought processes of such individuals were deteriorated in the same manner as persons with the senility of old age (M. Bleuler, 1978). These younger individuals seemed to have an ability to split off their emotions from their thoughts. Bleuler indicated that he thought the condition was essentially incurable. However, his son, Manfred Bleuler, discovered that his father was wrong because he had only seen the patients who returned for treatment and had not tracked the ones who never returned, as Manfred Bleuler ultimately did (M. Bleuler, 1978). Today, the view within psychiatry and psychology is overwhelmingly in favor of the biological explanation, and until recently, anyone who rejected that view was seen as naïve, uninformed, or unscientific.

Schizophrenia is the most perplexing of the psychological states studied in abnormal psychology because the individuals seem so incomprehensible to most of us that we wish to see them as entirely alien to our own life experience. Although only about 1% of the population is diagnosed as schizophrenic at any time in their life, because of the bizarre nature of the symptoms, the topic of schizophrenia receives an enormous amount of attention in both professional publications and the media. In everyday speech, when someone seriously calls another person "crazy," "insane," or "out of his or her mind," the behavior that is being referred to is probably what a mental health professional would diagnose as schizophrenia. In recent years, the popular press and media have repeatedly highlighted stories involving seemingly random acts of mass murders by persons said to be either psychotically depressed or schizophrenic (e.g., shootings at a Newtown school, Columbine High School, a Colorado movie theater). This not only highlights the importance of this relatively rare disorder but also creates a sense of urgency concerning public safety and calls for greater restraints (gun controls, forced medications, return to lengthy involuntary hospitalizations) on the freedoms of such individuals living with the rest of the community.

Because of the conceptual confusion in the field of clinical psychology and the other mental health professions, there is much confusion in terminology related to schizophrenia. Fundamentally, to receive a diagnosis of schizophrenia, one must appear to be highly disruptive in normal social relationships in one's culture and must be so in a manner that does not seem rational or does not make sense to others. Psychosis is similar to those aspects of schizophrenia that are most dramatic—hallucinations, delusions of thought, extreme panic, emotionality, and/or aggressiveness. However, people can be "psychotic" with depression, drug overdoses (e.g., stimulants), posttraumatic stress disorder, and the intense sleep deprivation that goes with stress. Acute psychosis is a challenge to deal with, but if dealt with compassionately and effectively, it can completely resolve and may never recur. When the psychosis lasts for more than 6 months, the diagnosis is converted to schizophrenia.

The *Diagnostic and Statistical Manual of Mental Disorders* (5th ed.; DSM-5; American Psychiatric Association, 2013) discusses different manifestations of schizophrenia. In *catatonic* states a person alternates between being completely immobile (*waxy inflexibility*) and highly physically aggressive. *Paranoia* may include hallucinations and delusions; the individual may seem to live in a reality different from the rest of human society, seeing, hearing or believing aspects of reality others do not sense or believe to be true or real. Delusions may be grandiose (e.g., "I am Jesus Christ") or persecutory (e.g., "The FBI is bugging my phone and implanting electrodes in my brain to control me"). Disorganized symptoms involve being unable to communicate coherently, having bizarre forms of speech, and being unable to function in the simplest aspects of daily life or self-care.

Chronic schizophrenia has a preponderance of the typical negative symptoms associated with the diagnosis. *Negative* does not mean bad or undesirable here, because all the symptoms of schizophrenia are generally thought to be undesirable; it means that the symptoms are the absence of social skills and behaviors that we would hope a person would engage in—for example, self-care, interest in the world, motivation, and so forth. Negative symptoms are seen in chronic schizophrenia as a general absence of involvement in the world—sitting for hours staring into space, not asleep but not really aware and awake. The positive symptoms are behaviors and experiences that are present in an individual that typically would not be present in a person who was not having significant psychological problems: hallucinations, delusions, belligerence, and overt sexual expression that is unwelcome and intrusive. These are more prevalent in acute stages of schizophrenia and tend to lessen, at least for a short time, with medication.

The medical model assumes that most people with schizophrenic symptoms will end up becoming chronic schizophrenics, and in fact, under the current system of ineffective treatment, that is usually the case. Loren Mosher's work (Mosher et al., 1975) showed that this is not necessarily the inevitable outcome of schizophrenia. However, the most recent U.S. government–backed research on the "atypical antipsychotic" drugs revealed that the side effects of these new "safer" drugs are as bad or worse than those of the first-generation antipsychotic drugs (Lieberman et al., 2005). The "atypicals" are no more helpful than the original antipsychotics, though they may produce slightly less brain damage in terms of tardive dyskinesia; however, they have much worse effects on the hormonal and circulatory system. It is believed that the average patient taking the atypicals is likely to lose over 20 years of life expectancy. This is due to increased rates of diabetes and heart disease among the chronic schizophrenic population on atypical antipsychotic drugs (Lieberman et al., 2005). These often disabling substances actually cost about 50 times as much as the first-generation antipsychotics while they were on patent. This is much worse than the already bad situation of the selective serotonin reuptake inhibitors (SSRIs) because the serious side effects are more common and people are on them for more years. However, what is the same is that the large drug corporations are promoting the use of both SSRIs and atypicals and increasingly getting U.S. Food and Drug Administration approval for prescribing the drugs to children of younger ages (3, 4, and 5 years of age). R. Whitaker (2005, 2011) is right: It is the shame of a nation. Or maybe we are just a shameless nation.

INTERSECTION WITH THE LEGAL SYSTEM

Insanity is a legal term, not a psychological concept or term. When one is insane, one is seen, depending on state law, as either incapable of (a) knowing right from wrong, (b) knowing the consequences of one's behavior, or (c) controlling one's behavior in accordance with reason. It is a defense used by lawyers to keep their clients out of jail; if one is found "not guilty by reason of insanity," one is sentenced to a state mental hospital for treatment and can then be released without jail time in most states. For this to happen, one must be shown to be "insane" at the time the crime was committed.

Incompetent to stand trial is another legal term often used with individuals diagnosed with a schizophrenic disorder. Lawyers may plead that their client, after committing a crime, is incompetent to stand trial, meaning they do not have the mental capacity to understand the charges against them and cannot participate in their own defense. In such circumstances a person may be found incompetent and sent to a state mental hospital until they are competent, at which time they can be tried. Thus, being found insane versus incompetent has different long-term consequences, though to begin with they have the same effect (being sent to a hospital, not a prison).

Involuntary commitment is another legal procedure that interconnects with psychiatric or psychological treatment. In this case, a state psychologist or psychiatrist can certify a patient as severely mentally ill and dangerous to himself or others. If that happens, the person can be forced to enter a hospital or, if an outpatient, can be forced to take antipsychotic and/or antidepressant medications. Forced treatment of outpatients is a relatively new social phenomenon in the United States, introduced only in the past 10 years or so, and many civil libertarians are horrified by its existence. It puts mental illness into the same category as highly contagious deadly diseases that the state has the right to intervene over, given public health concerns. With the exception of these concerns, it is unheard of in the West for citizens to lose control over the way medical professionals treat our bodies. That is, it is unheard of unless one is a person with a "severe and persistent mental illness" (i.e., schizophrenia), in which case it is regarded as perfectly legal and acceptable.

CONTEMPORARY MEDICAL MODEL OF SCHIZOPHRENIA

Little progress had been made in discovering the causes of serious mental illnesses when phenothiazine medications such as chlorpromazine and haloperidol (Thorazine and Haldol) were developed into behavior-altering psychiatric treatments in the early 1960s. Following this shift, the psychiatry profession, pharmaceutical companies, and increasingly influenced by those companies, state and federal governments have been united in an attempt to claim that these drugs, rather than just immobilizing a person in a chemical straightjacket, actually treat the underlying cause of schizophrenia in the brain—an excess of the neurotransmitter dopamine (Lieberman, Kinon, & Loebel, 1990). Thus, a psychophysiological conjecture became a dogma. Scientific medicine requires that an underlying physiological mechanism for the development of symptoms must be located and a medication or surgery designed to return that physiological mechanism back to normal functioning. Psychiatry needed such a theory to be accepted as a modern form of medicine. Today, the dopamine theory has been largely discredited (Moncrieff, 2009), but not before the hypothesis set in motion considerable research to find a genetic basis for the dysregulation in the dopamine pathways in the brain.

In the postwar era, even after the consequences of eugenics in Nazi Germany had been fully exposed, psychiatrists and conservative politicians and policy analysts maintained, despite a lack of evidence, that schizophrenia and all serious mental disorders were rooted in genetic inheritance. Although they no longer promoted sterilization of those who were supposedly unfit to pass along their genes, mainstream psychiatrists shifted their emphasis to incapacitating and confining the severely mentally ill. They would be locked up in prisons or mental hospitals, or if deinstitutionalized, they would be so heavily medicated that they would be unable to lead independent lives in which they might reproduce.

THE GENETIC EVIDENCE

To examine genetic evidence we must return to the world of statistical evidence for "heritability" and the probability of various gene variants referred to as *alleles* being found in a given sample of the population. In familial and adoption studies, findings have been extremely diverse. Early studies claimed that heritability was between 50% and 80% (Gottesman & Shields, 1982), and the key adoption study done in Denmark showed children who grow up to become schizophrenic are much more concordant for that diagnosis with their biological parents than with adoptive parents (Kety, Rosenthal, Wender, Schulsinger, & Jacobsen, 1976). However, J. Joseph (2006) found evidence suggesting that the criteria for concordance were altered in the study when the first data analysis did not show a higher rate of concordance with biological parents. In addition, Walker, Kestler, Bollini, and Hochman (2004) noted that subsequent research has found that children of schizophrenic mothers adopted at birth only had a higher rate of schizophrenia than controls when reared in "highly disruptive environments"; an elevated rate of schizophrenia was not found in adoptees who were raised in healthy family environments.

The research of the last decade on molecular genetics is parallel to that discussed in Chapter 5 on anxiety and depression. Initial excitement about gene polymorphisms (alleles) that are statistically overrepresented in groups of patients with schizophrenia was followed by caution and confusion as further studies failed to replicate initial findings but turned up new alleles that are statistically overrepresented in the new patient group. A good example is the study by Q. Wang et al. (2013), which looked for common gene variants associated with reduced brain volume in schizophrenic patients but found instead "novel susceptibility loci for schizophrenia on 3 genes/intergenic regions" (p. 8). Attempting to reconcile the findings with the goals of the study, the authors offered the following seeming apologia:

> It is challenging to identify genes involved in the pathogenesis of schizophrenia due to its complex model of inheritance and the unknown pathophysiology of the disorder. Furthermore, phenotypic heterogeneity, such as various clinical presentation and duration of illness, complicated the genetic study of schizophrenia. (p. 8)

The authors were essentially saying (a) we do not have a clear pattern of genetic inheritance within families; (b) even though we are convinced that schizophrenia must be a brain disease, we have no idea what the physiological factors are in the body or brain that produce the symptoms; (c) the symptoms of the illness are ill-defined and diverse; and (d) the outcomes of patients with the same diagnosis are also extremely diverse. Faced with similar confusion when looking at the genetic research on schizophrenia, Walker et al. (2004) suggested that "unexpressed genetic vulnerabilities may be common in the general population" (p. 410). This is reminiscent of the "one genus postulate" by the American psychiatrist H. S. Sullivan (1892–1949), who was seen as a master clinician when it came to working with schizophrenic patients: "We are all much more simply human than otherwise." (Sullivan, 1953/1968, p. 32)

BRAIN STRUCTURE AND FUNCTION

The Hypothalamic–Pituitary–Adrenal Axis

With the demise of the dopamine hypothesis, researchers have been searching for the pathophysiology (physiological disorder) that explains schizophrenia. They have settled in on three areas of research. One is already familiar to us: the hypothalamic–pituitary–adrenal (HPA) axis linking the prefrontal cortex to the glandular and hormonal system of the body, which may be critical in how the body responds to environmental stress. Walker, Mittal, and Tessner (2008) identified four lines of evidence that link HPA activity and psychosis: (a) physical illnesses with elevated cortisol or corticosteroids can produce psychotic symptoms, (b) patients with schizophrenia and other psychoses show both HPA dysregulation and shrinking of the hippocampus, (c) HPA activation alters dopamine pathways in the brain, and (d) prenatal factors thought to be associated with schizophrenia are known to alter HPA functioning.

This is an interesting theory in that it offers a clear diathesis–stress model of schizophrenia focusing on a physiological system that we all share that may be altered by stress. It also lends itself to a Gene × Environment explanation, in that HPA axis is thought to affect the expression of genes that influence brain development during adolescence, the prime period for the emergence of schizophrenic symptoms. Although the authors focused on all the ways medication may be used to alter the functioning of the HPA axis, it is clear that reducing environmental stress during adolescence is another viable approach to reducing symptoms.

Brain Volume

Early positron-emission tomography (PET) and magnetic resonance imaging (MRI) studies of the brain claimed to have shown diminished brain volume in some schizophrenic patients. Critics have claimed that the loss of brain matter was due to the use of antipsychotic medications. Haijma et al. (2013) conducted a meta-analysis of 317 brain volume studies of schizophrenic patients. In 33 of the studies patients had never been treated with antipsychotic medications. White matter of the brain was decreased to a similar extent in both the medicated and unmedicated groups. Gray matter loss was associated with both duration of symptoms and the dosage of antipsychotic medications received in treatment. Patients who had never been treated with medication had 25% loss of gray matter. However, an internationally renowned research team, Button et al. (2013), specifically pointed to the brain imaging studies on brain volume in schizophrenia as evidence of the overreporting of significant findings due to selective reporting, selective analyses of data, and general bias in favor of finding a biological cause of schizophrenia. In addition, if the Haijma et al. (2013) finding is confirmed by other replication studies, it will only provide proof of a correlation between schizophrenia and brain volume. One can imagine that the stimulus-deprived, internally conflicted, and isolated world of many psychotic patients might produce changes in the brain, rather than loss of brain volume producing the schizophrenia.

Psychopharmacology

There is a wealth of data from two multinational World Health Organization studies (Hopper, Harrison, Janca, & Sartorius, 2007; Sartorius, Jablensky, Shapiro, 1977; the second a deliberate replication of the first) and a well-documented and researched treatment program in Finland, the Open Dialogue program (Seikkula, Alakare, & Aaltonen, 2011), that uses minimal medication in the treatment of schizophrenia and has found that patients treated without antipsychotic medication do far better in their long-term outcomes than patients who are medicated. This is supported as well by historical data (beginning in the late 1700s) on the success of the Quaker community's manner of dealing with neighbors who showed signs of what then was called "madness"–namely, what came to be called *moral treatment* (see the next section). The NIMH-sponsored Clinical Antipsychotic Trials of Intervention Effectiveness (Lieberman & Stroup, 2011) found that the newer atypical antipsychotics that alter dopamine and serotonin pathways in the brain are no more effective than the first generation antipsychotics that primarily targeted dopamine. Nor do the atypicals have fewer or less-debilitating overall side effects. In fact, schizophrenic patients treated with atypical antipsychotic medications that cost over $12,000 a year per patient for the first 20 years they were available experienced a reduced average life expectancy of over 20 years. They also found that 75% of the patients pre-scribed antipsychotic medications discontinued taking their medication.

MORAL TREATMENT

Moral treatment, developed in the mid 1800s, was a social movement aimed at humanizing the terrible conditions in public mental hospitals. It was led by a social reformer, Dorothea Dix, who may have been inspired by the earlier work of the Quaker community of York, England, in the late 1780s. They had discovered that a home-like setting that provided a kind and benevolent but firm approach to "mad" patients was far superior in its effects than the insane asylums of the day. They kept meticulous records and reported that two thirds of patients were well enough to return to their homes after a year. Dix encouraged a similar approach to state mental hospitals—they should be small enough to provide a sense of community (less than 200 patients) and should be staffed with people who were able to implement something akin to the Quaker approach (R. Whitaker, 2005).

The reforms were successful, again reporting that about two thirds of the patients were sufficiently recovered to return to their own communities and resume their lives. However, this success was short-lived. The Civil War, a massive influx of immigrants, a cycle of post-war boom and bust, led to a ten-fold increase in patients. Simultaneously, budgets were cut by state governments, staff became demoralized, and care reverted to custodial and penal practices of the 18th century (Luchins, 1988). Under these conditions, the patients became increasingly chronic, and the institutions became targets of political and professional criticism. First neurologists, then social workers, and finally psychologists attempted to convince state officials they had the answers to madness and insanity (Luchins, 1988).

The psychosocial model of schizophrenia essentially states that *schizophrenia* is the label we give to behaviors and experiences that reflect a human being under the most severe stress to which he or she can be exposed. In extreme conditions of combat, shelling, or prisoner of war or concentration camps, human beings who have never before experienced psychotic symptoms do so (Frankl, 1946/2006; Herman, 1995). Breggin (1994) called this *psychological overwhelm*. The experience is of being almost continuously terrified, with no way to stop the source of the terror from returning. Studies in stimulus and sleep deprivation have shown that high percentages of college student volunteers in such experiments begin to hallucinate. We also know that people who live at the bottom of the social ladder are always more prone to psychosis than individuals in the upper tiers (Read, 2010).

PSYCHOANALYTIC APPROACHES

Another important influence on the treatment of schizophrenia from outside of medicine is the diversification of psychoanalytic approaches and the spread of psychoanalysis to the rest of Europe, the United Kingdom, and the United States. Beginning with some of Freud's earliest followers, particularly the Hungarian Sandor Ferenzi (1873–1933), psychoanalytic thinkers explored the psychological meaning of psychotic symptoms (Fromm-Reichmann, 1950; Perry, 2005; Rosen, 1966; Sullivan, 1953/1968). They confirmed Manfred Bleuler's (1978) finding that up to two thirds of patients with schizophrenia make either a partial or full recovery and are able to live symptom-free and/or independently after a psychotic episode. The humanistic psychologist Carl Rogers, having served as the president of the American Psychological Association in 1960, also attempted to treat schizophrenics at Mendota State Hospital in Wisconsin with his approach to psychotherapy that emphasized empathy, positive regard, and authentic connection or genuineness. His student Gary Prouty (2003) continued to develop this into a more effective approach than the study had demonstrated. The psychoanalytic innovator Bertram Karon (Karon & VandenBos, 1981) demonstrated in clinical and research studies that intensive psychotherapy could be effective in producing a complete and permanent remission of symptoms in some patients and, in a controlled NIMH-sponsored study, showed that at 1- and 2-year follow-ups it was superior to hospital treatment with medication.

In the 1950s and 1960s, family therapy began to emerge as an innovative form of psychotherapy in which multiple family members were seen conjointly by a therapist or team of therapists. Murray Bowen (1991) and Carl Whitaker (1976) pioneered the application of this approach in clients with schizophrenic symptoms, and although the approach ran afoul of managed care restrictions in the United States in the 1980s, it has survived among those treating children and adolescents in the United States and has flourished in Western Lapland, Finland, where it has been incorporated into the Open Dialogue hospitalization prevention program for psychotic patients (Seikkula et al, 2011). Western Lapland now has the lowest rate of schizophrenia in the Western world, and as a result, within 2 years of first psychotic break, 80% of patients recover from schizophrenia without the need for ongoing medication. The program is based on humanistic, social-democratic values of community and the unwavering belief that symptoms are a response to a personal crisis of meaning. Once the meaning is discerned, the underlying interpersonal problems can be addressed with the cooperation of the family. The family therapy approach of encouraging open communication about topics that have been taboo in the family, and at the same time showing respect for all family members' beliefs and feelings, is critical to the success of the program (Seikkula et al., 2011).

In my doctoral education in clinical psychology and subsequent training and study over a period of 15 years of active participation in my profession, I had never encountered any information that schizophrenia could be so effectively treated through psychotherapeutic methods that individuals would completely recover. It was through the work of Bertram Karon that I first encountered this extraordinary proposition. What follows is Karon's most extensively reported and detailed published case study (Karon, 2008). It has been abbreviated by the author (R. Miller) and edited from the first to the third person to allow smoother transitions between the abbreviated sections of the case study. Except for this editing the case study appears with the permission of the author as it was written.

AN INCURABLE SCHIZOPHRENIC: THE CASE OF MR. X
BERTRAM P. KARON[1,2]

Dr. Karon is a Harvard graduate who took his PhD at Princeton University in the 1950s, studying under Silvan Tomkins, who pioneered the study of emotions as a legitimate topic for psychological research. Karon's clinical internship was at a hospital that specialized in treating with psycho-analytic therapy chronic schizophrenics who had previously failed to respond to treatment at the most prestigious and expensive psychiatric hospitals in the United States. He found he had an ability to work effectively with this population and published several early case studies based on this work. Subsequently, he worked as chief psychologist at a minimum-security reformatory for male adolescents and did a postdoctoral research fellowship at a more traditional

[1]From "An 'Incurable' Schizophrenic: The Case of Mr. X," by B. P. Karon, 2008, *Pragmatic Case Studies in Psychotherapy, 4*, pp. 1–24. Copyright 2008 by B. P. Karon. Adapted with permission.
[2]With the editorial assistance of Anmarie Widener, MA, MSW.

psychiatric hospital that practiced psychoanalytic therapy, supportive therapy, medication, and electroshock treatment, alone and in combination.

In 1962, Karon secured an academic appointment at Michigan State University in the psychology department and published a paper asserting that in treating acute schizophrenics, psychoanalytic therapy was the treatment of choice over either medication or electroconvulsive therapy (ECT), which were the widely accepted treatments of the day. Karon formulated a theory of schizophrenia as a chronic terror syndrome based on the individual's life history, including both perceived life experiences and fantasies (both conscious and unconscious) and the child's attempt to give life meaning in the context of these events and fantasies. The initial paper and his subsequent book, *Psychotherapy of Schizophrenia: The Treatment of Choice* (Karon & VandenBos, 1981), gave specific instructions on how to conduct such psychoanalytic psychotherapy with patients in extreme distress and included a discussion of relevant outcome research.

His early work with this population in Michigan was hampered by the general hostility to practicing clinical psychologists among physicians, psychiatrists, and psychiatric hospitals. Even the state university where he worked banned psychologists from practicing clinical psychology from their academic offices, on the grounds that it would be a form of socialized medicine.

The Referral and Framework

In 1963, Karon, who was now known at the university as a proponent of psychoanalytic treatment of schizophrenia, was approached by a graduate student in experimental psychology who was concerned about his friend, a university professor ("Mr. X") who had been recently hospitalized and appeared to be heading toward ECT. Karon advised against ECT and offered to speak with the man's wife, if she so desired.

The wife called and indicated that Mr. X had previously been treated for several years as an outpatient with both therapy and medication, first in the Northeastern city where they had previously lived and then for a year locally since they moved to the Midwest. They had sought treatment from a well-respected psychiatrist, but her husband's condition deteriorated, his medication was increased, and he finally needed to be hospitalized. In the hospital, his medication was increased further and combined with new prescriptions, but he continued to deteriorate, at which point his wife was told by his psychiatrist and the hospital staff that he was an "incurable schizophrenic" and that the only hope was ECT, which probably would not cure him, but was the only treatment left to try.

On the basis of Karon's advice, the wife withdrew the permission for ECT, which was scheduled for the next morning, and withdrew him from the hospital, against medical advice. The staff warned her that she was "killing him" by removing him from their care. She took him to Karon's office immediately on discharge. He was not eating, he was not sleeping, he had trouble standing, and he was continuously hallucinating and largely incoherent.

Karon advised that Mr. X immediately stop all medications and start intensive psychoanalytic treatment—7 days the first week; 6 the second; a 5-day-a-week schedule for several months; then a 4-session-per-week regimen; and eventually, a regular 3-day-a-week schedule came to be the routine. After the third year, he was seen on a once-per-week basis. His wife and friends of the family took turns being with him for the first 2 months of treatment.

Karon allowed Mr. X or his wife to call him at any time, day or night, if there was an emergency, and this proved beneficial for Mr. X when he was having disturbing experiences. After one confidential session with his wife, all other discussions with her were described to Mr. X, though his own sessions were not discussed with her unless he chose to disclose the content of his sessions to her.

Following Freud's advice on technique, Karon rarely took notes during the sessions, because the note taking interfered with careful listening. Rather, he made notes after the session.

During the early months of outpatient psychoanalytic psychotherapy, two deans from the university asked Karon what could be done to help their psychotic faculty member and when he might be expected to return to work. In both instances Karon involved Mr. X in responding to the deans so as not to diminish Mr. X's status as a responsible person. Mr. X indicated that he thought he might not be ready to return to work the next term but would perhaps be ready for the one after that.

First Session and Initial Family Background

In the first hour of psychotherapy, when Karon asked the patient what he wanted help with, Mr. X said,

> I don't want to have this scared feeling, can't hold up straight. I don't know what it means to have tension in the head. I don't want to have to hang around my wife's apron strings. I can't leave her by a foot. I don't want to be nauseated when my wife steps out of the room.

Also in the first session, Karon commented to Mr. X something that he routinely found helpful to tell people having their first psychotic episode, but which most other people, including therapists, found inexplicable: "I won't kill you or let anyone else kill you." This was meant to acknowledge and address both the conscious and unconscious abject terror a person experiences in a psychotic episode. Karon noted that Mr. X "neither acted as if that were very helpful nor as if it were strange. Probably he did not believe me, but he did not say so."

The Client's Family Background

Gradually, as Mr. X became more coherent, his family history emerged. Mr. X was from an intact middle-class Jewish family consisting of his father, mother, and an older brother. He spoke highly of his parents, particularly his mother. As an adult, he could not remember his childhood before the second year of high school and did not think that odd.

He was not a religious person. His father had been treated with ECT some years earlier, and was disabled. His mother still worked. Neither of his parents had gone to college, but both he and his brother had. His brother was in business for himself. Mr. X had generally been more successful academically than his brother.

Anticipating the criticism that if Mr. X made a complete recovery, he could not have been a true schizophrenic and was more likely manic-depressive (or severely bipolar), Karon noted that at the time Mr. X was hospitalized, there was a clear consensus among the psychiatrists treating him that he was indeed schizophrenic in terms of the diagnostic criteria of the era, and that even at the time of publication he would have met *DSM–IV* (American Psychiatric Association, 1994) criteria for schizophrenia.

The Course of Therapy: Refusal to Eat

Because not eating can kill you in 30 days, Karon's treatment started with that symptom. The second session was at 7:00 a.m. at an all-night restaurant, the kind that looks like the men's room on the subway—all white tiles.

He said, "I can't go in there. They'll think I'm crazy."

"No," Karon responded, "They'll think you're drunk."

"I'll throw up."

"Do you think you're the first drunk who threw up here tonight?"

Karon discussed food, the fear of poisoning, and its possible origins while he (Karon) ate—most importantly that Mr. X's mother may have resented feeding him and, therefore, felt angry whenever she fed him, which hurts a child. This was interpreted symbolically: Poison, after all, is simply something you eat and you get hurt afterwards. For a baby, an angry mother is like being hit with a sledgehammer. The patient reported nausea while watching Karon eat. But by the second restaurant session, he took some coffee for himself. Then coffee and toast at the third session. Finally, he ate breakfast, but he objected, "I'm paying for therapy and all I do is watch you eat. I've got a right to be listened to!" At that point, they returned to the office for more traditional treatment.

Life History

Karon allowed family members, like spouses or parents, one confidential session; any other sessions, if they wish, or contacts would be discussed with the patient. He also makes himself available to spouses or parents for advice. In his initial talks with his wife, she told Karon they had met when they were both on Fulbright scholarships to Paris. They began living together. Karon got the impression of two very anxious young people clinging to each other. She said he was the most interesting man she ever met. She had finished a master's degree but stopped her education and was not currently working. She had grown up in the South and was, and felt she ought to be, a stay-at-home wife who was taking care of their 5-year-old son. She did mention that their son was an accident.

The patient had first taken a job at a prestigious small college, but socializing with the members of his department and other faculty and administrators seemed to be a required part of the job, and he found it uncomfortable. Taking a job at a larger research university seemed to them as if they would have more choice about their private lives and more privacy. Nonetheless, things did not go well. Karon suggested that since Mr. X was incapacitated, she needed to resume working. This advice was helpful: she actually resented not working, but did not say so at the time because this was the early 1960s, and she felt obliged to be a traditional wife and mother. Nonetheless, she got a job teaching high school and eventually finished a PhD and became a successful faculty member and assistant dean at a "Big Ten" research university. (It should be noted that she did go into psychoanalytic therapy herself before accomplishing these career moves.)

The details of Mr. X's life emerged in therapy, at first in fragments, later coherently. Mr. X described meeting his wife on the Fulbright in Paris. She was very bright and very attractive, but she was not Jewish. He had been told by someone she was "wild," but he did not know whether to believe it or not, and this still troubled him in the early years of the analysis. His mother literally told him, like the apocryphal Jewish mother stories, that he did not have to worry about the wedding because she would not be there. She would commit suicide. Right up to the day of the wedding, he was terrified that she would carry out her threat.

His previous experiences with women were not good. He both felt that he ought to be sexually active and attractive and, at the same time, any interest in sexuality or sexual activity was bad. He was intensely guilty about masturbating, feeling as many disturbed people do, that his body and his penis really did not belong to him. Karon told him that his parents were wrong, that his penis and his body belonged to him and that he had a right to enjoy them; his penis did not belong to his mother but to him.

The year before he went to Paris, he had been seeing a woman seriously and they took a trip to Mexico together. She met another man on the trip and had sex with the new man in the room next to his in the motel where he could hear them. This was repeated on several nights. He described his feelings of humiliation and, with Karon's help, rage.

At the beginning of treatment, he could not read, which is a serious problem for an academic, which needed to be helped before he could consider going back to work. Taking seriously the analytic writers who relate reading inhibition to a defense against learning about sexual matters (e.g., Fenichel, 1945), when he raised this issue, Karon decided to give him advice. "Don't try to read professional writings or even good literature. Forget about it for now. I want you to buy a copy of Playboy and try to read it, and we'll talk about your difficulties."

It turned out he had never read *Playboy*, and all his life had always read what was highly thought of. He protested his therapist's lousy taste and how awful the magazine was. Karon insisted Mr. X try to read it and talk about his difficulties, without explaining the choice of material. Within a few sessions, he was able to read it, while protesting all the while that it was a terrible, "pandering" magazine. While throughout the therapy, Karon always emphasized the importance of being able to think about anything, what seemed to make a difference was having an authority figure tell him to read sexy material, and being able to continually denounce it, and denounce the therapist's poor taste in suggesting it, and talk about the sexual ideas that came to mind. Karon responded by talking about the normality of sexual curiosity and interest. After being able to read one issue, Mr. X discovered he could read ordinary books and his professional reading without trouble.

Memories of Childhood

As they worked, Mr. X recalled more of his childhood. His mother, whom he idealized, used to dress him in white clothes when he was around five years old and send him out to play and then punish him for getting dirty. He felt that was all right because it was his fault. Of course, any parent knows that if you put a little boy in all white clothes in a hermetically sealed room, he would still manage to get dirty in half an hour or less. Karon pointed out how his mother set Mr. X up for this, that any child would get dirty, and that she probably enjoyed punishing him. He got mad at Karon, as most patients do when a therapist makes uncharitable comments about a client's parents. They often defend their parents by admitting defects that they earlier denied but which are less derogatory than the therapist's suggestions; at which point, Karon usually tells them they are right and he is wrong, unless they leave out something that is not speculation, but facts that they already know.

Although the patient and his family were Jewish, they lived in an Italian neighborhood in New York City. His mother, ostensibly for his safety, told him to go out and play, but not to play with those Italian kids because they are very dangerous. Of course, in an Italian neighborhood in New York City all the kids are Italian, and this advice prevented him from having friends.

All his life, he had wanted his parents' approval, and made extraordinary efforts to gain it, but nothing was enough. His parents continually cut him and his brother down. His older brother was a businessman, and when they talked to his brother, the parents talked about how brilliant Mr. X was and, when Mr. X published, what he had published. When his parents talked to Mr. X, they only talked about how much money his brother made and how little he did. Of course, his parents were neither brilliant nor wealthy, but they could always make him feel inadequate instead of feeling inadequate themselves. It was necessary to point out that both he and his brother were unusually bright and competent, but that time is limited and there is not time enough to do everything. If you decide to become a businessman, you are not going to write or get a PhD. If you become an academic you will write and get a PhD, but you're not going to make a lot of money. There just isn't time to do everything, but to do either one is an achievement.

This is particularly relevant because his psychotic break came when he finished his PhD. He had the fantasy that this would finally earn him the love and respect of his parents. He started teaching while completing his dissertation. When he finally finished, he was given a promotion, a raise, and tenure. He had finally done it. He called his parents to tell them the good news. They did not react. His father only asked him how much he was making. He told them he was getting a raise. Their response was that they were telling people he made more than that already.

From that point, his defenses unraveled until he was finally psychotic. Medication could not replace the triumph through acceptance that never would be. One of his initial terrifying hallucinations was burning in hell. This was not a verbal or abstract thought, nor a fear of eventual punishment. It was a horrible and apparently real experience. The friend who had first referred him for treatment asked Karon if Mr. X had ever talked about the scar on his hand and suggested that Karon ask him about it. When he asked the patient whether he had a scar on his hand, he indicated that he did, and there was a story his mother told about the scar. According to her, they were in a store when he was 5. She saw him with a toy in his hand, and asked him where he had gotten it. He said a lady had given it to him. She asked the lady, who had not given it to him. His mother made him put it back and apologize to the lady. Then she took him by the hand, walked him home (four or five blocks), up the stairs to the third floor to their apartment, turned on a gas burner, and held his hand in the burner to teach him not to steal. The burn left a permanent scar. However, he maintained that it had no effect on him because he could not remember it. Karon told him that he had a different opinion, that what you cannot remember has the most profound effect on you. Karon added further, "Most of us can only imagine what it would be like to burn in Hell. But you've actually been there." Even correct interpretations do not always lead to dramatic improvement. This one did. His hallucination of burning in hell disappeared after that session.

Early Progress

Early in his treatment, as Mr. X began to improve, he began to interact with people again. However, at a social gathering a physician told him that he was killing himself by seeing a psychologist, and that he should stop immediately and see a psychiatrist if he wanted to get any help at all. This set him back abruptly. His symptoms got considerably worse, and we had to spend weeks to work through the meaning of this encounter and the feelings of inevitable doom it produced, relating it not only to the present situation and the physician's lack of knowledge, but to the bad advice his mother regularly gave him, and that he needed to learn to trust his own experience, especially his own experience with people outside the family. Interestingly enough, a year later that physician developed a psychotic depression and called for help to a psychoanalytic psychiatrist in New York, who then referred the physician to the Chair of Psychiatry at the best medical school in the state, who then made a referral to a psychologist in the local area. The Chair said that he did not like referring to psychologists, but this one had done her internship in his department and was a remarkable therapist and the only professional in our local area he would trust. This psychologist, who for personal reasons was at that time confining her practice to evaluations, in turn referred the physician to Karon. The physician recovered with therapy. Karon resisted with difficulty the temptation to tell the physician how destructive that conversation had been to Mr. X, or even to mention that he (Karon) knew of that conversation. (Of course, Karon did not mention the physician's symptoms or treatment to Mr. X.)

When it was time for the patient to go back to work, 6 months after he began treatment, it was possible to schedule an appointment just before his first class. Needless to say he was scared, but they talked about it. Karon then walked Mr. X to his class, and waited outside the classroom until it was over. He said, "It was OK," and Karon left and saw him at his next appointment the next day. Several months later he reported that his colleagues said to him, "You're not still seeing that guy, are you? You're the healthiest guy in this department." After recounting this interchange, Mr. X said to Karon, "You know how sick I am."

On hearing this Karon responded, "Yes, I know how sick you are, but they may be right anyway."

Even though he never kept his hospitalization or diagnosis or psycho-analytic treatment a secret, he was offered the chairmanship of his department several times in the ensuing years. He turned it down each time because he would have rather been a scholar than an administrator. He also had an extremely helpful effect on students. "You don't have to suffer like that," he told students with problems, "There are competent people out there who can help you. I know. I really know. I was schizophrenic." They did not believe he was ever schizophrenic, but he assured them he was and added, "If I could get help, you can get help."

A year after treatment began, Karon could say to him: "Anyone can go crazy under enough stress, but under the stresses of ordinary life, you will never be psychotic again." Mr. X said, "This is better than I have ever been, better than what I used to call normality, but if you think this is good enough for me, you're crazy." This patient continued in psychotherapy for 14 years, although it was on a once-per-week basis after the third year. He kept raising new issues.

The Move Toward Traditional Psychoanalytic Psychotherapy With Broadening Interests

At this point, Karon began working psychoanalytically with Mr. X on the problems in living that most of us who are not incapacitated by psy-chotic symptoms experience. This part of the case makes fascinating reading in understanding the process of psychoanalytic psychotherapy with neurotic and interpersonal problems, and can be found in the original source (Karon, 2008). Briefly summarized here are the topics Karon covered with Mr. X in the remaining 14 years of his psychodynamic psychotherapy: (a) writer's block at work; (b) feelings of guilt when he allowed himself enjoyment of any kind, including music and playing the piano; (c) occasional psycho-somatic symptoms and rare but frightening hallucinations; (d) adaptation to a heart attack; (e) marital problems and his wife's breast cancer, surgery, and complications of the surgery; (f) fear of his wife's surgical scars, a subsequent affair, and his fear of castration; and (g) reconciliation with his son whom he had neglected during his psychotic period, his subsequent heart attack, his wife's cancer, and the period of the affair.

In dealing with each of these issues in psychoanalytic psychotherapy, the client was ultimately successful. He wrote a book that became a classic in his field; he recovered from the psychosomatic symptoms and his heart attack, and the hallucinations faded away. He and his wife reconciled, and he developed a good relationship with his teenage son who graduated from college, married, and was delighted to provide his parents with a grandson. Granted, along the way Karon stumbled a bit in attempting to treat Mr. X's spouse in separate individual therapy, and he sought consultation for how to extricate himself from the situation, which he then did successfully. In his workshops and writing he has freely admitted when he does not understand a client's symptoms and that he is open to seeking consultation from colleagues in the field. Karon summarized the outcome of the case as follows:

> The patient is now internationally renowned in his field. He is an outstanding scholar and teacher, as well as a good husband and father. His therapy did not make him a bright man or a kind man, but it did keep his brightness and kindness from being destroyed. It did allow him to feel safe, perceive and think realistically and creatively, and use his intelligence and kindness to make his own and other people's lives more interesting.
>
> A few years ago (more than 20 years after the completion of treatment) the patient sent me a copy of a magazine article about a prestigious award that he had received, with a note saying that he had never properly thanked me for giving him back a life. Remembering the role of his parents never acknowledging his achievements had in producing his problems, I wrote back that, "From time to time I have heard from people in your field about your accomplishments and from your students about your teaching, and it has always been a source of satisfaction that I was available when you needed me."

AFTERWORD

Karon's (2008) case of Mr. X is astounding in a number of respects: A person regarded as an "incurable schizophrenic" by respected community psychiatrists is indeed "cured"; there is a 20-year follow-up demonstrating that Mr. X continued to thrive subsequent to the termination of treatment; and the success was achieved without the use of antipsychotic medication. Although there are numerous reports of both case studies and empirically informed research of similar successes from many different sources both in the United States and Europe (going back to the Quakers in York, England, in the late 18th century), undergraduate and graduate departments in clinical psychology, nursing, medicine, psychiatry, social work, and counseling continue to teach that schizophrenia is an incurable disorder, with antipsychotic medication the treatment of choice for managing its symptoms.

In the context of the earlier chapters of this book that covered other forms of psychological suffering commonly referred to as anxiety, depression, internalizing and externalizing childhood disorders, and personality disorders,

http://dx.doi.org/10.1037/14693-009
Not So Abnormal Psychology: A Pragmatic View of Mental Illness, by R. B. Miller

Karon's work with Mr. X is impressive, but not quite so astounding. We have seen in both extensive case reports and cited empirical literature evidence of remarkable improvements in difficult cases in which psychotropic medications were not used. This included cases of young children, college students, and middle-aged individuals with diagnoses that often prove unresponsive to treatment (including posttraumatic stress disorder, autism, severe antisocial personality, narcissistic personality, oppositional defiant disorder, and extreme separation anxiety). When psychotherapists understand and treat symptoms not as physical illnesses and disorders, but instead as the client's attempt to cope with unbearable life circumstances, symptoms tend to gradually abate, and healthy development is more likely to ensue. In the present climate dominated by the biomedical (and to a lesser extent the cognitive–behavioral) model, these cases seem as though they must be either random outliers or miraculous cures beyond rational explanation. Particularly when we encounter intense psychological suffering, we are often in the realm of the mysteries of human existence, and claims to certain knowledge should be met with skepticism. Yet there are a number of psychological principles that tie together the disparate cases that are described in detail in the preceding chapters and that suggest that there is a coherent and pragmatic way of understanding and working with these forms of psychological suffering.

PRINCIPLE ONE: THE SEARCH FOR SELF-UNDERSTANDING IS PARAMOUNT

Once we understand ourselves, even if that self-understanding involves seeing clearly harsh realities we have attempted to avoid, we are able to use this new information to accept ourselves, make more realistic decisions, and gain a sense of control over our lives. When we are denied actionable knowledge and understanding of our world, our sense of anxiety, powerlessness, hopelessness, and anger are greatly increased. The experience is like seeing the pieces of a puzzle fall into place once a missing element that was concealed is discovered. Having all the relevant information changes not only how one appreciates that single piece of information but ultimately also one's understanding of all of the other pieces.

PRINCIPLE TWO: RECOGNIZE THE UBIQUITY OF HUMAN SUFFERING

Human existence is perilous, with opportunities for great joy and great sorrow. Even when living in an idyllic environment, the unpredictability of human health and sudden death gives rise to tremendous anxieties.

Regrettably, few of us live in idyllic environments. For some, families can at times be a refuge from such suffering, but although they expand our opportunities for love and support, they can also be sources of great conflict and inevitable losses. Our larger communities, whether geographical, religious, occupational, or recreational, all extend our sense of belonging, connectedness, influence, or even power, while also expanding our vulnerability to conflict, loss, displacement, and even violence. Complex modern societies offer many advantages for the individual in terms of personal freedom, geographic and job mobility, education, and social networks. Yet there are also the inescapable increased anxieties from greater exposure to potential trauma, stress, and conflict. It is no wonder that we have seen an exponential growth in mental health services of all kinds, public and private, for adults and children, individuals and couples or families, medical and psychotherapeutic.

So too is the process of human development bittersweet as we move through the phases of life from infancy to old age. Gradual and sudden shifts in both our capabilities and environmental demands keep us challenged, stimulated, and at times overwhelmed. When these stresses come in bunches or cascade into one another, life can seem unbearable. The experience of unbearable suffering is not a sign that we are weak or have failed; rather, it is a sign of the inevitable challenges of human development and the inevitable interpersonal and intrapersonal conflicts of everyday life.

PRINCIPLE THREE: HUMAN ACTIONS ARE LADEN WITH MEANING, PURPOSE, AND INTENTION

A not so abnormal psychology begins with the assumption that all thought, emotion, and action, whether "symptomatic" or not, carry meaning and serve the goals and purposes of the individual. These meanings, purposes, and reasons are seen as the bedrock of human understanding. Human action at times also reflects concern with the ultimate goals and meaning of life in the spiritual, existential, or metaphysical realm.

When the actions of another human being seem bizarre, irrational, childish, incomprehensible, or "sick"—that is, without meaning—it is as much our own failure to understand the world of the other as it is the other's failure to understand what to do or how to act. This is not to say that scientific approaches do not also have a place in assisting us in understanding a person's physiological reactions to stress, trauma, and loss. But there are other important vantage points that can help to clarify perplexing human actions. The search for meaning and understanding consists of highly personal, subjective, even private experiences and often reflects aspects of ourselves that we have great difficulty articulating to others or even to ourselves.

Somewhat paradoxically, we require authentic, open and safe dialogue with another person to make this realm of our existence coherent and manageable. It is in this dialogue that we can begin to unravel the defense mechanisms our unconscious mind has mobilized to contain the unbearable pain and anguish from earlier experiences in our lives. It is these defense mechanisms that both helped us to survive in the past, and now keep us a confusing mystery to others and even ourselves. To be effective, defense mechanisms must also be convincing. We can, without realizing it, cry tears to hide our rage, or express rage to hide our intense feeling of vulnerability to fear or loss. We can convince ourselves that we actually want to do something we really despise doing, only to find ourselves mysteriously bungling our attempt to do it. Armed with the understanding of defense mechanisms we are able to make sense out of what would otherwise seem to be the senseless, meaningless, actions of ourselves or others.

PRINCIPLE FOUR: APPRECIATE THE PRESENCE OF A SAFE GUIDE

By the time most of us seek help with our own psychological suffering, we are feeling raw, confused, and vulnerable. In that emotional and cognitive state, we are not likely to risk encountering the painful source of our problems unless those offering help do so in a manner that is (a) compassionate, respectful, kind, and loving (in the sense of *agape*—love for humanity) and (b) informed by sufficient understanding of psychological suffering in her- or himself and other people. Both the ability to form such a relationship and the ability to guide the search for psychological self-understanding must be present.

Being such a psychotherapeutic guide is labor-intensive and difficult work. Such a guide must carry hope for us even if we have mostly given up having any hope for ourselves; a guide must understand that life-transforming change can be a painstakingly slow and uneven process. It may be that for extended periods the positive changes are almost imperceptible to another person or that periods of positive change are followed by backsliding. In these periods the guide is often being tested to see whether she or he will abandon the client when times get tough.

It is often claimed that because of the more long-term nature of this work, it is not cost-effective. This seems obviously true, but only if one considers short-term benefits. Numerous sources cited in Chapters 6, 7, and 8 have demonstrated that in complex, difficult cases of depression, personality disorder, and schizophrenia, the long-term outcome of relation-based psychotherapy is just as cost-effective, or more cost-effective, than treatment that merely attempts to manage symptoms with medication over a lifetime, with no promise of recovery.

Participating in such a process of self-discovery and self-understanding is a deeply moving process for not only the client but also for the mental health professional. It gives great meaning to one's work and contributes to the possibility of a lifelong career in which one is always learning and growing as both a professional and as a human being.

PRINCIPLE FIVE: WHEN IN DOUBT, BE A JAMESIAN PRAGMATIST

In the realm of human affairs, difficult life choices, confusing relationships, and existential nightmares, there are always friends, family, and experts who have conflicting visions of what we should think, feel, or do to make our lives better. In the end we must decide which intuitive psychotherapist, body of controversial research, received wisdom, or gut feeling we will listen to. I take the message of William James's pragmatism to be a rather simple but profound idea that we must always be guided by our practical experience in implementing any idea. If one cannot decide on a big decision, one must take a small step in one direction and carefully observe its consequences. Does such a step shift one's immediate environment in a positive or negative direction? Does one feel steadier—more grounded—after taking such a step or more shaky and vulnerable? Does what seemed like the right thing to do now feel empty or tawdry? Does it feel like one has made a small dent in making the world a better place or as though one is now feeling slimy and ashamed? Many of these questions are questions about us as moral agents, people who feel better and more whole when we know we are acting for good in the world—our own world and the world we share with others.

If the answers to these questions after this first small step are mostly positive, we take another step in the same direction. If the answers to our questions come back in a negative direction, we must learn from our mistakes and try a new direction. Pragmatism is an iterative and self-corrective process of seeing what difference it makes to believe one idea or another. It is an inductive process of learning from our own experience. This is true whether the idea is about whether to change the sweater we are wearing out to dinner, change the time of a meeting with a friend, change our view of the trustworthiness of a partner, or change the direction of our lives. There are no certain answers, but through a process of trial and error that is carefully monitored for results, answers can be found. Over time we learn inductively which of our intuitive feelings are more or less trustworthy and which of our judgments of other people and situations are more or less accurate, and we make more trials with less error. In the process, we reach a degree of self-understanding that allows us to make a life for ourselves that is meaningful and fulfilling and at times even transformative.

REFERENCES

Aanstoos, C. M. (2012). A phenomenology of sexual experiencing. In P. J. Kleinplatz (Ed.), *New directions in sex therapy: Innovations and alternatives, Second Edition* (pp. 51–67). New York, NY: Routledge/Taylor & Francis Group.

Abbass, A., Sheldon, A., Gyra, J., & Kalpin, A. (2008). Intensive short-term dynamic psychotherapy for *DSM–IV* personality disorders: A randomized controlled trial. *Journal of Nervous and Mental Disease, 196,* 211–216. http://dx.doi.org/10.1097/NMD.0b013e3181662ff0

Achenbach, T. M. (1992). Developmental psychopathology. In M. H. Bornstein & M. E. Lamb (Eds.), *Developmental psychology: An advanced text* (3rd ed., 629–676). Hillsdale, NJ: Erlbaum.

Adler, A. (1959). *Understanding human nature.* New York, NY: Premier Books.

Ainsworth, M. D. (1969). Object relations, dependency, and attachment: A theoretical review of the infant–mother relationship. *Child Development, 40,* 969–1025. http://dx.doi.org/10.2307/1127008

Albee, G. W., & Joffe, J. M. (2004). Mental illness is NOT "an illness like any other." *The Journal of Primary Prevention, 24,* 419–436. http://dx.doi.org/10.1023/B:JOPP.0000024799.04666.8b

Alcoholics Anonymous. (2014). *A.A. Fact File.* Retrieved from http://www.aa.org/pdf/products/m-24_aafactfile.pdf

Allport, G. W. (1937). *Personality: A psychological interpretation.* Oxford, England: Holt.

American Psychiatric Association. (1968). *Diagnostic and statistical manual of mental disorders* (2nd ed.). Washington, DC: Author.

American Psychiatric Association. (1980). *Diagnostic and statistical manual of mental disorders* (3rd ed.). Washington, DC: Author.

American Psychiatric Association. (1994). *Diagnostic and statistical manual of mental disorders* (4th ed.). Washington, DC: Author.

American Psychiatric Association. (2013). *Diagnostic and statistical manual of mental disorders* (5th ed.). Washington, DC: Author.

Angel, M. (2005). *The truth about the drug companies.* New York, NY: Random House.

Anonymous. (2001). *Alcoholics anonymous: The story of how many thousands of men and women have recovered from alcoholism.* New York, NY: A.A. World Services.

Arons, M. (1993). Philosophy, psychology and the moral crisis: Reflections on compassion, "between tradition and another beginning." *The Humanistic Psychologist, 21,* 296–324. http://dx.doi.org/10.1080/08873267.1993.9976925

Baldessarini, R. J., Tondo, L., & Viguera, A. C. (1999). Discontinuing lithium maintenance treatment in bipolar disorders: Risks and Implications. *Bipolar Disorders, 1,* 17–24.

Banaschewski, T., Becker, K., Scherag, S., Franke, B., & Coghill, D. (2010). Molecular genetics of attention-deficit/hyperactivity disorder: An overview. *European Child & Adolescent Psychiatry, 19*, 237–257. http://dx.doi.org/10.1007/s00787-010-0090-z

Bandura, A. (1969). *Principles of behavior modification*. New York: Holt, Rinehart and Winston.

Barlow, D. H. (2004). Psychological Treatments. *American Psychologist, 59*, 869–878.

Barrett, C. L., Hampe, I. E., & Miller, L. (1978). Research on psychotherapy with children. In S. L. Garfield & A. E. Bergin (Eds.), *Handbook of psychotherapy and behavior change: An empirical analysis* (pp. 411–435). New York, NY: Wiley.

Bateson, G., Jackson, D. D., Haley, J., & Weakland, J. (1956). Toward a theory of schizophrenia. *Behavioral Science, 1*, 251–264. http://dx.doi.org/10.1002/bs.3830010402

Baumrind, D. (1991). Effective parenting during the early adolescent transition. In P. A. Cowan & E. M. Hetherington (Eds.), *Advances in family research* (Vol. 2, pp. 111–163). Hillsdale, NJ: Erlbaum.

Beck, A. T. (1991). Cognitive therapy: A 30-year retrospective. *American Psychologist, 46*, 368–375. http://dx.doi.org/10.1037/0003-066X.46.4.368

Beck, A. T., Ward, C. H., Mendelson, M., Mock, J., & Erbaugh, J. (1961). An inventory for measuring depression. *Archives of General Psychiatry, 4*, 561–571. http://dx.doi.org/10.1001/archpsyc.1961.01710120031004

Beck, J. (2011). *Cognitive behavior therapy: Basics and beyond*. New York, NY: Guilford Press.

Belsky, J., Bakermans-Kranenburg, M., & van IJzendoorn, M. H. (2007). For better and for worse: Differential susceptibility to environmental influences. *Current Directions in Psychological Science, 16*, 300–304. http://dx.doi.org/10.1111/j.1467-8721.2007.00525.x

Benton, S. A., Robertson, J. M., Tseng, W., Newton, F. B., & Benton, S. L. (2003). Changes in counseling center client problems across 13 years. *Professional Psychology: Research and Practice, 34*, 66–72. http://dx.doi.org/10.1037/0735-7028.34.1.66

Bergin, A. E., & Garfield, S. L. (1971). *Handbook of psychotherapy and behavior change: An empirical analysis*. New York, NY: Wiley.

Biglan, A., Flay, B. R., Embry, D. D., & Sandler, I. N. (2012). The critical role of nurturing environments for promoting human well-being. *American Psychologist, 67*, 257–271. http://dx.doi.org/10.1037/a0026796

Black, S. A., Gallaway, M. S., Bell, M. R., & Ritchie, E. C. (2011). Prevalence and risk factors associated with suicides of army soldiers 2001–2009. *Military Psychology, 23*, 433–451. http://dx.doi.org/10.1037/h0094766

Blanck, G., & Blanck, R. (1994). *Ego psychology: Theory and Practice* (2nd ed.). New York, NY: Columbia University Press.

Bland, H. W., Melton, B. F., Welle, P., & Bigham, L. (2012). Stress tolerance: New challenges for millennial college students. *College Student Journal, 46*, 362–375. Retrieved from http://search.ebscohost.com/login.aspx?direct=true&db=psyh&AN=2012-19556-013&site=ehost-live&scope=site

Blatt, S. J. (2004). *Experiences of depression: Theoretical, clinical, and research perspectives*. Washington, DC: American Psychological Association. http://dx.doi.org/10.1037/10749-000

Blaxill, M. F. (2004). What's going on? The question of time trends in autism. *Public Health Reports, 119*, 536–551.

Bleuler, M. (1978). *The schizophrenic disorders: Long-term patient and family studies*. New Haven, CT: Yale University Press.

Block, J. H., & Block, J. (1980). The role of ego-control and ego-resiliency in the organization of behavior. In W. A. Collins (Ed.), *Development of cognition, affect, and social relations: The Minnesota symposia on child psychology* (Vol. 13, pp. 39–101). Hillsdale, NJ: Erlbaum.

Bohart, A., & Watson, J. (2011). Person centered/experiential therapies. In S. B. Messer & A. S. Gurman (Eds.), *Essential psychotherapies: Theory and practice* (pp. 223–260). New York, NY: Guilford Press.

Bonnie, R. J. (2002). Political abuse of psychiatry in the Soviet Union and in China: Complexities and controversies. *The Journal of the American Academy of Psychiatry and the Law, 30*, 136–144.

Boulind, M., & Edwards, D. (2008). The assessment and treatment of post-abortion syndrome: A systematic case study from southern Africa. *Journal of Psychology in Africa, 18*, 539–548.

Bowen, M. (1991). *Family therapy in clinical practice*. New York, NY: Jason Aronson.

Bowlby, J. (1969). *Attachment and loss: Vol. 1. Attachment*. New York, NY: Basic Books.

Bratton, S. C., Ray, D., Rhine, T., & Jones, L. (2005). The efficacy of play therapy with children: A meta-analytic review of treatment outcomes. *Professional Psychology: Research and Practice, 36*, 376–390. http://dx.doi.org/10.1037/0735-7028.36.4.376

Breggin, P. (1994). *Toxic psychiatry: Why therapy, empathy and love must replace the drugs, electroshock, and biochemical theories of the "new psychiatry."* London, England: St. Martin's Griffin.

Breggin, P. R., & Cohen, D. (2007). *Your drug may be your problem: How and why to stop taking psychiatric medications* (2nd ed.). Cambridge, MA: Perseus Books.

Bruch, H. (2001). *The golden cage: The enigma of anorexia nervosa*. Cambridge, MA: Harvard University Press. (Original work published 1978)

Bühler, C., & Massarik, F., (Eds.). (1968). *The course of human life: A study of goals in the humanistic perspective*. New York, NY: Springer.

Burston, D., & Frie, R. (2006). *Psychotherapy as a human science*. Pittsburgh, PA: Duquesne University Press.

Butcher, J. N., Dahlstrom, W. G., Graham, J. R., Tellegen, A., & Kaemmer, B. (1989). *Manual for the restandardized Minnesota Multiphasic Personality Inventory: MMPI–2.* Minneapolis: University of Minnesota Press.

Button, K. S., Ioannidis, J. P. A., Mokrysz, C., Nosek, B. A., Flint, J., Robinson, E. S. J., & Munafò, M. R. (2013). Power failure: Why small sample size undermines the reliability of neuroscience. *Nature Reviews Neuroscience, 14,* 365–376. http://dx.doi.org/10.1038/nrn3475

Calisto, V., & Esteves, V. I. (2009). Psychiatric pharmaceuticals in the environment. *Chemosphere, 77,* 1257–1274. http://dx.doi.org/10.1016/j.chemosphere.2009.09.021

Casey, R. J., & Berman, J. S. (1985). The outcome of psychotherapy with children. *Psychological Bulletin, 98,* 388–400. http://dx.doi.org/10.1037/0033-2909.98.2.388

Caspi, A., Sugden, K., Moffitt, T. E., Taylor, A., Craig, I. W., Harrington, H., . . . Poulton, R. (2003). Influence of life stress on depression: Moderation by a polymorphism in the 5-HTT gene. *Science, 301,* 386–389. http://dx.doi.org/10.1126/science.1083968

Centers for Disease Control and Prevention. (2014). Attention-deficit/hyperactivity disorder (ADHD): Data and statistics. http://www.cdc.gov/ncbddd/adhd/data.html

Chessick, R. D. (1993). The outpatient psychotherapy of the borderline patient. *American Journal of Psychotherapy, 47,* 206–227.

Christopher, J. (2006). Hermeneutics and the moral dimension of psychotherapy. In L. Hoshmand (Ed.), *Culture, psychotherapy, and counseling: Critical and integrative perspectives* (pp. 179–204). Thousand Oaks, CA: Sage. http://dx.doi.org/10.4135/9781483328942.n9

Christopher, J. C., Wendt, D. C., Marecek, J., & Goodman, D. M. (2014). Critical cultural awareness: Contributions to a globalizing psychology. *American Psychologist, 69,* 645–655. http://dx.doi.org/10.1037/a0036851

Churchill, S. D. (2006). Phenomenological analysis: Impression formation during a clinical assessment interview. In C. T. Fischer (Ed.), *Qualitative research methods for psychologists: Introduction through empirical studies* (pp. 79–110). San Diego, CA: Elsevier Academic Press. http://dx.doi.org/10.1016/B978-012088470-4/50007-7

Cohen, D. (2010). Psychopharmacology and clinical social work practice. In J. R. Brandell (Ed.), *Theory and practice of clinical social work* (2nd ed., pp. 763–810). Newbury Park, CA: Sage.

Collins, C., Hewson, D. L., Munger, R., & Wade, T. (2010). *Evolving models of behavioral health integration in primary care.* New York, NY: Milbank Memorial Fund.

Conners, C. K., Sitarenios, G., Parker, J. D., & Epstein, J. N. (1998). The revised Conners' Parent Rating Scale (CPRS–R): Factor structure, reliability, and criterion validity. *Journal of Abnormal Child Psychology, 26,* 257–268. http://dx.doi.org/10.1023/A:1022602400621

Cooper, S. E. (2014). *DSM–5, ICD–10, ICD–11*, the psychodynamic diagnostic manual, and person-centered integrative diagnosis: An overview for college mental health therapists. *Journal of College Student Psychotherapy, 28*, 201–217. http://dx.doi.org/10.1080/87568225.2014.914828

Corrigan, P. W., Morris, S. B., Michaels, P. J., Rafacz, J. D., & Rüsch, N. (2012). Challenging the public stigma of mental illness: A meta-analysis of outcome studies. *Psychiatric Services, 63*, 963–973. http://dx.doi.org/10.1176/appi.ps.201100529

Costa, P. T., Jr., & McRae, R. R. (1988). From catalogue to classification: Murray's needs and the five-factor model. *Journal of Personality and Social Psychology, 55*, 258–265. http://dx.doi.org/10.1037/0022-3514.55.2.258

Costa, P. T., Jr., & VandenBos, G. R. (Eds.). (1996). *Psychological aspects of serious illness: Chronic conditions, fatal diseases, and clinical care*. Washington, DC: American Psychological Association. http://dx.doi.org/10.1037/10076-000

Couprie, W., Wijdicks, E. F. M., Rooijmans, H. G., & van Gijn, J. (1995). Outcome in conversion disorder: A follow up study. *Journal of Neurology, Neurosurgery & Psychiatry, 58*, 750–752. http://dx.doi.org/10.1136/jnnp.58.6.750

Cushman, P. (1996). *Constructing the self, constructing America: A cultural history of psychotherapy*. Reading, MA: Addison-Wesley/Addison Wesley Longman.

Dattilio, F. M., Edwards, D. J. A., & Fishman, D. B. (2010). Case studies within a mixed methods paradigm: Toward a resolution of the alienation between researcher and practitioner in psychotherapy research. *Psychotherapy: Theory, Research, Practice, Training, 47*, 427–441. http://dx.doi.org/10.1037/a0021181

Davanloo, H. (2001). *Intensive short-term dynamic psychotherapy: Selected papers of Habib Davanloo*. Chichester, England: Wiley.

Davies, N. (1994, March 1). The mad world of Parkhurst Prison. *The Guardian*. Retrieved from http://www.nickdavies.net/1994/03/01/the-mad-world-of-parkhurst-prison/

Day, P. (2008). *A new history of social welfare* (6th ed.). New York, NY: Pearson.

Della Selva, P. C. (1996). *Intensive short-term dynamic psychotherapy: Theory and technique*. Oxford, England: Wiley.

Derobertis, E. M. (2006). Charlotte Bühler's existential–humanistic contributions to child and adolescent psychology. *Journal of Humanistic Psychology, 46*, 48–76. http://dx.doi.org/10.1177/0022167805277116

Dickstein, D. P., Pescosolido, M. F., Reidy, B. L., Galvan, T., Kim, K. L., Seymour, K. E., . . . Barrett, R. P. (2013). Developmental meta-analysis of the functional neural correlates of autism spectrum disorders. *Journal of the American Academy of Child & Adolescent Psychiatry, 52*, 279–289. http://dx.doi.org/10.1016/j.jaac.2012.12.012.

Dilalla, L. F., Kagan, J., & Reznick, J. S. (1994). Genetic etiology of behavioral inhibition among 2-year-old children. *Infant Behavior & Development, 17*, 405–412. http://dx.doi.org/10.1016/0163-6383(94)90032-9

Duncan, L. E., & Keller, M. C. (2011). A critical review of the first 10 years of candidate gene-by-environment interaction research in psychiatry. *The American Journal of Psychiatry*, 168, 1041–1049. http://dx.doi.org/10.1176/appi.ajp.2011.11020191

Eagle, Morris, N. (1989). *Recent developments in psychoanalysis: A critical evaluation*. Cambridge, MA: Harvard University Press.

Edvardsen, J., Torgersen, S., Røysamb, E., Lygren, S., Skre, I., Onstad, S., & Øien, P. A. (2009). Unipolar depressive disorders have a common genotype. *Journal of Affective Disorders*, 117, 30–41. http://dx.doi.org/10.1016/j.jad.2008.12.004

Edwards, D. A. (1998). Types of case study work: A conceptual framework for case-based research. *Journal of Humanistic Psychology*, 38, 36–70. http://dx.doi.org/10.1177/00221678980383003

Edwards, D. A. (2009). Treating posttraumatic stress disorder in South Africa: An integrative model grounded in case-based research. *Journal of Psychology in Africa*, 19, 189–198.

Eells, T. D. (2007). Generating and generalizing knowledge about psychotherapy from *Pragmatic Case Studies*. *Pragmatic Case Studies in Psychotherapy*, 3, 35–54. http://dx.doi.org/10.14713/pcsp.v3i1.893

Eley, T. C., & Gregory, A. M. (2004). Behavioral genetics. In T. L. Morris & J. S. March (Eds.), *Anxiety disorder in children and adolescents* (2nd ed., pp. 71–97). New York, NY: Guilford Press.

Elkins, D. N. (2012, August). A brief history of the recent *DSM–5* effort. In Brent D. Robbins (Chair), The *DSM–5* controversy. President's symposium conducted at the APA Annual Convention, Orlando, FL.

Ellenberger, H. F. (1974). Psychiatry from ancient to modern times. In S. Arieti (Ed.), *American handbook of psychiatry* (2nd ed., Vol. 1, pp. 3–27). New York, NY: Basic Books.

Elliott, R., Greenberg, L. S., & Lietaer, G. (2004). Research on experiential psychotherapies. In M. J. Lambert (Ed.), *Bergin and Garfield's handbook of psychotherapy and change* (5th ed., pp. 493–539). New York, NY: Wiley.

Engel, G. L. (1977). The need for a new medical model: A challenge for biomedicine. *Science*, 196, 129–136. http://dx.doi.org/10.1126/science.847460

Eppel, A. B. (2013). Paradigms lost and the structure of psychiatric revolutions. *Australian and New Zealand Journal of Psychiatry*, 47, 992–994. http://dx.doi.org/10.1177/0004867413492222

Erickson, M., Rossi, L., & Rossi, S. I. (1976). *Hypnotic realities: The induction of clinical hypnosis and forms of indirect suggestion*. New York, NY: Irvington.

Erikson, E. (1963). *Childhood and society* (2nd ed.). New York, NY: Norton.

Evans, R. I. (1975). *Carl Rogers: The man and his ideas*. New York, NY: Dutton.

Exner, J. E. (1993). *The Rorschach: A comprehensive system: Vol. 1. Basic foundations* (3rd ed.). New York, NY: Wiley.

Eysenck, H. J. (1952). The effects of psychotherapy: An evaluation. *Journal of Consulting Psychology*, 16, 319–324. http://dx.doi.org/10.1037/h0063633

Eysenck, H. J., & Eysenck, M. W. (1985). *Personality and individual differences*. New York, NY: Plenum.

Faraone, S. V., Perlis, R. H., Doyle, A. E., Smoller, J. W., Goralnick, J. J., Holmgren, M. A., & Sklar, P. (2005). Molecular genetics of attention-deficit/hyperactivity disorder. *Biological Psychiatry, 57*, 1313–1323. http://dx.doi.org/10.1016/j.biopsych.2004.11.024

Farberow, N. L. (1963). Introduction. In N. L. Farberow (Ed.), *Taboo topics* (pp. 1–7). New York, NY: Prentice Hall.

Felitti, V. J., Anda, R. F., Nordenberg, D., Williamson, D. F., Spitz, A. M., Edwards, V., . . . Marks, J. S. (1998). Relationship of childhood abuse and household dysfunction to many of the leading causes of death in adults. The Adverse Childhood Experiences (ACE) Study. *American Journal of Preventive Medicine, 14*, 245–258. http://dx.doi.org/10.1016/S0749-3797(98)00017-8

Fenichel, O. (1945). *The psychoanalytic theory of neurosis*. New York, NY: W. W. Norton.

Fischer, C. T. (2000). Collaborative, individualized assessment. *Journal of Personality Assessment, 74*, 2–14. http://dx.doi.org/10.1207/S15327752JPA740102

Fisher, D. B., & Ahern, L. (2000). Personal assistance in community existence (PACE): An alternative to PACT. *Ethical Human Sciences & Services, 2*, 87–92. Retrieved from http://search.ebscohost.com/login.aspx?direct=true&db=psyh&AN=2001-14426-001&site=ehost-live&scope=site

Fishman, D. (1999). *The case for pragmatic psychology*. New York, NY: NYU Press.

Fishman, D. B. (2013). L'etude de cas pragmatique: Une method de recherché rigoureuse et systématique qui parle aux praticiens. [Pragmatic case study: One method for creating rigorous and systematic, practitioner-friendly research]. *Psychothérapies, 33*, 3–12.

Fonagy, P. (2010). Psychotherapy research: Do we know what works for whom? *The British Journal of Psychiatry, 197*, 83–85. http://dx.doi.org/10.1192/bjp.bp.110.079657

Fowers, B. J. (2005). *Virtue and psychology: Pursuing excellence in ordinary practices*. Washington, DC: American Psychological Association.

Fox, D. R. (1993). Psychological jurisprudence and radical social change. *American Psychologist, 48*, 234–241. http://dx.doi.org/10.1037/0003-066X.48.3.234

Frankl, V. (2006). *Man's search for meaning*. Boston, MA: Beacon Press. (Original work published 1946)

Freeman, M. (1997). Why narrative? Hermeneutics, historical understanding, and the significance of stories. *Journal of Narrative and Life History, 7*, 169–176.

Freud, A. (1946). *The ego and the mechanisms of defense*. New York, NY: International Universities Press.

Freud, S. (1905). Three essays on the theory of sexuality. In J. Strachey (Ed. & Trans.), *The standard edition of the complete psychological works of Sigmund Freud* (Vol. 7, pp. 123–231). London, England: Hogarth Press.

Freud, S. (1966). *Introductory lectures on psychoanalysis* (J. Stachey, Trans. & Ed.). New York, NY: Norton. (Original work published 1920)

Friedman, M., Breall, W. S., Goodwin, M. L., Sparagon, B. J., Ghandour, G., & Fleischmann, N. (1996). Effect of type A behavioral counseling on frequency of episodes of silent myocardial ischemia in coronary patients. *American Heart Journal, 132*, 933–937.

Fromm-Reichmann, F. (1950). *The principles of intensive psychotherapy*. Chicago, IL: University of Chicago Press.

Gatchel, R. J., & Oordt, M. S. (2003). *Clinical health psychology and primary care: Practical advice and clinical guidance for successful collaboration*. Washington, DC: American Psychological Association.

Gatz, M., Pederson, N. L., Plomin, R., & Nesselroade, J. R. (1992). Importance of shared genes and shared environments for symptoms of depression in older adults. *Journal of Abnormal Psychology, 101*, 701–708. http://dx.doi.org/10.1037/0021-843X.101.4.701

Gendlin, E. T. (1996). *Focusing-oriented psychotherapy: A manual of the experiential method*. New York, NY: Guilford Press.

Gergen, K. J. (1985). The social constructionist movement in modern psychology. *American Psychologist, 40*, 266–275. http://dx.doi.org/10.1037/0003-066X.40.3.266

Ghaemi, S. N. (2009). The rise and fall of the biopsychosocial model. *The British Journal of Psychiatry, 195*, 3–4. http://dx.doi.org/10.1192/bjp.bp.109.063859

Giorgi, A. (2010). Phenomenological psychology: A brief history and its challenges. *Journal of Phenomenological Psychology, 41*, 145–179. http://dx.doi.org/10.1163/156916210X532108

Goldberg, L. R. (1993). The structure of phenotypic personality traits. *American Psychologist, 48*, 26–34. http://dx.doi.org/10.1037/0003-066X.48.1.26

Goldfried, M. R. (1995). Toward a common language for case formulation. *Journal of Psychotherapy Integration, 5*, 221–244.

Gottesman, I. I., & Shields, J. (1982). *Schizophrenia: The epigenetic puzzle*. Cambridge, England: Cambridge University Press.

Gottman, J. M. (1999). *The marriage clinic: A scientifically based marital therapy*. New York, NY: Norton.

Graham, J. (1993). *MMPI–2: Assessing personality and psychopathology* (2nd ed.). New York, NY: Oxford University Press.

Gregory, A. M., Lau, J. Y. A., & Eley, T. C. (2008). Finding gene–environment interactions for generalised anxiety disorder. *European Archives of Psychiatry and Clinical Neuroscience, 258*, 69–75. http://dx.doi.org/10.1007/s00406-007-0785-4

Haijma, S. V., Van Haren, N., Cahn, W., Koolschijn, P. C., Hulshoff Pol, H. E., & Kahn, R. S. (2013). Brain volumes in schizophrenia: A meta-analysis in over 18,000 subjects. *Schizophrenia Bulletin, 39*, 1129–1138. http://dx.doi.org/10.1093/schbul/sbs118

Haley, J. (1993). *Uncommon therapy: The psychiatric techniques of Milton Erickson.* New York, NY: Norton.

Hall, S. S. (2010). Revolution postponed. *Scientific American, 303,* 60–67. http://dx.doi.org/10.1038/scientificamerican1010-60

Hare, R. D., & Neumann, C. S. (2008). Psychopathy as a clinical and empirical construct. *Annual Review of Clinical Psychology, 4,* 217–246. http://dx.doi.org/10.1146/annurev.clinpsy.3.022806.091452

Hare-Mustin, R. T. (2004). Can we demystify theory? Examining masculinity discourses and feminist postmodern theory. *Journal of Theoretical and Philosophical Psychology, 24,* 14–29. http://dx.doi.org/10.1037/h0091235

Hare-Mustin, R. T., & Marecek, J. (1988). The meaning of difference: Gender theory, postmodernism, and psychology. *American Psychologist, 43,* 455–464. http://dx.doi.org/10.1037/0003-066X.43.6.455

Harré, R. (1998). *The singular self: An introduction to the psychology of personhood.* Thousand Oaks, CA: Sage.

Hawkins, R. M. F. (2001). A systematic meta-review of hypnosis as an empirically supported treatment for pain. *Pain Reviews, 8,* 47–73.

Hayes, S. C., Follette, V. M., & Linehan, M. M. (2004). *Mindfulness and acceptance: Expanding the cognitive–behavioral tradition.* New York, NY: Guilford Press.

The Health Insurance Portability and Accountability Act of 1996 (HIPPA). Public L. No. 104-191 (1996).

Healy, D. (2004). *Let them eat Prozac: The unhealthy relationship between the pharmaceutical industry and depression.* New York, NY: NYU Press.

Healy, D. (2009). *Psychiatric drugs explained.* Edinburgh, Scotland: Churchill Livingstone Elsevier.

Held, B. S. (1995). *Back to reality: A critique of postmodern theory in psychotherapy.* New York, NY: Norton.

Held, B. S. (2007). *Psychology's interpretive turn: The search for truth and agency in theoretical and philosophical psychology.* Washington, DC: American Psychological Association. http://dx.doi.org/10.1037/11588-000

Herman, E. (1995). *The romance of American psychology: Political culture in the age of experts.* Berkeley, CA: University of California Press.

Hilgard, E. R. (1965). *Hypnotic susceptibility.* New York, NY: Harcourt, Brace, & World.

Hiller, W., Rief, W., & Brähler, E. (2006). Somatization in the population: From mild bodily misperceptions to disabling symptoms. *Social Psychiatry and Psychiatric Epidemiology, 41,* 704–712. http://dx.doi.org/10.1007/s00127-006-0082-y

Hoffman, L. (2001). *Family therapy: An intimate history.* New York, NY: Norton.

Hopper, K., Harrison, G., Janca, A., & Sartorius, N. (2007). *Recovery from schizophrenia: An international perspective. A report from the WHO collaborative project, the International Study of Schizophrenia.* New York, NY: Oxford University Press.

Horgan, J. (2013). Psychiatry in crisis! Mental health director rejects psychiatric "bible" and replaces with . . . nothing. *Scientific American*. Retrieved from http://blogs.scientificamerican.com/cross-check/2013/05/04/psychiatry-in-crisis-mental-health-director-rejects-psychiatric-bible-and-replaces-with-nothing/

Horney, K. (2013). *Self-analysis*. New York, NY: Norton. (Original work published 1942)

Hoshamond, L. T. (1992). *Orientation to inquiry in a reflective professional psychology*. Albany: State University of New York Press.

Houghton, K., Schuchard, J., Lewis, C., & Thompson, C. K. (2013). Promoting child-initiated social-communication in children with autism: Son-Rise Program intervention effects. *Journal of Communication Disorders, 46*, 495–506. http://dx.doi.org/10.1016/j.jcomdis.2013.09.004

Howard, G. (1986). *Dare we develop a human science?* Notre Dame, IN: Academic Publications.

Institute of Medicine. (2007). *Treatment of PTSD: An assessment of the evidence*. Washington, DC: National Academy of Sciences.

Jacobson, E. (1976). *You must relax* (5th ed.). New York, NY: McGraw-Hill.

James, W. (1966). *Is life worth living? Essays on faith and morals*. New York, NY: New American Library. (Original work published 1896)

James, W. (1975). *Pragmatism: A new name for some old ways of thinking*. Cambridge, MA: Harvard University Press. (Original work published 1907)

James, W. (1983). *Essays in psychology*. Cambridge, MA: Harvard University Press. (Original work published 1892)

Jansz, J., & van Drunen, P. (2004). *A social history of psychology*. Oxford, England: Blackwell.

Johns, L. C., & van Os, J. (2001). The continuity of psychotic experiences in the general population. *Clinical Psychology Review, 21*, 1125–1141. http://dx.doi.org/10.1016/S0272-7358(01)00103-9

Johnson, R. (2005). *Emotional health: What emotions are and how they cause social and mental diseases* (2nd rev. ed.). Isle of Wight, England: Truth Consent.

Joint Commission on Mental Illness and Health. (1961). *Action for mental health: Final report*. New York, NY: Basic Books.

Jones, B. T., Corbin, W., & Fromme, K. (2001). A review of expectancy theory and alcohol consumption. *Addiction, 96*, 57–72. http://dx.doi.org/10.1046/j.1360-0443.2001.961575.x

Joseph, A. J. (2013). Empowering alliances in pursuit of social justice: Social workers supporting psychiatric-survivor movements. *Journal of Progressive Human Services, 24*, 265–288. http://dx.doi.org/10.1080/10428232.2010.540748

Joseph, J. (2006). *The missing gene: Psychiatry, heredity, and the fruitless search for genes*. New York, NY: Algora.

Josselson, R., & Lieblich, A. (Eds.). (1993). *The narrative study of lives, Volume 1*. Thousand Oaks, CA: Sage.

Jourard, S. M. (1964). *The transparent self*. New York, NY: Van Nostrand.

Judd, L., & Akiskal, H. S. (2003). The prevalence and disability of bipolar spectrum disorders in the U.S. population: Re-analysis of the ECA database taking into account subthreshold cases. *Journal of Affective Disorders, 73*, 123–131. http://dx.doi.org/10.1016/S0165-0327(02)00332-4

Kant, I. (1929). *The critique of pure reason* (N. Kemp Smith, Trans.). London, England: McMillan. (Original work published 1781)

Kaplan, H. I., & Sadock, B. J. (Eds.). (1989). *Comprehensive textbook of psychiatry* (5th ed.). Baltimore, MD: Williams and Wilkins.

Karon, B. P. (2004). Insights, hope, kindness, and confusion: Odyssey of a psychoanalyst. *Psychoanalytic Psychology, 21*, 541–553. http://dx.doi.org/10.1037/0736-9735.21.4.541

Karon, B. P. (2008). An "incurable" schizophrenic: The case of Mr. X. *Pragmatic Case Studies in Psychotherapy, 4*, 1–24. Retrieved from http://jrul.libraries.rutgers.edu/index.php/pcsp/article/view/923/2325

Karon, B. P., & VandenBos, G. R. (1981). *Psychotherapy of schizophrenia: The treatment of choice*. New York, NY: Jason Aronson.

Katz, L. S., & Epstein, S. (2005). The relation of cancer-prone personality to exceptional recovery from cancer: A preliminary study. *Advances in Mind-Body Medicine, 21*, 6–20.

Kaufman, B. N. (1995). *Son-rise: The miracle continues*. Tiburon, CA: HJ Kramer.

Keen, E. (1970). *Three faces of being: Toward an existential clinical psychology*. New York, NY: Appleton-Century-Crofts.

Kessler, R. C., Berglund, P., Demler, O., Jin, R., Merikangas, K. R., & Walters, E. E. (2005). Lifetime prevalence and age-of-onset distributions of DSM–IV disorders in the National Comorbidity Survey Replication. *Archives of General Psychiatry, 62*, 593–602. http://dx.doi.org/10.1001/archpsyc.62.6.593

Kessler, R. C., Chiu, W. T., Demler, O., & Walters, E. E. (2005). Prevalence, severity, and comorbidity of 12-month DSM–IV disorders in the National Comorbidity Survey Replication. *Archives of General Psychiatry, 62*, 617–627. http://dx.doi.org/10.1001/archpsyc.62.6.617

Kety, S. S., Rosenthal, D., Wender, P. H., Schulsinger, F., & Jacobsen, B. (1976). Mental illness in the biological and adoptive families of adopted individuals who have become schizophrenic. *Behavior Genetics, 6*, 219–225. http://dx.doi.org/10.1007/BF01065721

Kirsch, I., Deacon, B. J., Huedo-Medina, T., Scoboria, A., Moore, T. J. & Johnson, B. T. (2008). Initial severity and antidepressant benefits: A meta-analysis of data submitted to the Food and Drug Administration. *Plos Medicine, 5*(2), e45–e45.

Kirsch, I., & Sapirstein, G. (1998). Listening to Prozac but hearing placebo: A meta-analysis of antidepressant medication. *Prevention & Treatment, 1*, Article 2a. http://dx.doi.org/10.1037/1522-3736.1.1.12a

Kirschner, S. R. (1996). *The religious and romantic origins of psychoanalysis: Individuation and integration in post-Freudian theory.* New York, NY: Cambridge University Press.

Kleinman, A. A. (1988). *The illness narratives: Suffering healing and the human condition.* New York, NY: Basic Books.

Kotzalidis, G. D., Patrizi, B., Caltagirone, S. S., Koukopoulos, A., Savoja, V., Ruberto, G., . . . Girardi, P. (2007). The adult SSRI/SNRI withdrawal syndrome: A clinically heterogeneous entity. *Clinical Neuropsychiatry, 4*, 61–75.

Kramer, P. (1993). *Listening to Prozac: Antidepressants and the remaking of the self.* New York, NY: Penguin Books.

Laing, R. D. (1959). *The divided self: An existential study in sanity and madness.* New York, NY: Penguin Books.

Lambert, N. M. (1988). Adolescent outcomes for hyperactive children: Perspectives on general and specific patterns of childhood risk for adolescent educational, social, and mental health problems. *American Psychologist, 43*, 786–799. http://dx.doi.org/10.1037/0003-066X.43.10.786

Lanyon, R. I. (2007). Utility of the Psychological Screening Inventory: A review. *Journal of Clinical Psychology, 63*, 283–307. http://dx.doi.org/10.1002/jclp.20344

Lazarus, A. A. (1976). *Multi-modal behavior therapy: Behavior, affect, sensation, imagery, cognition, interpersonal relations.* New York, NY: Springer.

Legrand, L. N., McGue, M., & Iacono, W. G. (1999). A twin study of state and trait anxiety in childhood and adolescence. *Journal of Child Psychology and Psychiatry, 40*, 953–958. http://dx.doi.org/10.1111/1469-7610.00512

Levine, A. G., & Levine, M. (2014). Research in the real world: Social context and its effects. *American Journal of Orthopsychiatry, 84*, 164–171. http://dx.doi.org/10.1037/h0099389

Levine, M., Perkins, D. D., & Perkins, D. V. (2005). *Principles of community psychology: Perspectives and applications* (3rd ed.). New York, NY: Oxford University Press.

Levit, K. R., Mark, T. L., Coffey, R. M., Frankel, S., Santora, P., Vandivort-Warren, R., & Malone, K. (2013). Federal spending on behavioral health accelerated during recession as individuals lost employer insurance. *Health Affairs, 32*, 952–962. http://dx.doi.org/10.1377/hlthaff.2012.1065

Lieberman, J. A., Kinon, B. J., & Loebel, A. D. (1990). Dopaminergic mechanisms in idiopathic and drug-induced psychoses. *Schizophrenia Bulletin, 16*, 97–110. http://dx.doi.org/10.1093/schbul/16.1.97

Lieberman, J. A., & Stroup, T. S. (2011). The NIMH-CATIE Schizophrenia Study: What did we learn? *The American Journal of Psychiatry, 168*, 770–775. http://dx.doi.org/10.1176/appi.ajp.2011.11010039

Lieberman, J. A., Stroup, T. S., McEvoy, J. P., Swartz, M. S., Rosenheck, R. A., Perkins, D. O., . . . Hsiao, J. K. (2005). Effectiveness of antipsychotic drugs in patients with chronic schizophrenia. *The New England Journal of Medicine, 353,* 1209–1223. http://dx.doi.org/10.1056/NEJMoa051688

Lifton, R. (1988). *The Nazi doctors: Medical killing and the psychology of genocide.* New York, NY: Basic Books.

Lilienfeld, S. O., Lynn, S. J., & Lohr, J. M. (Eds.). (2004). *Science and pseudoscience in clinical psychology.* New York, NY: Guilford Press.

Lilienfeld, S. O., Wood, J. M., & Garb, H. N. (2000). The scientific status of projective techniques. *Psychological Science in the Public Interest, 1,* 27–66. http://dx.doi.org/10.1111/1529-1006.002

Lindsley, C. W. (2012). The top prescription drugs of 2011 in the United States: Antipsychotics and antidepressants once again lead CNS therapeutics. *ACS Chemical Neuroscience, 3,* 630–631. http://dx.doi.org/10.1021/cn3000923

Linehan, M. M. (2013). What psychiatrists should know about dialectical behavior therapy. *Psychiatric Annals, 43,* 148–148. http://dx.doi.org/10.3928/00485713-20130403-02

Litschge, C. M., & Vaughn, M. G. (2009). The mentally ill offender treatment and crime reduction act of 2004: Problems and prospects. *Journal of Forensic Psychiatry & Psychology, 20,* 542–558. http://dx.doi.org/10.1080/14789940802434675

Losh, M., Sullivan, P. F., Trembath, D., & Piven, J. (2008). Current developments in the genetics of autism: From phenome to genome. *Journal of Neuropathology and Experimental Neurology, 67,* 829–837. http://dx.doi.org/10.1097/NEN.0b013e318184482d

Luborsky, L., Rosenthal, R., Diguer, L., Andrusyna, T. P., Berman, J. S., Levitt, J. T., . . . Krause, E. D. (2002). The dodo bird verdict is alive and well—Mostly. *Clinical Psychology: Science and Practice, 9,* 2–12.

Luchins, A. S. (1988). The rise and decline of the American asylum movement in the 19th century. *The Journal of Psychology: Interdisciplinary and Applied, 122,* 471–486. http://dx.doi.org/10.1080/00223980.1988.10542952

Luthar, S. S., Cicchetti, D., & Becker, B. (2000). The construct of resilience: A critical evaluation and guidelines for future work. *Child Development, 71,* 543–562.

Mahler, M., Pine, F., & Bergman, A. (1975). *The psychological birth of the human infant: Symbiosis and individuation.* New York, NY: Basic Books.

Malan, D. H. (1995). *Individual psychotherapy and the science of psychodynamics* (2nd ed.). London, England: Butterworth-Heineman.

Malan, D. H. (1997). *Anorexia, murder, & suicide.* Oxford, England: Read Educational and Professional Publishing.

Malan, D. H., & Della Selva, P. (2006). *Lives transformed: A revolutionary method of dynamic psychotherapy* (Rev. ed.). London, England: Karnac Books.

Marecek, J., & Hare-Mustin, R. T. (2009). Clinical psychology: The politics of madness. In D. Fox, I. Prilleltensky, & S. Austin (Eds.), *Critical psychology: An introduction* (2nd ed., pp. 75–92). Thousand Oaks, CA: Sage.

Martin, J., & Sugarman, J. (2000). Between the modern and the postmodern: The possibility of self and progressive understanding in psychology. *American Psychologist, 55,* 397–406. http://dx.doi.org/10.1037/0003-066X.55.4.397

Maslow, A. (1971). *The farther reaches of human nature.* New York, NY: Viking.

McAdams, D. P. (2006). The role of narrative in personality psychology today. *Narrative Inquiry, 16,* 11–18. http://dx.doi.org/10.1075/ni.16.1.04mca

McGuffin, P., Katz, R., Watkins, S., & Rutherford, J. (1996). A hospital-based twin registery study of the heritability of *DSM–IV* unipolar depression. *Archives of General Psychiatry, 53,* 129–136. http://dx.doi.org/10.1001/archpsyc.1996.01830020047006

McKeon, R. (1941). *The basic works of Aristotle.* New York, NY: Random House.

McLeod, J. (2010). *Case study research in counselling and psychotherapy.* London, England: Sage.

McWilliams, N. (2011). *Psychoanalytic diagnosis: Understanding personality structure in the clinical process* (2nd ed.). New York, NY: Guilford Press.

Meehl, P. (1962). Schixotaxia, schizotypy, schizophrenia. *American Psychologist, 17,* 827–838. http://dx.doi.org/10.1037/h0041029

Menand, L. (2001). *The metaphysical club: A story of ideas in America.* New York, NY: Farrar, Strauss & Giroux.

Messer, S. B. (1986). Behavioral and psychoanalytic perspectives at therapeutic choice points. *American Psychologist, 41,* 1261–1272. http://dx.doi.org/10.1037/0003-066X.41.11.1261

Messer, S. B. (2013). Three mechanisms of change in psychodynamic therapy: Insight, affect, and alliance. *Psychotherapy, 50,* 408–412. http://dx.doi.org/10.1037/a0032414

Miller, M., Barber, C., Young, M., Azrael, D., Mukamal, K., & Lawler, E. (2012). Veterans and suicide: A reexamination of the National Death Index-Linked National Health Interview Survey. *American Journal of Public Health, 102,* S154–S259.

Miller, R. B. (1983). A call to armchairs. *Psychotherapy: Theory, Research, & Practice, 20,* 208–219. http://dx.doi.org/10.1037/h0088492

Miller, R. B. (2004). *Facing human suffering: Psychology and psychotherapy as moral engagement.* Washington, DC: American Psychological Association.

Miller, W. R. (1996). Motivational interviewing: Research, practice, and puzzles. *Addictive Behaviors, 21,* 835–842. http://dx.doi.org/10.1016/0306-4603(96)00044-5

Minuchin, S., & Nichols, M. (1993). *Family healing: Strategies for hope and understanding.* New York, NY: Free Press.

Mitchell, S. A. (1988). *Relational concepts in psychoanalysis: An integration* (Vol. 102). Cambridge, MA: Harvard University Press.

Moene, F. C., Spinhoven, P., Hoogduin, K. A. L., & Van Dyck, R. (2003). A randomized controlled clinical trial of a hypnosis-based treatment for patients with conversion disorder, motor type. *International Journal of Clinical and Experimental Hypnosis, 51*, 29–50. http://dx.doi.org/10.1076/iceh.51.1.29.14067

Moeschler, J. B., Shevell, M., & the Committee on Genetics. (2006). Clinical genetic evaluation of the child with mental retardation or developmental delays. *Pediatrics, 117*, 2304–2316. http://dx.doi.org/10.1542/peds.2006-1006

Moncrieff, J. (2009). A critique of the dopamine hypothesis of schizophrenia and psychosis. *Harvard Review of Psychiatry, 17*, 214–225. http://dx.doi.org/10.1080/10673220902979896

Moore, D. (2003). *The dependent gene: The fallacy of "nature vs. nurture".* New York, NY: Henry Holt and Company.

Moos, R. H., & Moos, B. S. (1994). *Family environment (FES).* Menlo Park, CA: Consulting Psychologists Press.

Moreno, C., Laje, G., Blanco, C., Jiang, H., Schmidt, A. B., & Olfson, M. (2007). National trends in the outpatient diagnosis and treatment of bipolar disorder in youth. *Archives of General Psychiatry, 64*, 1032–1039. http://dx.doi.org/10.1001/archpsyc.64.9.1032

Morris, A. S., Cui, L., & Steinberg, L. (2013). Parenting research and themes: What we have learned and where to go next. In R. E. Larzelere, A. S. Morris, & A. W. Harrist (Eds.), *Authoritative parenting: Synthesizing nurturance and discipline for optimal child development* (pp. 35–58). Washington, DC: American Psychological Association. http://dx.doi.org/10.1037/13948-003

Mosher, L. R., Menn, A., & Matthews, S. M. (1975). Soteria: Evaluation of a home-based treatment for schizophrenia. *American Journal of Orthopsychiatry, 45*, 455–467. http://dx.doi.org/10.1111/j.1939-0025.1975.tb02556.x

Moustakas, C. (1997). *Relationship play therapy.* Northvale, NJ: Jason Aronson.

Munafò, M. R., Durant, C., Lewis, G., & Flint, J. (2009). Gene X environment interactions at the serotonin transporter locus. *Biological Psychiatry, 65*, 211–219. http://dx.doi.org/10.1016/j.biopsych.2008.06.009

Murray, H. (1943). *The Thematic Apperception Test: Manual.* Cambridge, MA: Harvard University Press.

Myers, J. E. B. (2008). A short history of child protection in America. *Family Law Quarterly, 42*, 449–463.

Nutt, D. J., King, L. A., & Phillips, L. D. (2010). Drug harms in the UK: A multi-criteria decision analysis. *The Lancet, 376*, 1558–1565. http://dx.doi.org/10.1016/S0140-6736(10)61462-6

O'Hara, M. (1997). Emancipatory therapeutic practice in a turbulent transmodern era: A work of retrieval. *Journal of Humanistic Psychology, 37*, 7–33. http://dx.doi.org/10.1177/00221678970373002

Osbeck, L. M., Nersessian, N. J., Malone, K. R., & Newstetter, W. C. (2011). *Science as psychology: Sense-making and identity in science practice.* New York, NY: Cambridge University Press. http://dx.doi.org/10.1017/CBO9780511933936

Papp, P. (1994). *The process of change*. New York, NY: Guilford Press.

Parcesepe, A. M., & Cabassa, L. J. (2013). Public stigma of mental illness in the United States: A systematic literature review. *Administration and Policy in Mental Health and Mental Health Services Research, 40*, 384–399. http://dx.doi.org/10.1007/s10488-012-0430-z

Patient Protection and Affordable Care Act, 42, U.S.C. § 18001 (2010).

PDM Task Force. (2006). *Psychodynamic diagnostic manual*. Silver Spring, MD: Alliance of Psychoanalytic Organizations.

Perry, J. W. (2005). *The far side of madness* (2nd ed.). Dallas, TX: Spring.

Peterson, D. R. (1976). Need for the doctor of psychology degree in professional psychology. *American Psychologist, 31*, 792–798. http://dx.doi.org/10.1037//0003-066X.31.11.792

Polkinghorne, D. (2004). *Practice and the human sciences: The case for a judgment-based practice of care*. Albany, NY: State University of New York Press.

Prilleltensky, I. (1989). Psychology and the status quo. *American Psychologist, 44*, 795–802. http://dx.doi.org/10.1037/0003-066X.44.5.795

Prilleltensky, I., Prilleltensky, O., & Voorhees, C. (2009). Psychopolitical validity in counselling and therapy. In D. Fox, I. Prilleltensky, & S. Austin (Eds.), *Critical psychology: An introduction* (2nd ed., pp. 355–372). Thousand Oaks, CA: Sage.

Prouty, G. (2003). Pre-therapy: A newer development in the psychotherapy of schizophrenia. *Journal of the Academy of Psychoanalysis and Dynamic Psychiatry, 31*, 59–73.

Rampell, K. (2013, July 2). Most U.S. health spending is exploding—But not for mental health. *The New York Times*. Retrieved from http://economix.blogs.nytimes.com/2013/07/02/most-u-s-health-spending-is-exploding-but-not-for-mental-health/

Read, J. (2010). Can poverty drive you mad? "Schizophrenia," socio-economic status and the case for primary prevention. *New Zealand Journal of Psychology, 39*, 7–19.

Reilly, P. R. (1987). Involuntary sterilization in the United States: A surgical solution. *The Quarterly Review of Biology, 62*, 153–170. http://dx.doi.org/10.1086/415404

Richardson, F. C., Fowers, B. J., & Guignon, C. B. (1999). *Re-envisioning psychology: Moral dimensions of theory and practice*. San Francisco, CA: Jossey-Bass.

Risch, N., Herrell, R., Lehner, T., Liang, K. Y., Eaves, L., Hoh, J., . . . Merikangas, K. R. (2009). Interaction between the serotonin transporter gene (5-HTTLPR), stressful life events, and risk of depression: A meta-analysis. *JAMA, 301*, 2462–2471. http://dx.doi.org/10.1001/jama.2009.878

Robinson, D. (1995). *An intellectual history of psychology* (3rd ed.). Madison: University of Wisconsin Press.

Robinson, D. N. (2008). *Consciousness and mental life*. New York, NY: Columbia University Press.

Roe, D., & Davidson, L. (2008). Recovery. In K. T. Mueser & D. V. Jeste (Eds.), *Clinical handbook of schizophrenia* (pp. 566–574). New York, NY: Guilford Press.

Rogers, C. (1951). *Client-centered therapy: Its current practice, implications and theory.* London, England: Constable.

Rogers, C. R. (1960). *On becoming a person.* Boston, MA: Houghton Mifflin.

Rogers, C. R. (1961). The process equation of psychotherapy. *American Journal of Psychotherapy, 15,* 27–45.

Rorschach, H. (1942). *Psychodiagnostics: A diagnostic test based on perception.* New York, NY: Grune & Stratton. (Original work published 1921)

Rosen, J. D. (1966). *Direct analysis: Selected papers.* New York, NY: Grune & Stratton.

Rossignol, D. A., & Frye, R. E. (2012). A review of research trends in physiological abnormalities in autism spectrum disorders: Immune dysregulation, inflammation, oxidative stress, mitochondrial dysfunction and environmental toxicant exposures. *Molecular Psychiatry, 17,* 389–401. http://dx.doi.org/10.1038/mp.2011.165

Runyan, W. (1982). *Life histories and psychobiography: Explorations in theory and method.* New York, NY: Oxford University Press.

Rychlak, J. F. (1981). *A philosophy of science for personality theory* (2nd ed.). Malabar, FL: Krieger.

Safran, J. D. (2012). *Psychoanalysis and psychoanalytic therapies.* Washington, DC: American Psychological Association.

Saltzman, N., & Norcross, J. C. (1990). *Therapy wars: Contention and convergence in differing clinical approaches.* San Francisco, CA: Jossey-Bass.

Sartorius, N., Jablensky, A., & Shapiro, R. (1977). Two-year follow-up of the patients included in the WHO International Pilot Study of Schizophrenia. *Psychological Medicine, 7,* 529–541. http://dx.doi.org/10.1017/S0033291700004517

Sass, L. A., & Parnas, J. (2003). Schizophrenia, consciousness, and the self. *Schizophrenia Bulletin, 29,* 427–444. http://dx.doi.org/10.1093/oxfordjournals.schbul.a007017

Satir, V. (1983). *Conjoint family therapy.* Palo Alto, CA: Science and Behavior Books.

Schienle, A., Hettema, J. M., Caceda, R., & Nemeroff, C. (2011). Neurobiology and genetics of generalized anxiety disorder. *Psychiatric Annals, 41,* 113–123.

Schneider, K. J., Bugental, J. T., & Pierson, J. (2001). *The handbook of humanistic psychology: Leading edges in theory, research, and practice.* Thousand Oaks, CA: Sage.

Schön, D. A. (1987). *Educating the reflective-practitioner.* San Francisco, CA: Jossey-Bass.

Schuyler, D. (1974). *The depressive spectrum.* New York, NY: J. Aronson.

Seikkula, J., Alakare, B., & Aaltonen, J. (2011). The comprehensive open-dialogue approach in Western Lapland: II. Long-term stability of acute psychosis outcomes in advanced community care. *Psychosis: Psychological, Social and Integrative Approaches, 3,* 192–204.

Shedler, J. (2012). The efficacy of psychodynamic psychotherapy. In R. A. Levy, J. S. Ablon, & H. Kächele (Eds.), *Psychodynamic psychotherapy research: Evidence-based practice and practice-based evidence* (pp. 9–25). Totowa, NJ: Humana Press.

Siegel, B. (1998). *Love, medicine and miracles*. New York, NY: William Morrow.

Silverman, D. K. (2005). What works in psychotherapy and how do we know? What evidence-based practice has to offer. *Psychoanalytic Psychology, 22*, 306–312. http://dx.doi.org/10.1037/0736-9735.22.2.306

Silverman, L. H., & Lachmann, F. M. (1985). The therapeutic properties of unconscious oneness fantasies: Evidence and treatment implications. *Contemporary Psychoanalysis, 21*, 91–115. http://dx.doi.org/10.1080/00107530.1985.10745770

Skinner, B. F. (1953). *Science and human behavior*. New York, NY: Free Press.

Skinner, B. F. (1971). *Beyond freedom and dignity*. Indianapolis, IN: Hackett.

Skinner, H. A., Steinhauer, P. D, & Santa-Barbara, J. (1983). The family assessment measure. *Canadian Journal of Community Mental Health, 2*(2), 91–105.

Slife, B. D., Reber, J. S., & Richardson, F. C. (2005). *Critical thinking about psychology: Hidden assumptions and plausible alternatives*. Washington, DC: American Psychological Association.

Smink, F. R. E., van Hoeken, D., & Hoek, H. W. (2012). Epidemiology of eating disorders: Incidence, prevalence, and mortality rates. *Current Psychiatry Reports, 14*, 406–414. http://dx.doi.org/10.1007/s11920-012-0282-y

Smith, D. F., & Jakobsen, S. (2013). Molecular neurobiology of depression: PET findings on the elusive correlation with symptom severity. *Frontiers in Psychiatry*. Retrieved from http://journal.frontiersin.org/Journal/10.3389/fpsyt.2013.00008/full

Spiegel, D., & Classen, C. (2000). *Group therapy for cancer patients: A research based handbook of psychosocial care*. New York, NY: Basic Books.

Sroufe, L. A., Egeland, B., Carlson, E. A., & Collins, W. A. (2005). *The development of the person: The Minnesota study of risk and adaptation from birth to adulthood*. New York, NY: Guilford Publications.

Stein, M. B., Ford, D. R., Anderson, G., & Walker, J. R. (1997). Obsessive–compulsive disorder in the community: An epidemiological survey with clinical reappraisal. *American Journal of Psychiatry, 154*, 1120–1126.

Steinmetz, J. E. (2013). The changing landscape for research and education. *Association for Psychological Science Observer*. Retrieved from http://www.psychologicalscience.org/index.php/publications/observer/2013/may-june-13/the-changing-landscape-for-research-and-education-in-psychological-science.html

Sternberg, R. J. (2005). Unifying the field of psychology. In R. J. Sternberg (Ed.), *Unity in psychology: Possibility or pipedream?* (pp. 3–14). Washington, DC: American Psychological Association.

Stiles, W. B., Barkham, M., Twigg, E., Mellor-Clark, J., & Cooper, M. (2006). Effectiveness of cognitive–behavioural, person-centred and psychodynamic therapies as practised in UK National Health Service settings. *Psychological Medicine, 36*, 555–566. http://dx.doi.org/10.1017/S0033291706007136

Stolorow, R. D., Brandchaft, B., & Atwood, G. E. (1987). *Psychoanalytic treatment: An intersubjective approach*. Hillsdale, NJ: Analytic Press.

Stricker, G., & Trierweiler, S. J. (2006). The local clinical scientist: A bridge between science and practice. *Training And Education In Professional Psychology, S*(1), 37–46. http://dx.doi.org/10.1037/1931-3918.S.1.37

Substance Abuse and Mental Health Services Administration. (2009, September 17). *The NSDUH report: Suicidal thoughts and behaviors among adults*. Retrieved from http://www.ohiospf.net/files/SuicideHTML.pdf

Substance Abuse and Mental Health Services Administration. (2013). *Results from the 2012 national survey on drug use and health: Summary of national findings* (NSDUH Series H-46, HHS Publication No. SMA 13-4795). Retrieved from http://archive.samhsa.gov/data/NSDUH/2012SummNatFindDetTables/NationalFindings/NSDUHresults2012.pdf

Substance Abuse and Mental Health Services Administration. (2014). *Patient stress questionnaire*. Retrieved from http://www.integration.samhsa.gov/Patient_Stress_Questionnaire.pdf

Suffer. (2014). In *Oxford English dictionary*. Retrieved from http://www.oed.com/view/Entry/193523?redirectedFrom=suffer#eid

Suffering. (2014). In *Oxford English dictionary*. Retrieved from http://www.oed.com/view/Entry/193531?rskey=QcNI82&result=1#eid

Sugarman, J. (2005). Persons and moral agency. *Theory & Psychology, 15*, 793–811. http://dx.doi.org/10.1177/0959354305059333

Sullivan, H. S. (1968). *The interpersonal theory of psychiatry*. New York, NY: Norton. (Original work published 1953)

Szasz, T. (1984). *The myth of mental illness: Foundations of a theory of personal conduct* (Rev. ed.). New York, NY: HarperCollins. (Original work published 1960)

Tambs, K., Czajkowsky, N., Røysamb, E., Neale, M. C., Reichborn-Kjennerud, T., Aggen, S. H., . . . Kendler, K. S. (2009). Structure of genetic and environmental risk factors for dimensional representations of DSM–IV anxiety disorders. *The British Journal of Psychiatry, 195*, 301–307. http://dx.doi.org/10.1192/bjp.bp.108.059485

Teo, T. (2009). Philosophical concerns in critical psychology. In D. Fox, I. Prilleltensky, & S. Austin (Eds.), *Critical psychology: An introduction* (2nd ed., pp. 36–53). Thousand Oaks, CA: Sage.

Thomas, A., & Chess, S. (1977). *Temperament and development*. New York, NY: Brunner-Routledge.

Thompson, R. A., Winer, A. C., & Goodvin, R. (2010). The individual child: Temperament, emotion, self, and personality. In M. Bornstein & M. E. Lamb (Eds.), *Developmental science: An advanced textbook* (6th ed., pp. 423–464). New York, NY: Psychology Press/Taylor & Francis.

Tjeltveit, A. C. (1999). *Ethics and values in psychotherapy*. Florence, KY: Taylor & Frances/Routledge. http://dx.doi.org/10.4324/9780203360453

Tjeltveit, A. C. (2006). To what ends? Psychotherapy goals and outcomes, the good life, and the principle of beneficence. *Psychotherapy: Theory, Research, Practice, Training, 43*, 186–200. http://dx.doi.org/10.1037/0033-3204.43.2.186

Toulmin, S. (2003). *Return to reason*. Cambridge, MA: Harvard University Press.

Ullmann, L. P., & Krasner, L. (Eds.). (1965). *Case studies in behavior modification*. New York, NY: Holt.

U.S. Department of Health and Human Services. (2013). *Child maltreatment, 2012*. Retrieved from http://www.acf.hhs.gov/sites/default/files/cb/cm2012.pdf#page=31

U.S. Department of Labor. (2012). *Occupational employment statistics*. Retrieved from http://www.bls.gov/oes/current/oes_nat.htm#19-0000

Valenstein, E. S. (1998). *Blaming the brain*. New York, NY: Free Press.

Valle, R. (Ed.). (1998). *Phenomenological inquiry in psychology: Existential and transpersonal dimensions*. New York, NY: Plenum Press. http://dx.doi.org/10.1007/978-1-4899-0125-5

Visser, S. N., Danielson, M. L., Bitsko, R. H., Holbrook, J. R., Kogan, M. D., Ghandour, R. M., . . . Blumberg, S. J. (2014). Trends in the parent-report of health care provider-diagnosed and medicated attention-deficit/hyperactivity disorder: United States, 2003–2011. *Journal of the American Academy of Child & Adolescent Psychiatry, 53*, 34–46. http://dx.doi.org/10.1016/j.jaac.2013.09.001

Wachtel, P. L. (1997). *Psychoanalysis, behavior therapy, and the relational world*. Washington, DC: American Psychological Association. http://dx.doi.org/10.1037/10383-000

Wakefield, J. C. (1992). The concept of mental disorder. On the boundary between biological facts and social values. *American Psychologist, 47*, 373–388. http://dx.doi.org/10.1037/0003-066X.47.3.373

Walker, E., Kestler, L., Bollini, A., & Hochman, K. M. (2004). Schizophrenia: Etiology and course. *Annual Review of Psychology, 55*, 401–430. http://dx.doi.org/10.1146/annurev.psych.55.090902.141950

Walker, E., Mittal, V., & Tessner, K. (2008). Stress and the hypothalamic pituitary adrenal axis in the developmental course of schizophrenia. *Annual Review of Clinical Psychology, 4*, 189–216. http://dx.doi.org/10.1146/annurev.clinpsy.4.022007.141248

Wallis, D., Russell, H. F., & Muenke, M. (2008). Review: Genetics of attention deficit/hyperactivity disorder. *Journal of Pediatric Psychology, 33*, 1085–1099. http://dx.doi.org/10.1093/jpepsy/jsn049

Wang, P. S., Lane, M., Olfson, M., Pincus, H. A., Wells, K. B., & Kessler, R. C. (2005). Twelve-month use of mental health services in the United States: Results from the National Comorbidity Survey Replication. *Archives of General Psychiatry, 62*, 629–640. http://dx.doi.org/10.1001/archpsyc.62.6.629

Wang, Q., Xiang, B., Deng, W., Wu, J., Li, M., Ma, X., . . . Li, T. (2013). Genome-wide association analysis with gray matter volume as a quantitative phenotype in first-episode treatment-naïve patients with schizophrenia. *PLoS ONE, 8*(9), e75083–e75083. http://dx.doi.org/10.1371/journal.pone.0075083

Watson, J. B. (1924). *Behaviorism.* New York, NY: People's Institute.

Watson, J. C., Goldman, R. N., & Greenberg, L. S. (2011). Humanistic and experiential theories of psychotherapy. In J. C. Norcross, G. R. VandenBos, & D. K. Freedheim (Eds.), *History of psychotherapy: Continuity and change* (2nd ed., pp. 141–172). Washington, DC: American Psychological Association.

Wechsler, D. (1981). The psychometric tradition: Developing the Wechsler Adult Intelligence Scale. *Contemporary Educational Psychology, 6,* 82–85. http://dx.doi.org/10.1016/0361-476X(81)90035-7

Weisz, J. R. (2014). Building robust psychotherapies for children and adolescents. *Perspectives on Psychological Science, 9,* 81–84. http://dx.doi.org/10.1177/1745691613512658

Weisz, J. R., Weiss, B., Alicke, M. D., & Klotz, M. L. (1987). Effectiveness of psychotherapy with children and adolescents: A meta-analysis for clinicians. *Journal of Consulting and Clinical Psychology, 55,* 542–549. http://dx.doi.org/10.1037/0022-006X.55.4.542

Weisz, J. R., Weiss, B., Han, S. S., Granger, D. A., & Morton, T. (1995). Effects of psychotherapy with children and adolescents revisited: A meta-analysis of treatment outcome studies. *Psychological Bulletin, 117,* 450–468. http://dx.doi.org/10.1037/0033-2909.117.3.450

Wertz, F. J. (1986). Common methodological fundaments of the analytic procedures in phenomenological and psychoanalytic research. *Psychoanalysis & Contemporary Thought, 9,* 563–603.

Wertz, F. J., Charmaz, K., McMullen, L. M., Josselson, R., Anderson, R., & McSpadden, E. (2011). *Five ways of doing qualitative analysis: Phenomenological psychology, grounded theory, discourse analysis, narrative research, and intuitive inquiry.* New York, NY: Guilford Press.

Whitaker, C. A. (1976). The technique of family therapy. In G. P. Sholevar (Ed.), *Changing sexual values and the family* (pp. 144–157). Springfield, IL: Charles C Thomas.

Whitaker, R. (2005). *Mad in America: Bad science, bad medicine, and the enduring mistreatment of the mentally ill.* New York, NY: Basic Books.

Whitaker, R. (2011). *Anatomy of an epidemic: Magic bullets, psychiatric drugs, and the astonishing rise of mental illness in America.* New York, NY: Broadway Books.

White, R. W. (1992). Exploring personality the long way: The study of lives. In R. A. Zucker, A. I. Rabin, J. Aronoff, & S. J. Frank (Eds.), *Personality structure in the life course: Essays on personology in the Murray tradition* (pp. 3–21). New York, NY: Springer.

Whitehead, A. N. (1925). *Science and the modern world.* Cambridge, England: Cambridge University Press.

Williams, K. R. (2006). The Son-Rise Program intervention for autism: Prerequisites for evaluation. *Autism, 10*, 86–102. http://dx.doi.org/10.1177/1362361306062012

Williams, K. R., & Wishart, J. G. (2003). The Son-Rise Program intervention for autism: An investigation into family experiences. *Journal of Intellectual Disability Research, 47*, 291–299. http://dx.doi.org/10.1046/j.1365-2788.2003.00491.x

Wolpe, J. (1969). *The practice of behavior therapy.* London, England: Pergamon Press.

Woolfolk, R. (1998). *The cure of souls: Science, values, and psychotherapy.* San Francisco, CA: Jossey-Bass.

World Health Organization. (2005). *WHO multi-country study on women's health and domestic violence against women summary report—Initial results on prevalence, health outcomes and women's responses.* New York, NY: Author.

Zubin, J., & Spring, B. (1977). Vulnerability—A new view of schizophrenia. *Journal of Abnormal Psychology, 86*, 103–126. http://dx.doi.org/10.1037/0021-843X.86.2.103

INDEX

PDDs (pervasive developmental
disorders), 115–119
Permissive parents, 108–109
Personality patterns and disorders,
165–183
antisocial, 98, 169–170, 180–183
borderline, 172–174
in *DSM–5*, 167, 169, 171–176
early history of, 165
introversion and extroversion,
165–166
and neurotic trends, 166–172
in psychodynamic theory, 73–74
and psychological suffering,
107–108
and psychosomatic disorders, 132
treatment case example, 177–180
treatment of, 176–177
Personality testing, 82
Person-centered approaches, 11–12,
119
Pervasive developmental disorders
(PDDs), 115–119
PET scans. *See* Positron-emission
tomography scans
Pharmaceutical industry
and medicalization of anxiety
disorders, 123
patents in, 148–149
psychiatric research in, 63
scandals in, 51
and schizophrenia, 186–187
Phenomenological psychology, 14
Phenothiazine medications, 192
Phillips, L. D., 142
Philosophical psychology, 12–13
Phobias, 129
Physical abuse, 110, 138–139
Pine, F., 173
Piven, J., 116
Play therapy, 50, 103, 113–115
Positive symptoms (schizophrenia),
190–191
Positron-emission tomography (PET)
scans, 63, 127, 148, 195. *See also*
Brain research
Posttraumatic stress disorder (PTSD),
134–137
Pragmatism, 22–24, 213
Preschool education, 88

Prisoners, 180–181
"Problems in living," 6
Process of Experiencing Scale, 87
Projection (defense mechanism), 72
Prouty, Gary, 197
Prozac, 19–20, 54, 128
Psychiatric disorders (term), 5–6
Psychiatric medication. *See also specific
medication types*
for anxiety and related disorders,
128
costs of, 43
history of, 19–21
side effects of, 105, 146, 191
Psychiatry
biomedical model in, 19, 47, 54, 62
dominance of, 65
history of, 34
psychology's emulation of, 39
research in, 41
Psychoanalytic psychology
and eating disorders, 158
history of, 13–14, 68–70
psychopathology in, 5–6
schizophrenia in, 197–198
Psychodynamic Diagnostic Manual, 75
Psychodynamic psychology, 68–75
approaches to schizophrenia in, 187
childhood personality in, 107–108
defense mechanisms in. *See* Defense
mechanisms
diagnosis in, 73–75
history of, 68–71
lack of attention paid to, *vii*
personality patterns in, 177
theories of mania in, 156
Psychological abuse, 110
"Psychological birth," 173
"Psychological overwhelm," 197
Psychological Screening Inventory—
2, 82
Psychological suffering. *See also specific
forms of suffering*
childhood. *See* Childhood
psychological suffering
epidemiology of, 41–42
in history of American psychology,
40–42
ubiquity of, 210–211
as unifying theme in psychology, 5–7

ABOUT THE AUTHOR

Ronald B. Miller, PhD, is professor of psychology at Saint Michael's College, where he has also directed the master's program in clinical psychology for 30 years. He is the author of *Facing Human Suffering: Psychology and Psychotherapy as Moral Engagement* (2004), an associate editor for the *Encyclopedia of Psychology* (2000), and the editor of *The Restoration of Dialogue: Readings in the Philosophy of Clinical Psychology* (1992). He is a founding associate editor of the journal *Pragmatic Case Studies in Psychotherapy* and the former editor of *The Journal of Theoretical and Philosophical Psychology*. A fellow of the American Psychological Association, Dr. Miller is currently the chair of the Vermont Board of Psychological Examiners.